ABSENT

FROM SCHOOL

ABSENT

FROM SCHOOL

Understanding and Addressing
Student Absenteeism

MICHAEL A. GOTTFRIED
ETHAN L. HUTT

Editors

HARVARD EDUCATION PRESS
Cambridge, Massachusetts

Second Printing, 2019

Paperback ISBN 978-1-68253-277-5
Library Edition ISBN 978-1-68253-278-2

Library of Congress Cataloging-in-Publication Data

Names: Gottfried, Michael A., editor. | Hutt, Ethan L., editor.
Title: Absent from school : understanding and addressing student absenteeism / Michael A. Gottfried, Ethan L. Hutt, editors.
Description: Cambridge, Massachusetts : Harvard Education Press, [2019] | Includes bibliographical references and index.
Identifiers: LCCN 2018047000| ISBN 9781682532775 (pbk.) | ISBN 9781682532782 (library edition)
Subjects: LCSH: School attendance—United States. | Academic achievement—United States. | Education and state—United States. | School improvement programs—United States. | School environment—United States. | Parent-teacher relationships. | Teacher-student relationships. | Education—Parent participation—United States.
Classification: LCC LC143 .A23 2019 | DDC 371.2/94—dc23 LC record available at https://lccn.loc.gov/2018047000

Published by Harvard Education Press,
an imprint of the Harvard Education Publishing Group

Harvard Education Press
8 Story Street
Cambridge, MA 02138

Cover Design: Endpaper Studio
Cover Image: iStock.com/narloch-liberra

The typefaces used in this book are Adobe Garamond and Gotham.

CONTENTS

PART I

Measuring Absenteeism

FOREWORD

THIS IS A TIMELY VOLUME. Its publication occurs just as the majority of school districts in the United States will begin to regularly measure and publish the percentage of students who miss 10 percent or more of the school year (about 18 days in a typical 180-day school year). As a result of the federal Every Students Succeeds Act, passed in 2015, thirty-six states plus the District of Columbia have included measures of chronic absenteeism in their school accountability systems. The first school and district report cards to include a school's chronic absenteeism rate will be released during the 2018–19 school year. As a result, interest in learning more about what chronic absenteeism is, what is known about it, and what can be done to reduce it will be as high as it has ever been.

That makes this an important volume, as current knowledge and understanding of chronic absenteeism is low. Attendance has been recorded and reported ever since schooling became universal. Students typically receive report cards that list total days absent to date, and states have had compulsory school attendance laws on the books for over a hundred years. It was not until 2016, however, that the US Department of Education released the first data it ever published on chronic absenteeism. Thus, it remains the rare principal who can tell you from memory what percent of his or her students are chronically absent.

What most principals will be able to tell you is their school's average daily attendance. This is a measure that shows the percent of enrolled students present in school on a typical day and, historically, is the attendance measure used to determine school funding and accountability. It is typical for schools to have attendance rates around 90 percent. That *seems* OK, as schooling has taught us that anything in the 90s equals an A, which is good. But an attendance rate of 90 percent means the typical student is missing 10 percent of class time, or almost a month of learning.

It may sound obvious to say that student attendance and engagement in schoolwork is a mandatory part of learning, but it is constantly overlooked as a primary mechanism for improving student achievement. Policy makers and educators often view increasing attendance as a low-level goal, claiming it's not enough to just get students to show up and what matters is what they're being taught. However, there is increasing recognition that a focus on content and curriculum do not matter if students are not fully engaged in the lessons teachers prepare. It can seem okay for students to miss class now and then, but you never know when a student will miss something—information or a key assignment—that makes them fall behind. And catching up is much harder than keeping up.

Thus, until recently chronic absenteeism has been hiding in plain sight as a key mechanism for understanding differences in student achievement and for changing practice to improve it. This volume does a great service by pulling back the covers. It shows both what we know about chronic absenteeism, what we are learning, and what remains to be understood. Each of these is important.

What we know, and what this volume reinforces, is that being in school on a regular basis matters. This may seem self-evident, but decades of disparagement of the public education system have created a sense that not much of value is going on in schools. This volume clearly shows that being in school leads to student learning and educational advancement, and being chronically absent undermines student success. Every missed day matters, whether the student's absence was formally excused, unexcused, or the result of the school's actions via a suspension.

What we are learning is two-fold. First, though attendance is easy to measure, whether the student is in school or not, how we define chronic absenteeism and measure it is complex. This volume shows that we must thoughtfully approach what might seem like simple measurement issues. Second, solutions to chronic absenteeism will need to involve educators working collaboratively with students, families, and the community. This will be nearly as big a change for some schools as measuring chronic absenteeism is. A long-standing belief that will need to be overcome is that it is the school's responsibility to teach those students who attend and that it is the responsibility of families and the students themselves to do what is needed to attend school regularly. Yet, research shows that educators can influence student attendance through the ways that they engage with students and their families. And there are issues that cut across schools, families, and community, such as transportation and health, that can induce chronic absenteeism and must be combated through integrated efforts.

The research on chronic absenteeism is young, and there is much work that remains to be done. We know that students who are chronically absent in one year, absent effective intervention, are more likely to be chronically absent in future years. Yet, few studies have been able to document and understand these patterns and their relationship with student achievement. School, district, and state data systems are rarely designed to record patterns of absenteeism over multiple years or the amount of school time lost when students transfer between districts or between schools within the same district. Finally, and perhaps uncomfortably for both scholars and school administrators, we need to understand how the evaluation of effective and ineffective school reforms has been biased by not measuring attendance. That means learning the extent to which students attended school regularly enough to benefit from the reform, whether the intervention itself influenced attendance in ways which had potentially adverse effects that undermined it, or beneficial effects that explain the real success of the program. Hopefully this is the first of many scholarly volumes on the measurement, impact, and solutions for chronic absenteeism.

Now that the cover has been pulled back, it's time to fully discover what we have been missing.

Elaine Allensworth
Lewis-Sebring Director of the University of
Chicago Consortium on School Research

Robert Balfanz
Research Professor at the Center for the Social
Organization of Schools at Johns Hopkins
University School of Education

Introduction

MICHAEL A. GOTTFRIED AND ETHAN L. HUTT

REDUCING INEQUALITY and improving academic achievement has been an explicit goal of state and federal policy for more than half a century. While public attention has been directed at policies ranging from financial expenditures and academic standards to teacher training and class size reduction, these issues have often come with a hefty price tag. Improving curricular quality has been of particular interest given the rise of the modern standards and accountability movement. Implementing America's Choice in Rochester, New York, for instance, cost $90,000 for every thirty teachers, and that is before including additional classroom expenses.[1] While potentially effective, these programs are expensive and complex, and so the prospect of using them to close the achievement gap becomes remote: the schools that need them the most are the least likely to be able to afford them or implement them effectively over the long term.

As a contrast to these complex interventions, research is finding a far simpler means of closing educational gaps: boosting student attendance. Unlike classroom-based reforms that require procuring new materials, securing teacher buy-in, and adapting instructional practice, efforts to improve school attendance seek a much more concrete outcome and possess a much simpler (if not simplistic) theory of improvement. This theory was succinctly explained to us by a teacher in a large urban school district who said that "students who miss school are 'ABT'—ain't been taught."[2] In other words, scholars, reformers, and policy makers can dream up the most effective educational programs or ways to improve teacher quality, but if the students are not in their seats, what's the point?

Right now we are at a juncture in our nation's history where addressing absenteeism is critically important. Indeed, addressing absenteeism has recently become a matter of interest to federal, state, and local lawmakers and advocates. In late 2015, the Obama administration released Every Student, Every Day: A National Initiative to Address and Eliminate Chronic Absenteeism, whose goals were to better monitor attendance data and to reduce chronic absenteeism. The initiative did not solely reflect the priorities of educational stakeholders. Rather, it represented a joint partnership between the White House and the Departments of Education, Health and Human Services, Housing and Urban Development, and Justice. Addressing school absenteeism also extends beyond the federal level. State policy agencies, including the California attorney general's office under (now Senator) Kamala Harris, had also been invested in reducing absenteeism in recent years. And community-based organizations, such as Attendance Works, have also been involved in understanding and preventing who is absent and why.

Perhaps even more consequentially, the flexibility within the Every Student Succeeds Act (ESSA) had led many states to develop new ways to define and measure school quality. And while, as expected, many indicators of school accountability in ESSA focus on test scores, states are also now incorporating a measure of school-level chronic absenteeism as an indicator of performance. As of the start of 2018, thirty-six states and the District of Columbia had approved ESSA plans to use an absenteeism metric in their accountability rubrics.

This newfound interest in absenteeism is not without justification. Large-scale data collection, as well as more rigorous empirical techniques, have shown that missing school stunts the academic growth and cripples the development of our nation's students. Research also shows that absenteeism is more prevalent among students from students in our most under-resourced schools; children living in poverty are four times more likely to be chronically absent as compared to their more advantaged peers.[3]

The consequences of missing school are dire. Students with more school absences have lower test scores and grades, greater risk of dropping out of high school, and higher odds of future unemployment. Absent students are also more likely to use tobacco, alcohol, and other drugs, and they exhibit greater behavioral issues, including social disengagement and alienation. The most recent national estimates suggest that approximately 5–7.5 million students (out of a K–12 population of approximately 50 million) are missing at least 30 school days in a given academic year, translating into an aggregate 150–225 million days of instruction lost annually.[4] Also, a fifth of our nation's schools report that one-fifth of their students are missing 10 percent or more of the school year—an amount that would label them as chronically absent.[5] Truancy also exerts a financial strain on our schooling systems. Data from the California attorney general's office states that in the 2014–15 school year alone, absences cost California school districts $1 billion; and in the past four years, California school districts have lost a total of $4.5 billion due to absenteeism.[6] Hence, high absence rates have school finance implications. The "absenteeism crisis," a phrase often utilized by Kamala Harris, affects all corners of the country.

But while this research provides compelling evidence for trying to improve attendance rates for all children, incorporating attendance metrics into state accountability plans as part of ESSA is no simple matter. The idea that states should hold individual schools accountable for chronic absenteeism relies on two assumptions: that states/researchers can develop useful measures of tracking and assessing chronic absenteeism and that schools have the means and capacity to affect absenteeism. Around the first assumption there are many lingering questions: Can we use absenteeism to successfully identify students at risk for educational failure? What unsettled questions remain in the definition and application of "chronic absenteeism" measures? What lurking measurement measures are likely to arise as we move measures of absenteeism from descriptive statistics to the subject of accountability efforts? How should these issues shape future research and policymaking on measures of chronic absenteeism? The second assumption prompts different questions: What current/ongoing school-specific settings and existing programs could contribute to absence reduction? Is there evidence that absenteeism interventions are successful? How replicable and scalable are these interventions or ongoing practices? What best practices and learning lessons emerge?

Given these lingering questions, and given states' charges to hold schools accountable for missing students, it is important to take stock of what we know about the research, policy, and practice regarding absenteeism so that we might best support the efforts to reduce absences. This book is part of that effort.

To help facilitate a broader, more substantive conversation about the use of attendance policies and measures as mechanisms for addressing inequalities, we have assembled some of the experts in this field to produce a volume dedicated solely to the issue of school absenteeism. *Absent from School* presents a unique, multifaceted, multidisciplinary examination of what we have learned about how schools measure and reduce absenteeism and what we need to know going forward as policy charges that schools be held accountable for students' absences. The book's chapters take a critical look at numerous school structures and programs, exploring their links to address aspects of absenteeism and to ask what we can learn from ongoing efforts and what issues demand our further attention and exploration. The book also addresses measurement issues in absenteeism and how understanding the nuances of absenteeism is important as we move forward. Representing a multitude of disciplines and methodological approaches and geographic regions, the contributing authors provide a first critical, systematic look at our nation's current absenteeism crisis.

With the goal of preparing the way for a substantive, fruitful debate about chronic absenteeism, it is necessary first to clear away some of the existing underbrush that prevents new ideas from taking root. To that end, we address at the outset several myths about absenteeism and how the chapters in this book look beyond these misconceptions and disrupt our thinking about the causes, consequences, and possible means of redressing the effects of absenteeism.

MYTH 1: Measuring (and Worrying About) Missing School Is New

School reform ideas move in cycles. Ideas that were once considered state of the art eventually come to be seen as faddish or old-fashioned and fall out of favor before being rediscovered decades later as the newest solution to our education ills.[7] Concerns around absenteeism are no different. While the flexibility provided by ESSA has increased interest in absentee policies, it is hardly the first time that it has been a matter of public interest and policy makers' concern.

For most of the first century of public schooling in America—from the common school to the Progressive Era—measuring attendance was a major concern of school administrators and reformers.[8] Then, as now, measuring attendance was a key part of state calculations of school funding. But attendance records meant much more than that. Schools' average daily attendance (school records in those days were almost always collected and reported in aggregate) was seen to reflect a combination of the potency of its moral suasion, holding power, and administrative efficiency. Low attendance rates were understood to pose a high risk to communities in the form of high rates of child labor, incorrigibility, and, many assumed, poverty and crime. As the purposes of schooling grew beyond moral instruction and the three Rs to include the provision of a variety of social and vocational services, reformers spoke of the issue posed by irregular attendance in more alarmed tones. The passage of compulsory school laws in the late nineteenth century, along with the increasingly large attendance divisions and increasingly professionalized truancy officers, underscored the increasing concern with the student attendance. So, too, did the common practice of publishing league tables of school districts' average daily attendance: rates in the high 80s were applauded, rates below 80 were met with admonishment, and rates above 90 were treated with suspicion.[9]

While concern for student attendance rates was universal, views on how best to track and monitor it were not. Efforts to use rates of attendance to hold teachers, principals, and school administrators accountable for school performance were repeatedly undermined by the lack of agreement on basic definitions of truancy or methods of calculating average daily attendance.[10] In an era when students were mobile, school records were paper, and record-sharing capacities were limited, how schools counted the absences of students presumed to have transferred could have very large effects on attendance data. For instance, one common practice was to drop students from school rosters after a week of absences and retroactively drop the absences accrued during that period, a practice that led a district to report perfect attendance during an outbreak of the flu even though half the students were home sick.[11] While this account might well be apocryphal, it nevertheless served to communicate reformers' pervasive concern that districts were seizing every possible opportunity to burnish their statistics and avoid public scorn.

Today, as school attendance records once again move into the public spotlight, we should expect the return of all manner of efforts—some undertaken in good faith (e.g., varied definitions of chronic absenteeism) and others not—to interpret state rules and guidance in a way that is most beneficial to individual schools and school districts.[12] The decision of many states to increase attention on absenteeism beyond No Child Left Behind's (NCLB) reporting of average daily attendance is a potentially impactful one. But subsequent developments must be viewed in light of both the long history of efforts to define and evade attendance measures and the existing baseline of attendance data. Drawing on data from California's CORE districts, Heather Hough's and Kevin Gee's chapters in this volume offer insights on who chronically absent students are, how concentrated they are in schools, and how chronic absenteeism is associated with other academic and nonacademic risk factors. As the statistics, policies, and debates over chronic absenteeism inevitably evolve in response to newly adopted reporting requirements, Hough's and Gee's analyses provide an indispensable account of where we are and what we know about the current state of chronic absenteeism.

MYTH 2: Measuring Absenteeism Is a Straightforward Process

It is certainly true that in order to monitor absences and identify whether efforts to improve attendance are working, schools, districts, and states need access to data—on a regular basis. At the moment, however, the way states and districts collect and measure attendance data varies dramatically. As one example, absences are often delineated into "excused" and "unexcused," with the former generally falling into the "doctor's note" category and the latter being reasons a school finds unacceptable, such as missing school for recreational or extracurricular activities.[13] The result is measurement complexity concerning merely the *type* of absence a student has incurred. Making matters even more complicated, Hancock, Gottfried, and Zubrick show that absences can also be delineated into student- or parent-level reasons.[14] In other words, there is no set rubric for the type of information schools collect about types of absenteeism.

In recent years, the effort to establish cutoffs for measures like "chronically absent" has made matters slightly less complex in certain regards. Generally, "chronically absent" has been defined as missing 10 percent of the school year, regardless of the reason for absence. But, definitions of chronic absence can also vary. Work by Gottfried has tested for the effects of two or more weeks as "moderate" chronic absences and three or more weeks as "strong" chronic absence.[15] Jordan and Miller present a completely different rubric from the Office of Civil Rights: 0–5 percent of the school year is "low" chronic absence, 5–9 percent is "modest," 10–19 percent is "significant," 20–29 percent is "high," and 30 percent or more is "extreme." States also vary in their ESSA plans' definitions of chronic absence: for example, Alabama uses fifteen or more days, Colorado 10 percent of the school year, and Montana 5 percent of the school year.[16] Thus, even attempts to develop simplifying heuristics have propagated complexity.

The United States will likely see a surge in the collection and analysis of chronic absence data as states develop their plans for accountability under ESSA. In doing so, schools will need to collect the right information, which can then be used for research and school improvement efforts. However, without more definitive answers regarding absences metrics and how they impact students' outcomes, there may be unwanted variation in the collection, measurement, and analysis of chronic absence data.[17] Several chapters examine dimensions of these measurement issues in greater depth. Shaun Dougherty and Joshua Childs explore the implications of absences being quite unlike test scores in that absences are not normally distributed—that is, many students have zero absences. Kevin Gee examines whether we can detect where variation exists in student absences given that students are nested within classrooms and within schools. And Seth Gershenson, Jessica Rae McBean, and Long Tran explore the analysis of the effects of student absences on achievement, considering different modeling schematics to test for these impacts.

MYTH 3: To Solve Chronic Absenteeism, We Just Need to Focus on Teens Ditching Class

Contrary to what many believe, missing school begins very early. Ehrlich and colleagues found that in Chicago, almost half of three-year-olds and a third of four-year-olds were missing 10 percent of the preschool year.[18] Chang and Davis showed that in any given year, 10 percent of all kindergartners and first graders in the US are missing at least 10 percent of the school year.[19] Further, 14 percent of all US kindergartners were "at-risk" absentees, meaning they missed only one to six days fewer than the number that would have classified them as chronic absentees.[20] In sum, among children just starting out in formal education, one-quarter of our nation's students are chronically absent or just shy of being classified as such.

Research specifically around absenteeism in early education has found negative effects of such behavior on school outcomes, thereby highlighting that missing school is an issue that starts early and has immediate negative impacts. Ehrlich, Gwynne, and Allensworth found that preschoolers who missed more school were less prepared to attend kindergarten both academically and socioemotionally.[21] Chang and Romero linked absenteeism in kindergarten to lower first-grade academic performance.[22] Connolly and Olson linked early absenteeism in kindergarten to lower achievement, grade retention, and future chronic absenteeism.[23] Ehrlich and colleagues also showed that preschoolers who were chronically absent were much more likely to be chronically absent in kindergarten, and Gottfried linked absenteeism in kindergarten to lower academic achievement and socioemotional development at the end of that year.[24]

This is not to say that absenteeism is not also a problem as children become older—it is. Balfanz and Byrnes show that chronic absence rates in kindergarten are equivalent to those at the end of middle school and beginning of high school (there is a slight drop in late elementary school).[25] Therefore, this dire situation regarding absenteeism throughout preK–12 presents an opportunity for prevention at the very onset of schooling *as well as* in later years of education. By addressing absenteeism at numerous points in students' schooling careers, we can help students and schools develop positive habits and strategies around attendance for students at various life stages. Unique to this book, the chapter by Stacy Ehrlich and David Johnson focuses on addressing absenteeism at two major life points for students: prekindergarten and ninth grade. As described by the authors, both times represent major educational transitions, and both periods deserve equal attention and weight when considering how to combat missing school.

MYTH 4: The Ways Schools Can Reduce Absences Are Straightforward

As with so many things in education, what we wish were easy, straightforward, and monocausal turns out to be difficult, complex, and multicausal. First and foremost, students come through the school's front doors faced with numerous risk factors that are linked to more absences, ranging from lower socioeconomic status (SES) to social stress to disabilities.[26] Second, and often intertwined with SES, individual race moderates rates of absenteeism with students from underrepresented minority backgrounds cited as being absent more often.[27] And finally, health, having a cold or flu or any other illness, impacts school absenteeism.[28] To make matters more complex, it is not necessarily well understood why many individual factors of risk contribute to school absences.[29] Even when we can identify a set of factors we think are important for driving up absenteeism, the relationships among those factors are intricate and complex and can be among the factors themselves.[30]

The focus on individual risk factors is certainly critical, and there are many factors beyond a school's control. They help to identify children and families that require the most support in order to be successful in school. But identifying these factors may not directly lead to devising actionable items or levers for schools and policy makers. For instance, knowing how SES interplays with absenteeism is certainly important to document and address in order to reduce absenteeism gaps, but establishing this relationship on its own does not provide insight into what policy makers and school leaders can do to intervene. That said, Ehrlich and colleagues offer a three-pronged taxonomy for how schools might be able to play a role in reducing absenteeism by focusing on student health, school-going logistics, and school culture.[31] This taxonomy is useful in considering where schools can help to address absenteeism.

Around health, schools have traditionally addressed student illness and its link to absenteeism through their nurses.[32] Yet little work has explored beyond other ways schools can address student health in order to lower absenteeism. In their chapter, Jennifer Graves, Sarit Weisburd, and Christopher Salem explore whether schools can expand their capacity to address student health, looking at whether school-based health centers can play a role in reducing acute and chronic illnesses and thereby lower absenteeism. The role of the school is actionable: if schools can offer services that promote good health and address illness on campus, this can be a way for schools to take action to reduce absences.

Regarding logistics, students and their families can have difficulty setting routines and schedules around getting to school.[33] Failing to address issues such as transportation, packing lunches, and leaving the house does not instill good school-going behavior.[34] In their chapter, Sarah Cordes, Michele Leardo, Christopher Rick, and Amy Ellen Schwartz examine whether taking the school bus can help families better address such logistical issues. Schools offering busing is a straightforward policy lever: if a bus provides a reliable, cost-effective way for children to get school, then schools offering access to busing each and every day can promote school attendance.[35] This is another actionable way for schools to intervene in the attendance crisis.

Finally, we are at an important juncture in determining if school climate itself might exacerbate student absenteeism. For instance, Carolyn Sattin-Bajaj and Jacob Kirksey's chapter examines how the school's interplay with immigration enforcement activities can impact absenteeism for first- and second-generation immigrant-origin children. In their chapter, Kaitlin Andersen, Anna Egalite, and Jonathan Mills address the role of school disciplinary action programs and implementation and their effect on absenteeism and suggest that a shift in culture around at-risk students can influence school-going behavior. Stacy Ehrlich and David Johnson also examine school culture, looking at whether a school culture of data use links to higher or lower student absenteeism.

MYTH 5: Parents Understand That Missing School Is Bad

Too many parents are either unaware of or underestimate their child's absences.[36] This may be more true for low-SES families, where there is often less parental engagement and awareness.[37] However, when it comes to understanding the role of parents with regards to absenteeism, most research has been limited to studying family contextual factors or processes, such as family structure, father's occupation, mother's work status, and poverty status. Less is known about what parent-focused interventions might influence school attendance for our youngest schoolchildren.

What we do know is that high rates of absenteeism in elementary school are indicative of parents being absent from, unaware of, or uninvolved in their children's schooling.[38] Therefore, if patterns of absences serve as signals of family home environments, then it is possible that parents of children with high rates of absenteeism may be less involved in their children's schooling or less aware of the need for them to attend school regularly.[39] That is, parents of truant students may not be involved in their child's daily schooling and may not understand the negative consequences during early school years; they may believe that their children will catch up or that attendance in school is only important in later years.

The educational benefits of programs that improve the relationship between parents and schools, particularly for low-SES families, have been well documented.[40] Therefore, in determining how to allocate resources to reduce absenteeism, one potential way of reducing absenteeism may be through parent education and awareness interventions. In fact, for low-SES families, interventions mediated through parents have the potential to be more successful than purely school-based approaches. This is true because schools continue to make unrealistic demands on parents (e.g., mandatory volunteer hours at charter schools) without taking into account the daily constraints that low-SES families face.[41]

Chapters in this volume explore whether straightforward and easily scalable interventions can increase parental engagement and reduce absenteeism rates for families. Ken Smythe-Leistico and Lindsay Page focus on the role that text messages might play in the links between parent, student, and school, specifically for families in early education. Martha Mac Iver and Steven Sheldon examine an intervention that engages parents of students transitioning from eighth to ninth grades in better understanding the implications of good attendance. Finally, Rekha Balu's chapter takes a macro-level approach and synthesizes learning lessons from several parental engagement interventions.

* * *

When considering these issues, a multifaced, interdisciplinary focus on determining what drives absenteeism and how to measure it is justified. Being absent from school impacts academic performance, among other consequences.[42] In this book, we look to whether and how schools can impact and reduce absences to stop this damaging behavior in its tracks. There is growing evidence that reducing absences can improve student performance. The field generally agrees that one standard deviation reduction in absences can improve test scores by up to 0.10 standard deviations.[43] The importance of this comes into perspective when we consider the decades of time we've spent on improving test scores by other means. Schanzenbach reported that reducing class size from 22–25 to 13–17 students was associated with 0.15–0.20 standard deviations improvement in test scores.[44] And others have found the effect sizes of attendance to be similar in magnitude to one-third the effect of one standard deviation increase in teacher effectiveness.[45]

There is potential for absenteeism reduction to improve student achievement. But unlike many other school interventions, such as class size reduction or teacher quality improvement, there is potential for absenteeism reduction efforts to be replicable, scalable, and potentially more cost-effective than those programs that rely entirely on changes to or the increase of both capital and labor. In *Absent from School* we identify how these efforts and programs may reduce engaging in and the effects of such damaging behavior. This will allow researchers, policy makers, practitioners, and community members to consider how to develop scalable programs to reduce absenteeism. This first book on absenteeism should engage multiple stakeholders in considering how to more efficiently channel funds and resources in ways that reduce this high-risk schooling behavior, thereby boosting educational possibilities for all.

Measuring Absenteeism

1

Roll Call

Describing Chronically Absent Students, the Schools They Attend, and Implications for Accountability

---

HEATHER HOUGH

THE EVERY STUDENT SUCCEEDS ACT (ESSA) makes sweeping changes to the way school performance is measured and shifts to the states many of the decisions about what to measure, how to identify schools for support, and what types of support to provide. ESSA requires a more comprehensive approach to measurement than was required under No Child Left Behind (NCLB), with the intention of including more measures and moving away from adverse consequences of NCLB's measurement system, namely the narrowing of the curriculum toward tested subjects and content, strategic gaming of accountability structures, and cheating.[1] Specifically, ESSA requires states to include multiple measures of student achievement, including academic performance as measured by proficiency on English language arts (ELA) and math tests, academic growth, graduation rate, development of English learner (EL) proficiency, and at least one additional indicator of "School Quality or Student Success" (SQSS). This "fifth indicator" can include measures of student engagement, educator engagement, student access to and completion of advanced coursework, postsecondary readiness, or school climate and safety.

There is a growing understanding that chronic absenteeism can severely interfere with academic achievement and that increasing attendance rates among at-risk youth can help close achievement gaps.[2] The majority of states have chosen chronic absenteeism as their SQSS indicator, both due to the growing awareness of the importance of student attendance and because attendance data is something most schools, districts, and states have collected for many years as a way to track school enrollments.[3] However, chronic absence represents a very different approach to tracking attendance. Chronic absence as an indicator highlights the number of students missing a substantial amount of school, as opposed to how many students attend on average, which is what Average Daily Attendance has measured. Because reporting chronic absenteeism at the state level is so new, many questions remain about what such measures tell us about student and school performance.

Given the interest in measuring chronic absenteeism, there is much to learn from California's CORE districts about how such measures can be used to understand and improve school performance. The CORE districts—a network of school districts that serves nearly one million students in more than one thousand schools in California—are best known for the multiple measures accountability system they developed under an NCLB waiver. In this chapter, I analyze multiple years of chronic absence data in CORE's measurement system to better understand differences across students and schools, comparing these measures to a broader set of school performance indicators. I begin by describing attendance at the student level and how it varies by student characteristics. Then I illustrate how schools perform on this metric, by school type, by subgroup, and across time. And, finally, I explain how schools' performance on chronic absence metrics corresponds to other accountability metrics and the related implications for reporting school-level accountability measures under ESSA.

About the CORE Districts

The CORE Districts—Fresno, Garden Grove, Long Beach, Los Angeles, Oakland, Sacramento City, San Francisco, and Santa Ana unified school districts—are best known for the waiver they received from the US Department of Education that freed them from some of their federal obligations under NCLB. Under the terms of the waiver, six of these districts developed and are currently implementing an innovative measurement and shared accountability system that focuses on academic outcomes alongside non-academic measures of student success, including chronic absenteeism, suspension/expulsion, students' social-emotional skills, and school culture and climate.[4] As early adopters of the new focus on multiple measures, the CORE districts can provide lessons about how chronic absence can fit into a more comprehensive measurement system designed to build a deeper understanding of school performance.

The CORE districts represent nearly 20 percent of the students served in California. In my analysis, I use data from 2014–15, 2015–16, and 2016–17 for a subset of the CORE districts.[5] In total, the analysis includes 2,364,755 student-year records within 1,227 schools. The CORE districts have a combined 1,044 Title I schools, which is more than 28 of the 50 states.[6] For this reason, even though the CORE districts' data represent a consortium of a small number of school districts, the results from this analysis are likely generalizable to the types of schools that ESSA is intended to support. Furthermore, the CORE districts represent the kinds of demographic shifts taking place nationally. In 2015, 62 percent of the US population was White, but by 2065 this number is expected to decline to 46 percent.[7] In this way, the CORE districts, and California more generally, can provide advance lessons about how to support increasingly diverse populations elsewhere in the US. As shown in table 1.1, the CORE districts serve a large proportion of economically disadvantaged, EL, African American, Asian, and Hispanic/Latino students.[8]

In my analyses, I use CORE's student- and school-level measures to understand attendance patterns and explore how chronic absenteeism is related to other outcomes.[9] These measures include:

- *student attendance*, which is measured as the number of days attended out of the number of days enrolled over the whole school year. (In California, school districts are required to offer 180 days or more of instruction.[10] Students' absences were calculated by dividing the number of days they attended by the total number of days they were recorded as students in a given school. A student is considered chronically absent

TABLE 1.1

Demographics in CORE districts compared to California and the United States, 2016

	CORE DISTRICTS	CALIFORNIA	UNITED STATES
Economically disadvantaged*	78%	58%	52%
English learner	23%	21%	9%
Children with disabilities	12%	12%	13%
Hispanic/Latino	68%	54%	25%
White	9%	24%	50%
African American	9%	6%	16%
Asian/Pacific Islander	10%	12%	5%
Filipino	2%	3%	**
Pacific Islander	1%	1%	**
Asian	8%	9%	**
American Indian or Alaska Native	0%	1%	1%
Two or more races	3%	3%	3%
Number of students	808,490	6,228,236	50,313,000
Number of schools	1,227	10,680	98,176

Notes: *Eligible for free or reduced-price lunch.
**National data count Asian, Filipino, and Pacific Islander students as "Asian/Pacific Islander."

if they miss 10 percent or more of the days they were enrolled and is considered enrolled in the school if they have attended at least 45 days of school.)

- *academic performance*, which is measured by whether students tested at the "proficient" level for English language arts (ELA) and mathematics, based on Smarter Balanced Assessment Consortium (SBAC) test scores

- *academic growth*, which is measured as the extent to which students in a given school have improved their performance on ELA and math tests from one year to the next relative to demographically similar students who started the school year with similar prior achievement; the result is a growth percentile (0–100) comparing schools' contribution to student growth on ELA and math tests

- *graduation*, which is reported as the percentage of students who graduate in a four-year cohort compared with the number of students enrolled in the school (accounting for students who transfer into and out of the school)
- *English language proficiency*, which is represented as the percentage of students who are reclassified from EL status to "fluent English proficient," considering only students who have been in the US system at least five years.[11]

Understanding Chronic Absence at the Student Level

Before we can understand the implications of chronic absenteeism for accountability, we need to understand student attendance more broadly. To this end, it is important to understand how chronic absenteeism is defined, how many students are chronically absent, and how chronic absenteeism varies by student characteristics. Under ESSA, thirty-two states that have included chronic absenteeism use the same definition: missing 10 percent or more of enrolled days.[12] The research most often cited for this cut point is from a study designed to create a system of indicators (including poor attendance, misbehavior, and course failures in sixth grade) that can be used to identify 60 percent of the students who will not graduate from high school.[13] As shown in figure 1.1, the vast majority of students (89 percent) miss fewer than 10 percent of enrolled days. In fact, 19 percent of students only miss 1 percent of enrolled days (approximately two days of school per year). However, the 11 percent of students who are chronically absent produce a long tail, with 2 percent of students missing 25 percent or more of school days (approximately forty-five or more days of school).

There is a great deal of variation across rates of chronic absenteeism by grade level. As shown in figure 1.2, chronic absenteeism is highest in kindergarten, with 17 percent of students chronically absent. Chronic absenteeism declines in grades 1–6 and then increases again in the high school grades (with rates highest in grade 12 at 21 percent). The reasons for absence, and thus possible solutions for reducing it, are likely very different across grades. For example, the agent of student attendance changes from kindergarten, where the students are completely reliant on their parents and school is not yet compulsory, to high school, when students themselves make decisions about school attendance.[14]

FIGURE 1.1   Percentage of students at different absence levels

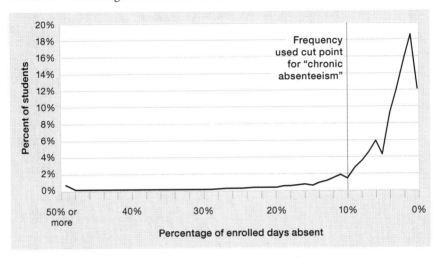

Note: N = 808,490 (2016–17)

FIGURE 1.2   Rates of chronic absenteeism by grade

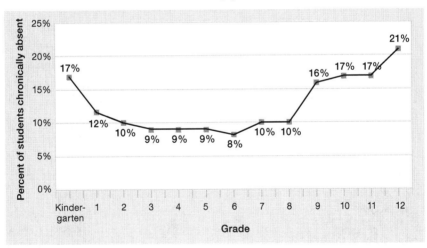

Note: N = 808,490 (2016–17)

There is also significant variation in rates of chronic absenteeism by student characteristics. ESSA requires disaggregation of results by subgroup, including: (1) economically disadvantaged students, defined in the sample

FIGURE 1.3   Rates of chronic absenteeism by demographic group

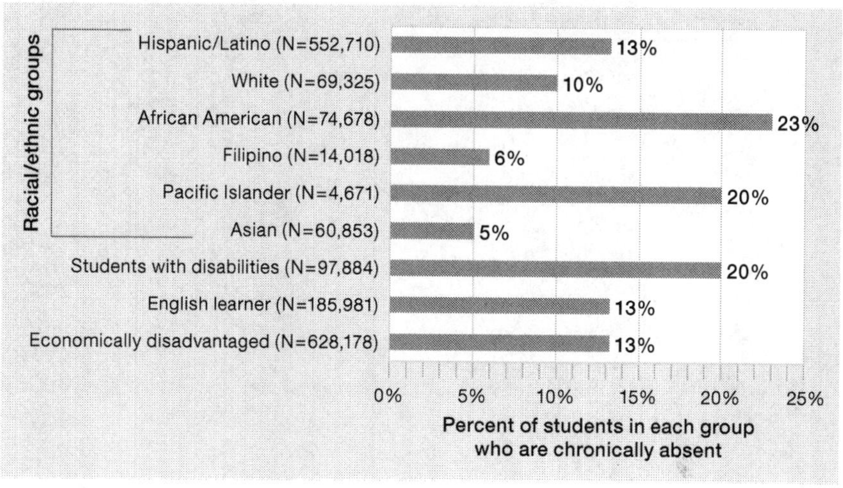

Percent of students in each group
who are chronically absent

as students eligible for free and reduced-price lunch; (2) students from major racial and ethnic groups; (3) students with disabilities; and (4) English learners. As shown in figure 1.3, African American students, Pacific Islander students, and students with disabilities have the highest rates of chronic absenteeism, at 23 percent, 20 percent, and 20 percent, respectively.

To think about potential solutions, it may be important to know how chronic absenteeism varies across time. In other words, is chronic absenteeism something that a student experiences just once (e.g., health or extenuating circumstance), or is it a problem that is repeated year after year (e.g., family situation, school environment)? The CORE data show that a chronically absent student in one year is ten times more likely to be absent in the following year. Figure 1.4 shows the probability of being chronically absent in the current year (2016–17) for students who were and were not chronically absent in the previous year.[15] As students progress through the grades, they are more likely to be chronically absent in one year if they were also chronically absent the year before. For example, a kindergartener who was chronically absent in one year has a .49 probability of being chronically absent in the next year. However, a chronically absent student in grade 9 has a .68 probability of being chronically absent in grade 10. Additionally, students' probability of being chronically absent increases as they progress through the grades, even without a prior attendance issue. This highlights two important

FIGURE 1.4   Predicted probability of being chronically absent, comparing students who were and were not chronically absent in the previous year

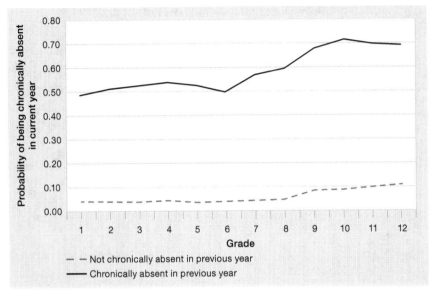

Note: N = 664,322 (2016–17)

problems of practice: educators addressing problems in student achievement as soon as they appear and paying particular attention to attendance of students in the upper grades, whether or not they have demonstrated attendance problems in the past.

Understanding Chronic Absenteeism at the School Level

With individual students' rates of chronic absenteeism varying greatly by grade, characteristic, and prior attendance, it is important to understand how these students are distributed across schools and what the resulting school metrics reveal about school performance. In this section I describe how schools perform on this metric, by school type and by subgroup.

Chronic Absenteeism by School Type

There is wide variation in the rates of chronic absenteeism by school type, reflecting the student-level differences by grade (figure 1.2). However, schools

FIGURE 1.5   Percentage of students chronically absent, by school type

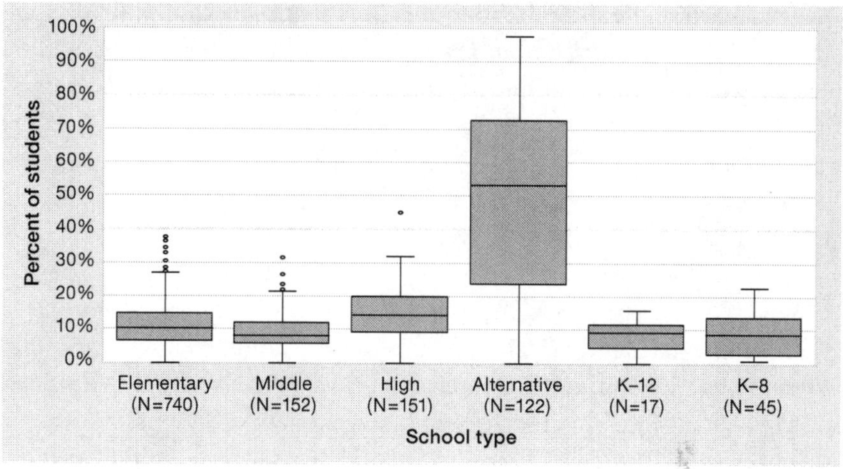

vary greatly in the rates of student absenteeism, even when they serve students in the same grades. The box-and-whisker plot in figure 1.5 shows the variation among schools in the percentage of students who are chronically absent. For example, in the median elementary school, 11 percent of students are chronically absent. The box itself represents the chronic absenteeism rates for schools between the twenty-fifth and seventy-fifth percentiles; in the case of elementary schools, this is a range of 7–15 percent of students who are chronically absent. The "whiskers," or the lines coming from the boxes, represent the interquartile range, or the expected range of rates of chronic absenteeism based on the distribution, with dots representing outlier schools outside this range.[16]

The plot enables an understanding of the variation in chronic absenteeism rates for different school types. For example, there is a bigger range of school-level rates of chronic absenteeism in high school than in elementary and/or middle schools. The range is even greater in alternative schools, where, in the median school, 53 percent of students are chronically absent, with a range of 20–73 between the twenty-fifth and seventy-fifth percentiles.[17] This makes sense, since alternative schools are specifically designed for students who have problems with academics and attendance or who are otherwise in danger of not graduating. Since these schools must also be held accountable under ESSA, it is important to observe their performance on the chronic absence metric separately from other high schools.[18]

Chronic Absence by Subgroup

New measures present new opportunities to understand how schools are serving diverse students and can prompt educators and stakeholders to have honest conversations about how to develop inclusive, equitable school environments. It is for this reason that ESSA requires disaggregation of results by subgroup. As with the gaps revealed in figure 1.3, there is wide variation in the rates of chronic absenteeism by subgroups. However, figure 1.6 also reveals that schools perform very differently with students in the same subgroups. This graph shows that schools on average see higher rates of chronic absenteeism among African American students than other racial/ethnic groups (at a median rate of 21 percent chronically absent) and that there is wide variation in the chronic absenteeism rates of African American students across schools. For schools with low rates of chronic absenteeism for African American students (at the twenty-fifth percentile), only 13 percent are chronically absent, and in the schools with the highest rates of chronic absenteeism (at the seventy-fifth percentile), 31 percent of African American students are chronically absent.[19]

Across schools, students perform differently by subgroup, but what about within schools? Do schools that perform well with one group tend to perform well with others, or are there substantial subgroup gaps within schools? Data show that it's the latter: there are very large gaps in chronic absenteeism rates by subgroup even within the same school, especially between racial/ethnic groups. Figure 1.7 compares chronic absence rates for students in the racial/ethnic subgroup with the highest level of chronic absence (y-axis) to the group with the lowest level (x-axis).[20] The diagonal line demarcates schools with no gap in chronic absence rates, or where chronic absence rates are the same for all racial/ethnic subgroups in the schools. The distance between the point for the school and the diagonal line shows the magnitude of the gap for each school. The two indicators are highly correlated (.85), indicating that school performance for different student groups is closely related within the same school for the majority of schools. However, the figure also reveals very substantial gaps between racial/ethnic groups for many schools. For example, in the elementary school with the largest gap (circled), 80 percent of African American students are chronically absent, compared to only 7 percent of the Hispanic/Latino students. These are places where there may be serious equity issues to be addressed. The question is what the situation and context are leading to such a substantial gap within schools, and then what the school can do to close those gaps.

FIGURE 1.6 Percentage of students chronically absent in each school by subgroup

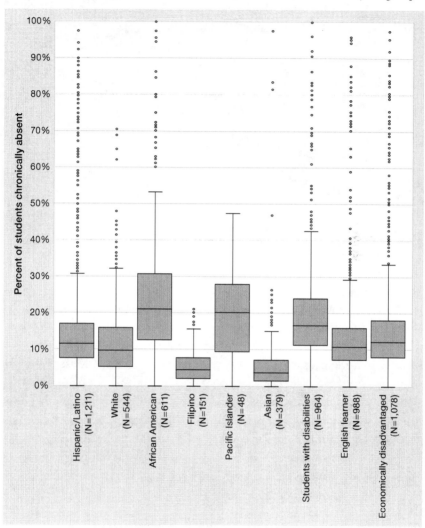

Using Measures of Chronic Absence in Accountability Systems

Ultimately, these measures will be used in state accountability systems, and so it is important to explore the ESSA requirements that any measures must allow for meaningful differentiation in school performance and must be used

FIGURE 1.7 Comparing rates of chronic absenteeism by racial/ethnic groups within the same school

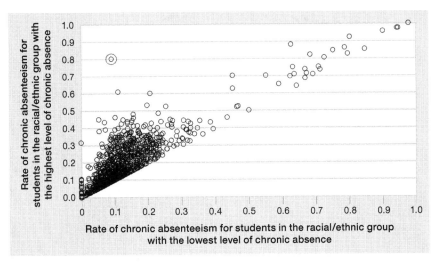

in a system of measures to identify schools for support and improvement. Within the CORE districts, educational leaders often say that a metric of school performance should be measurable, meaningful, and malleable.[21] We know that chronic absence is measurable, as it is now being measured fairly easily in nearly every state in the country. The fact that it's being reported alongside other, more traditional measures of school performance inherently makes it meaningful, along with the fact that there are substantial differences between student groups and schools that the metric highlights. But are chronic absence measures malleable? To what extent do school measures of chronic absenteeism change over time, and how can this information be included in accountability reporting?

Change in School-Level Chronic Absenteeism over Time

Because this issue of improvement is so important, it could be advantageous for states to report both the rate of chronic absenteeism in each year (the "status") and the change over time, as California does. With different cut points for each school level and each performance indicator, California's new school metric system, the California School Dashboard, determines a school's performance level based on both its performance in the current year and the change over time. The combination of these metrics then determines whether a school is "red" (the lowest level), "orange," "yellow," "green," or "blue" (the highest level). To illustrate the logic of this approach, I use a simple definition, separating schools into quintiles by status and change (from 2014–15 to 2016–17).

Figure 1.8 shows the distribution of schools across each of these performance levels. Overall, 16 percent of schools are in the lowest level and 28 percent in the highest level. Importantly, there are schools in nearly every cell, highlighting the importance of this kind of reporting strategy. A school with low chronic absenteeism but increasing rates should be flagged for intervention, just as a school with high chronic absenteeism but declining rates should be acknowledged for its progress. (Note that here I consider only Title I schools, since those are the only schools that must be included for identification under ESSA.)

Reporting the metric in this fashion attempts to take into account a school's performance alongside its progress. In this way, even if a school has very high chronic absenteeism, if it has improved significantly, it is not in the lowest performance category. However, if the school has a relatively low chronic absence rate but that rate is increasing over time, that school's indicator (a combination of status and change) will be lower than if the metric was based on status alone.

It is important to note that measuring change in this fashion is not the same as measuring a school's contribution to improvement in chronic

FIGURE 1.8 Approximating California's method for taking into account status and change

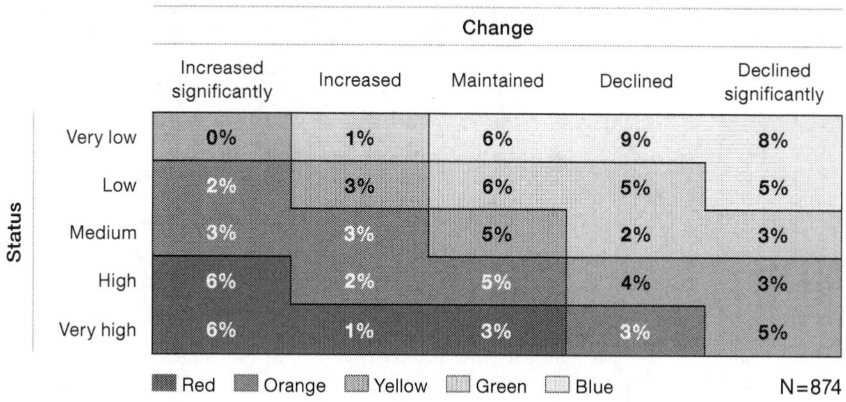

Status	Change				
	Increased significantly	Increased	Maintained	Declined	Declined significantly
Very low	0%	1%	6%	9%	8%
Low	2%	3%	6%	5%	5%
Medium	3%	3%	5%	2%	3%
High	6%	2%	5%	4%	3%
Very high	6%	1%	3%	3%	5%

■ Red   ■ Orange   ▨ Yellow   ▢ Green   ▢ Blue   N=874 absence, which would be done through the use of a school growth model.[22] An attendance growth model would take into account an individual student's prior attendance, economic disadvantage, disability status, EL status, homelessness, and foster care status and use this information to measure the extent to which their attendance improves relative to students similar to them in these same categories. In this way, a growth measure is constructed as a value-added model, estimating the school's impact on attendance relative to other schools serving similar students. The alternative, schoolwide change over time in chronic absenteeism does not account for changes in student population or the kinds of students a school serves. Nonetheless, incorporating change into a reporting system illuminates progress in a way that a status measure does not.

Additionally, reporting change over time by subgroup is another way to highlight equity problems within schools. Figure 1.9 shows how schools are performing with three different subgroups using a California-style metric: (1) the racial/ethnic group with highest rate of chronic absence (for schools with two or more racial/ethnic groups); (2) economically disadvantaged students; and (3) students with disabilities. Across all groups and school grade levels,

FIGURE 1.9   School performance with subgroups

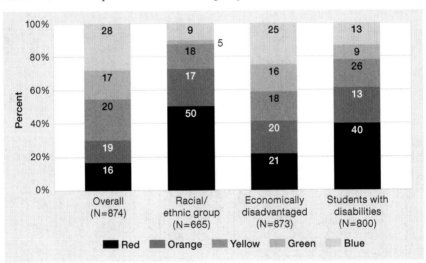

Notes:

Sample: Schools with valid CORE-aligned student attendance records, valid SQII scores, and Title I eligibility. 2016-2017 with linked 2014-2015 records only.

many more schools are in the lowest performance level for their subgroups than for their students overall. For example, 16 percent are in the red category overall, but 50 percent are in this lowest level for the racial/ethnic group in that school with the highest rate of chronic absenteeism; 21 percent are in the red category with economically disadvantaged students and 40 percent with students with disabilities.

Chronic Absence Related to Other Measures of School Performance

While it is certainly useful just knowing how schools are doing on chronic absence measures, schools will be identified for improvement under ESSA using a combination of *all* their performance metrics. How states do this will vary, but ESSA requires that states must identify at least 5 percent of Title I elementary, middle, and high schools for comprehensive support and improvement.[23] Each of the indicators must be included in identifying which schools are most in need of support, but the state may determine the relative priority of the measures.

Because chronic absence rates will be used in conjunction with these other metrics, it is important to understand how these metrics are related to one another. Because the bottom 5 percent is a meaningful cut point under ESSA, investigating which schools are identified by different metrics provides a useful comparison. It also helps us understand the extent to which chronic absenteeism is different from other accountability measures.

For example, figure 1.10 shows the relationship between chronic absenteeism and the percentage of students who are proficient on the ELA assessment for elementary schools; the dots in the bottom left quadrant represent schools that would be identified in the bottom 5 percent of all schools with both measures, the dots in the upper left quadrant represent schools that would only be identified using ELA proficiency, and the dots in the lower right quadrant represent schools that would only be identified in the bottom 5 percent of all schools using the indicator of chronic absenteeism. In the figure 62 schools are identified as being in the bottom 5 percent of all schools by either measure, but only 15 schools (24 percent) are similarly identified among the bottom 5 percent of all schools by both measures. (If the measures were identical, 100 percent of schools would be identified by both measures.)

FIGURE 1.10 Relationship between elementary school measures of chronic absenteeism and ELA achievement

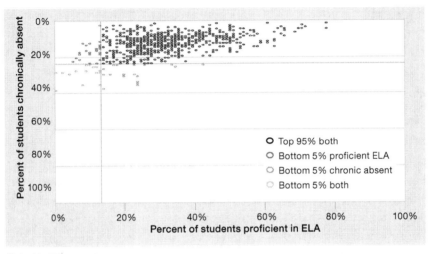

Note: N=670

While performance metrics are related in a multiple measures framework, schools are rarely low on all measures; they are high on some metrics and low on others.[24] This holds for chronic absence. Summarizing the relationships

TABLE 1.2
Percentage of schools similarly identified in pairwise comparisons

SIMILARITY		CHRONIC ABSENCE	ENGLISH LANGUAGE PROFICIENCY	GRADUATION RATES	ELA GROWTH	ELA PROFICIENCY
Chronic absence	%	100%				
	N	1,043				
EL proficiency	%	11%	100%			
	N	94	900			
Graduation rates	%	5%	0%	100%		
	N	63	56	173		
ELA growth	%	8%	4%	0%	100%	
	N	101	95	61	956	
ELA proficiency	%	19%	6%	1%	24%	100%
	N	98	101	68	90	977

Note: N=1,044

across all of the indicators, table 1.2 shows the percentage of schools that are similarly identified in pairwise comparisons across all indicators (math performance excluded for simplicity). When comparing chronic absenteeism to graduation, for example, sixty-three schools are identified as being in the bottom 5 percent of all schools by either graduation or chronic absence, but only 5 percent of those schools are similarly identified by both measures.

These analyses show that the different measures most states are developing and reporting under ESSA would identify dramatically different schools if used independently. Each of the indicators, including chronic absenteeism, appears to be measuring a different aspect of school performance, illuminating a different dimension of a school's strengths and weaknesses. This point is reinforced by the fact that not a single school is in the bottom 5 percent of all schools across all measures.

Making Use of Chronic Absence Measures Moving Forward

Because of ESSA's focus on using multiple measures of student outcomes to track school performance, most states are now including chronic absenteeism in their accountability systems. While districts in most states have been collecting attendance data for many years, chronic absence highlights critical attendance problems, thus focusing attention on the students who are most at risk. Given that tracking and reporting chronic absence data for accountability is new, I recommend the following actions.

Make measures actionable, conduct more fine-grained analysis and reporting. While state-level accountability indicators will certainly highlight problems of performance across a system of schools, these indicators are insufficient for understanding the true nature of the problem. School-level indicators will not be enough; educators should work to create more nuanced measures for use at the local level. For example, my analyses show that there is large variation by grade, which highlights the need to break down school-level measures by grade. In the development of these local systems, educators may also want to develop real-time indicators to catch attendance problems before it's too late. My findings show that students are more likely to be chronically absent in one year if they were chronically absent the year before. Local indicators can be developed that help educators intervene early and work to address chronic absence when it begins.

Focus on equity. On the chronic absence measure there are significant gaps between student groups, even within schools. This demonstrates
the need for schools to recognize these disparities and work to eliminate
them. New measures present new opportunities to understand how schools
are serving diverse students and can prompt educators and stakeholders to
have honest conversations about how to develop inclusive, equitable school
environments. For example, a large body of research has demonstrated that
African American students are treated differently than their peers, including higher rates of disciplinary action and special education designation and
lower expectations.[25] This differential treatment often has the effect of making such students feel less safe in school and less connected to their peers
and teachers.[26] Thus, in reviewing chronic absence data, educators need to
consider the inequitable treatment that may be related to absence and then
develop interventions that address this root cause.

Stress an improvement mind-set. The guiding principle of the CORE
districts in their use of multiple measures is that data should be used as a
"flashlight not a hammer."[27] What indicators reveal about school performance should be used to help them improve and not to scapegoat or punish.
Indeed, there is growing agreement among policy makers, school and district
leaders, and researchers that the most important use of school performance
measures should be in driving continuous improvement at both the local and
state levels.[28] However, for data to be truly used for improvement, all those
involved must approach its use with an improvement mind-set.[29] Without a
real, systemic focus on improvement, there will inevitably be pressure to game
the chronic absence metrics. While distortive practice is certainly possible on
academic outcomes as well, attendance indicators are arguably more sensitive
to manipulation given that they are locally reported.[30] Additionally, the fact
that the chronic absence indicator is driven by a relatively small number of
students makes it particularly sensitive. This targeted focus can be a powerful
motivator for improvement.[31] Yet, the focus on a small number of students
can encourage perverse incentives, such as misreporting or even expelling of
chronically absent students as a way to increase indicator scores.

Use multiple measures in concert. The inclusion of additional measures in an expanded accountability system is intended to provide a more
comprehensive picture of a school's successes and challenges that may be used
for many purposes by various stakeholders.[32] The move to multiple measures
under ESSA is undoubtedly better for students and schools, as all stakeholders

will now be able to support schools toward this more comprehensive view of performance. However, multiple measures also introduce complexity. As demonstrated, different indicators measure very different aspects of school performance, illuminating different dimensions of schools' strengths and weaknesses. If a central goal of ESSA is to broaden our conception of school performance in order to improve schools on all of these dimensions, system leaders will need to develop comprehensive approaches to school improvement that take into account all information provided by various metrics. These measurement systems being developed across the country will need to be paired with a strong, comprehensive approach to improvement at all levels of the system.

2

Variation in Chronic Absenteeism

The Role of Children, Classrooms, and Schools

KEVIN A. GEE

ACROSS THE EARLY ELEMENTARY YEARS, chronic absenteeism rates can vary considerably between schools as well as within schools. Take, for instance, a school district such as Alameda Unified School District (AUSD) in Alameda, California, which has ten elementary schools. Across those schools, chronic absenteeism rates (defined as missing 10 percent of the school year) for kindergarteners range from 2 percent to about 26 percent.[1] At the same time, within each school, certain children tend to be at higher or lower risk of being chronically absent as compared with their peers. Yet, where is most of the variation in chronic absenteeism? How much of that variability is between children versus between schools? Importantly, how much of that variation can be explained by factors we often associate with chronic absenteeism, such as children's health? Understanding where variability in chronic absenteeism lies, as well as the share of variability that certain factors explain, serves as a useful benchmark for gauging the relative importance of the kinds of factors that influence absenteeism. In general, factors that account for a larger share of the variability can be considered more relevant. By understanding which factors are more relevant than others, practitioners and policy makers can better prioritize which types of factors they should focus on when developing and investing in strategies to address absenteeism.

This chapter illustrates how variability in chronic absenteeism can be analyzed to yield important insights into the factors underlying absenteeism. It has two main objectives. First, it assesses differences in children's chronic absenteeism behaviors, quantifying the extent to which variability in chronic absenteeism in kindergarten through second grade is due to systematic differences between children relative to systematic differences between schools and classrooms. The focus is on children in their early elementary grades, a time when missing too much school can be especially disruptive to their formative learning. Second, the chapter describes and quantifies the extent to which a selected set of factors—attributes of children, their classrooms, and their schools—can help explain variability in chronic absenteeism. It draws on data from the Early Child Longitudinal Study, Kindergarten Class of 2010–11 (ECLS-K:2011), a large nationwide survey of children who started kindergarten in the fall of 2010.

Throughout the chapter, I use the term *variability* to describe the extent to which either children, their classrooms, or their schools systematically differ from each other in their propensities toward chronic absence. Some children, classrooms, and schools will have a higher propensity than others. Differences can be due to a range of circumstances that each child experiences in their lives as well as to the types of schools and classrooms they attend.

To illustrate the concept of variability, consider the children depicted in figure 2.1. Each child in School A faces the same chance of being chronically absent. In this case, children in School A do not vary in their probability of being chronically absent. Yet, each child in School B faces a different chance of being chronically absent. Thus, children in School B vary widely in their chances of being chronically absent.

Variability also exists between different classrooms in schools, as well as between different schools. This is because children who attend the same classes and schools can also share similar characteristics (e.g., socioeconomic level) and be exposed to similar experiences that may influence their absence behaviors. Thus, there could be some shared, common tendency toward being

FIGURE 2.1   Variability in the probability of chronic absenteeism

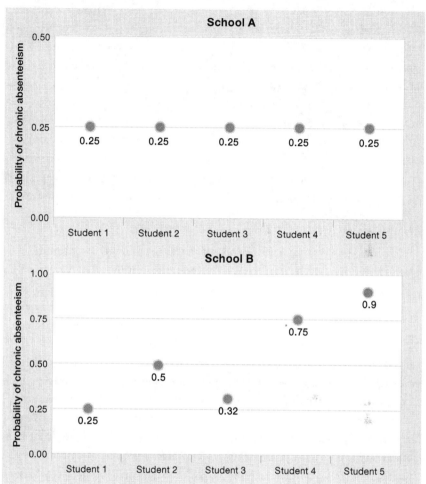

chronically absent among students within the same classrooms and schools. This shared propensity might look different between different classrooms as well as between different schools.

The total variability in chronic absenteeism consists of three components: (1) the variability that exists between children within a given classroom; (2) the variability that exists between classrooms within the same schools; and (3) the variability between different schools.

Analyzing variability can help us gauge how much a certain factor, or set of factors, matters for predicting variability in chronic absenteeism. Some factors will matter less, while others will matter more. In general, factors that explain a larger share of the variability can be considered more relevant than those factors that account for little to no variability. Imagine if we could explain all the variability in children's propensities for being chronically absent by just knowing one risk factor: their health. If we knew that health alone predicted chronic absenteeism, we could expect that if children's health risks changed, those changes would relate to all the changes in their attendance, and our knowledge other risk factors—such as their family background, achievement, and even their past behaviors—would not help explain absenteeism. From the perspective of schools and educational policy makers, this would highlight the importance of prioritizing and focusing on ways to address health-related drivers of absenteeism.

Of course, many factors simultaneously explain variability in chronic absenteeism, some more than others. Also, we may not readily observe or measure some factors (e.g., motivation). Yet, by systematically identifying which observable factors account for a large share of the variability, as well as the types of factors (i.e., individual, classroom, or school), we can gain a better understanding of which factors are more influential relative to others. Again, from a policy perspective, information about the relative influence of certain factors can help guide decisions about which factors to focus on and can help prioritize which factors to target when developing strategies to address chronic absenteeism.

Readers should keep in mind that, given the numerous factors we cannot observe or accurately measure, the factors I analyze in this chapter that help explain variability in absenteeism are *correlated* with but not causally linked to chronic absenteeism. As a result, these findings are not prescriptive and do not suggest that changing a certain set of factors will necessarily cause absenteeism to change.

Method

To analyze the variability in chronic absenteeism, I use data from the restricted-use version of ECLS-K:2011.[2] The survey tracks a large, nationally representative sample of children who entered kindergarten in the fall of 2010, and this study examines subsamples of children from the survey's first three waves: spring of kindergarten (n=6,810); spring of first grade (n=6,840); and spring of second grade (n=6,110). These include only the children in each grade who completed information across all measures in each of the analyses.[3] For this reason, the inferences drawn from these analyses are applicable only to these specific subsamples of children and are not generalizable more broadly to all children in the United States.

In the spring of a child's kindergarten, first, and second years in school, teachers were asked to report the total number of absences the child had for the current school year in one of six categories: no absences, 1–4 absences; 5–7 absences; 8–10 absences; 11–19 absences; or 20 or more absences. Consistent with earlier investigations of absenteeism using the ECLS-K dataset, this study uses 11 or more missed days as the threshold for chronic absenteeism.[4] Thus, the original six categories were collapsed into a binary variable that equaled 1 if a child experienced 11 or more absences and 0 otherwise.

Though there is no one agreed-on definition of chronic absenteeism, most states define it as 10 percent or more absences in a year (both excused and unexcused), which is typically 18 or more days.[5] In contrast, at the federal level, children are chronically absent if they miss 15 days of school for any reason.[6] Accordingly, given that this study's measure of chronic absenteeism includes students who are potentially below these state or federal thresholds, this measure should be interpreted as *moderate* chronic absenteeism.[7]

Table 2.1 summarizes predictors of the variability in chronic absenteeism included in these analyses, as organized into four groups: child attributes and demographics, parental characteristics, classroom (i.e., teacher) characteristics, and school characteristics. I selected these predictors for both their theoretical and practical importance and based largely on my earlier research on the socioecological determinants of absenteeism in the early elementary years.[8] While certainly not exhaustive, many of these factors have been shown to be strong drivers of chronic absenteeism.[9] From a practical standpoint, policy makers and practitioners have also often highlighted these factors to explain why absenteeism occurs and, subsequently, have taken these factors into account in developing interventions and policies to combat it.[10]

Table 2.2 shows descriptive statistics (means or proportions alongside their respective standard deviations) for characteristics of children, their parents, their classrooms, and the schools they attended during their kindergarten year. Characteristics are disaggregated by whether they were chronically absent or not. Several notable and statistically significant differences existed between students who were chronically versus not chronically absent.

TABLE 2.1

Predictors of chronic absenteeism

	CHILD ATTRIBUTES AND DEMOGRAPHICS
Approaches to learning	Average of 7 items rated on a scale of 1–4 (*never, sometimes, often*, or *very often*): keeps belongings organized; shows eagerness to learn new things; works independently; adapts easily to changes in routine; persists in completing tasks; pays attention well; follows classroom rules
Gender	Male or female
Health status	Excellent, very good/good, fair/poor
Home language	English or non-English
Prior chronic absenteeism	Chronically absent during the prior academic year (missing 11 or more days in the school year) or not*
Race/Ethnicity	White, black, Hispanic, Asian, other racial/ethnic background
	PARENTAL CHARACTERISTICS
Employment	Employment status in four categories: ≥35 hours per week; <35 hours per week; looking for work; not in the labor force
Parent-School engagement	Attended a parent teacher association (PTA) meeting and/or a parent-teacher conference
Socioeconomic status (SES)	NCES-constructed continuous index based on a composite of parents' education level, occupational prestige, and income
	CLASSROOM CHARACTERISTICS
Teacher experience & quality	Years of experience; qualifies as "highly qualified" based on state requirements
Teacher-Student relationship	Closeness and conflict scale based on the 15-item student-teacher relationship scale**
	SCHOOL CHARACTERISTICS
Aggressive behaviors	Extent to which student aggressive or disruptive behavior is a problem in the school: serious, moderate, minor/not a problem
Bullying	Frequency of bullying as a problem: daily/at least once a week, a least once a month, occasionally/never
School demographics	Percentages of nonwhite students and of students qualifying for free and reduced-price lunch
Teacher absenteeism	Extent to which teacher absenteeism is a problem: serious, moderate, minor/not a problem
Theft at school	Frequency of theft: daily/at least once a week, a least once a month, occasionally/never

Source: Robert C. Pianta, *Student-Teacher Relationship Scale* (Lutz, FL: Psychological Assessment Resources, 2001).

Note: *Applies to first- and second-grade analyses only.

TABLE 2.2

Sample descriptive statistics

	CHRONICALLY ABSENT (N=840)		NOT CHRONICALLY ABSENT (N=5,970)		TOTAL (N=6,810)	
	Mean	SD	Mean	SD	Mean	SD
CHILD ATTRIBUTES AND DEMOGRAPHICS						
Chronically absent					0.12	(0.33)
Health status						
excellent	0.49	(0.50)	0.63	(0.48)	0.61	(0.49)
very good or good	0.45	(0.50)	0.35	(0.48)	0.37	(0.48)
fair or poor	0.06	(0.24)	0.02	(0.12)	0.02	(0.14)
Home language is not English	0.16	(0.37)	0.14	(0.35)	0.15	(0.35)
Home language is English	0.84	(0.37)	0.86	(0.35)	0.85	(0.35)
Approaches to learning	2.99	(0.70)	3.16	(0.67)	3.14	(0.68)
Male	0.53	(0.50)	0.51	(0.50)	0.51	(0.50)
Female	0.47	(0.50)	0.49	(0.50)	0.49	(0.50)
Race/Ethnicity						
Asian	0.07	(0.25)	0.06	(0.24)	0.06	(0.24)
black	0.13	(0.33)	0.10	(0.30)	0.11	(0.31)
Hispanic	0.24	(0.42)	0.20	(0.40)	0.21	(0.40)
Native American, Pacific Islander, or multiracial	0.09	(0.29)	0.06	(0.23)	0.06	(0.24)
white	0.48	(0.50)	0.58	(0.49)	0.56	(0.50)
PARENTAL CHARACTERISTICS						
Socioeconomic status	-0.25	(0.79)	0.08	(0.81)	0.04	(0.81)
Parental employment status						
>=35 hours/week	0.30	(0.46)	0.43	(0.50)	0.41	(0.49)
<35 hours/week	0.21	(0.40)	0.22	(0.42)	0.22	(0.41)
looking for work	0.10	(0.30)	0.06	(0.24)	0.07	(0.25)
not in labor market	0.39	(0.49)	0.29	(0.45)	0.30	(0.46)
Attended a parent-teacher conference	0.89	(0.31)	0.92	(0.28)	0.91	(0.28)
Attended a PTA meeting	0.30	(0.46)	0.37	(0.48)	0.36	(0.48)

(continued)

TABLE 2.2 (*continued*)
Sample descriptive statistics

	CHRONICALLY ABSENT (N=840)		NOT CHRONICALLY ABSENT (N=5,970)		TOTAL (N=6,810)	
	Mean	SD	Mean	SD	Mean	SD
CLASSROOM (TEACHER) CHARACTERISTICS						
Years of experience	14.15	(10.05)	14.43	(9.68)	14.39	(9.72)
High-quality teacher	0.92	(0.27)	0.92	(0.26)	0.92	(0.26)
Closeness with teacher	4.31	(0.65)	4.41	(0.61)	4.40	(0.61)
Conflict with teacher	1.65	(0.82)	1.59	(0.76)	1.59	(0.77)
SCHOOL CHARACTERISTICS						
Aggressive behaviors						
serious	0.03	(0.16)	0.01	(0.11)	0.01	(0.12)
moderate	0.11	(0.31)	0.08	(0.28)	0.09	(0.28)
minor/not a problem	0.87	(0.34)	0.91	(0.29)	0.90	(0.30)
Bullying						
daily/once a week	0.15	(0.35)	0.12	(0.33)	0.12	(0.33)
once a month	0.21	(0.41)	0.24	(0.43)	0.24	(0.43)
occasionally/never	0.64	(0.48)	0.64	(0.48)	0.64	(0.48)
Percent nonwhite	42.22	(32.64)	40.22	(32.47)	40.46	(32.50)
Percent free and reduced-price lunch	46.39	(31.15)	39.92	(30.39)	40.72	(30.56)
Teacher absenteeism						
serious	0.00	(0.03)	0.00	(0.02)	0.00	(0.02)
moderate	0.04	(0.19)	0.05	(0.21)	0.05	(0.21)
minor/not a problem	0.96	(0.20)	0.95	(0.21)	0.95	(0.21)
Theft						
daily/once a week	0.00	(0.03)	0.00	(0.05)	0.00	(0.05)
once a month	0.04	(0.19)	0.03	(0.18)	0.03	(0.18)
occasionally/never	0.96	(0.19)	0.96	(0.19)	0.96	(0.19

In the comparison of parent-reported health ratings between chronic versus nonchronic absentees, a lower percentage of chronically absent children had excellent health, while a higher percentage had fair or poor health.

By racial and ethnic background, a higher proportion of chronically absent children were students of color, which reflects a broader nationwide trend in racial and ethnic disparities in absenteeism.[11] Just over half of chronic absentees (53 percent) were students of color (Asian, Black, Hispanic, Native American, Pacific Islander, or multiracial), while just 43 percent of those who were not chronically absent were students of color. Relative to their not chronically absent peers, chronically absent kindergarteners had parents who were more likely to be out of the labor market, while a lower proportion had parents who attended either a parent-teacher conference or a PTA meeting. Chronically absent kindergarteners had lower levels of closeness and higher levels of conflict with their teachers. Chronically absent children attended schools that were, on average, comparable to the schools their not chronically absent peers attended in terms of instances of aggressive behavior, bullying, teacher absenteeism, and theft. But they did attend schools with a higher proportion of students eligible for free and reduced-price lunch (FRPL) (46 percent versus 40 percent).

To quantify the variability in chronic absenteeism at different levels in the education system (e.g., between children versus between schools) and how much certain predictors explain of that variability, I used a statistical modeling procedure, multilevel logistic modeling, to quantify the relationship between the predictors at different levels of the educational system (child, classroom, and school) and the probability that a child is chronically absent. The model can be expressed in the form of an equation for child i in classroom k in school j:

$$Y^*ijk = \alpha + \gamma \mathbf{x} + vk + ujk + \varepsilon_{ijk}$$

where $\mathbf{x}$ is a vector of predictors (e.g., prior absenteeism and health) whose effects are represented by γ. In the equation, vk, and ujk are random effects for classroom and school, respectively, whose associated variances are denoted as τ_2^2 and τ_3^2; and εijk is the individual error that follows a logistic distribution with a constant variance $\frac{\pi^2}{3}$. Further, the assumption is that the observed outcome of whether a child is chronically absent or not, $Yijk$, takes on a value of either a 1 or 0 based on an underlying (unobserved) number of absences, Y^*ijk, that reach or exceed a threshold T:

$$Yijk = \begin{cases} 1 & \text{if } Y^*ijk \geq T \\ 0 & \text{if } Y^*ijk < T \end{cases}$$

For instance, when a child was absent eleven or more days during the school year (moderate chronic absenteeism), Y_{ijk} takes on the value of 1, 0 otherwise (a child missed fewer than eleven days).

To determine how much variability in chronic absenteeism was attributable to systematic differences between schools, classrooms, and students within classrooms (i.e., the intraclass correlation coefficient [ICC]), I estimated a null model, one that contained no predictors. After fitting the null model, I fit a series of models to data to determine the amount of variability that the predictors explained. Then, to parse out the importance of individual factors relative to groups of factors, I added predictors to the model (e.g., health status) individually and then in substantive groups: child attributes and behaviors (e.g., prior chronic absenteeism, health status[12]); child demographic characteristics (e.g., race/ethnicity); parental attributes (e.g., employment status); classroom attributes; and school-level characteristics. Finally, I included all predictors in one final model. Except for prior chronic absenteeism, I incorporated predictors specific to a particular year (e.g., second grade) into only the models for that year.

To estimate how much of the total variability in chronic absenteeism that each predictor or set of predictors explained, I calculated McKelvey and Zavoina's R^2 using a three-step approach.[13] First, for each model, I made linear predictions for the outcome for each child (based on the estimated model coefficients, **x**, the fixed effects). Second, I calculated the variance of these linear predictions, $\hat{\sigma}_F^2$, which represents the estimated *variation explained* by a predictor or set of predictors. Finally, I calculated how much of the total variation in chronic absenteeism consisted of variation explained by the predictors by dividing the variation explained by the total variability, as follows:

$$R^2_{MZ} = \frac{\text{variation explained by the model}}{\text{total variation in chronic absenteeism}} = \frac{\hat{\sigma}_F^2}{\hat{\sigma}_F^2 + \hat{\tau}_2^2 + \hat{\tau}_3^2 + \frac{\pi^2}{3}}$$

In this equation, the numerator $\hat{\sigma}_F^2$ is the variation explained by a particular model's predictors (e.g., health), while the denominator is the *total variability* in chronic absenteeism, which is the sum of four parts: (1) the explained variability, $\hat{\sigma}_F^2$; (2) between-school variability, $\hat{\tau}_2^2$; (3) between-classroom variability, $\hat{\tau}_3^2$; and (4) between-child variability in chronic absenteeism, which is fixed, $\frac{\pi^2}{3} \approx 3.29$. Thus, hypothetically, if the variation explained by health was 5 and the total variability was 100, we would know that 5 percent of the total variability in chronic absenteeism was attributed to the health of a child. Factors that account for a larger share of variability, and therefore are more relevant in explaining variation in chronic absenteeism, would be expressed as larger percentages.

Results

As shown in figure 2.2, the majority of the total variability in chronic absenteeism in kindergarten and first and second grades exists between students: 69 percent, 80 percent, and 73 percent, respectively. The remaining variability is between classrooms and schools. Thus, while schools and classrooms account for a nontrivial share of the total variability in chronic absenteeism, the majority is attributed to systematic differences between children rather than systematic differences between either classrooms or schools. Importantly, this larger proportion of the variability which exists at the student level indicates that accounting for variability in chronic absenteeism will depend largely on child-level factors relative to either classroom- or school-level factors.

Figures 2.3, 2.4, and 2.5 display the percentage of variability in chronic absenteeism each predictor explains by grade level. In kindergarten, among the child-level predictors, health status explains the highest proportion of variability followed by approaches to learning and then racial and ethnic background. Parental socioeconomic status explains roughly the same amount of variability, as do the child-level predictors as a whole. Predictors

FIGURE 2.2   Proportion of variability in chronic absenteeism

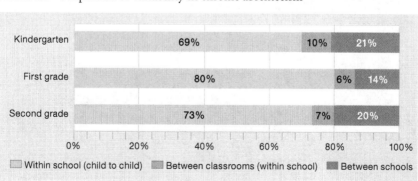

FIGURE 2.3 Explained variability in chronic absenteeism, kindergarten

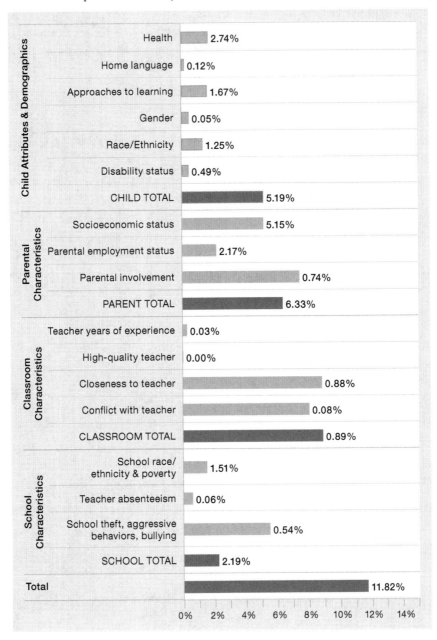

FIGURE 2.4 Explained variability in chronic absenteeism, first grade

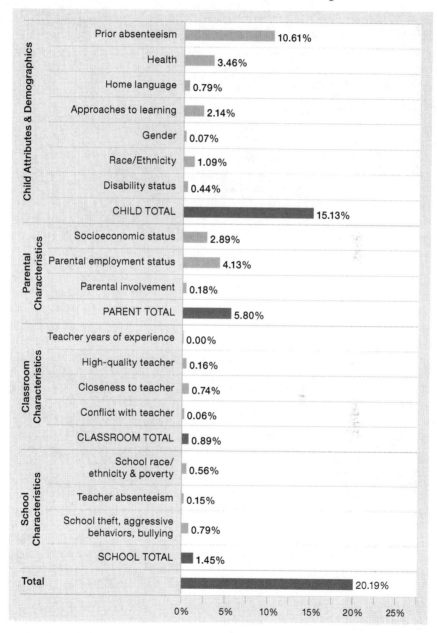

FIGURE 2.5 Explained variability in chronic absenteeism, second grade

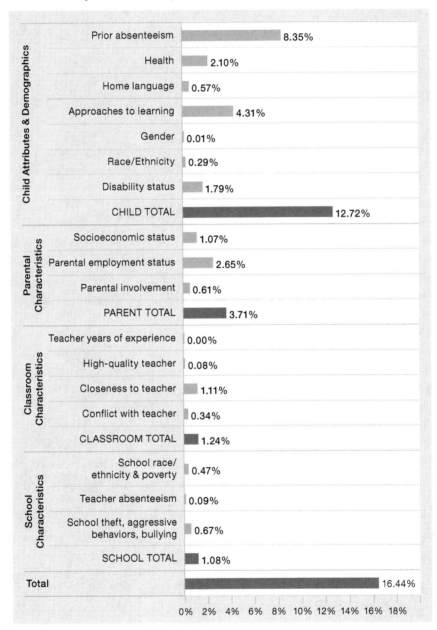

at the classroom and school levels account for relatively small shares of the total variability, ranging from almost no variability explained (e.g., if the child has a high-quality teacher) to school-level concentration of students of color and students eligible for free or reduced-price lunch. And we can collectively explain approximately 12 percent of the total variability; 88 percent remains unexplained. Note that the total percentage of variability explained with all predictors included is not cumulative, since some of predictors are correlated, so they jointly account for variability in chronic absenteeism.

In first grade, and consistent with the results for kindergarten, a child's health status, together with their approaches to learning scores and racial/ethnic backgrounds, helps explain variability. Collectively, these child-level attributes, in addition to prior chronic absenteeism, explain around 15 percent of the total variability. Parental SES and employment status continue to help explain variability in first graders' probability of being chronically absent. Collectively, these parent-level predictors account for a slightly higher degree of variability than was seen in kindergarten. Each of the classroom- and school-level predictors account for less than 1 percent of the variability; thus, they tend not to contribute much to our understanding of the total variability in chronic absenteeism. In contrast to the kindergarten results, more of the total variability in first grade can be explained by all of the model predictors, in part because chronic absenteeism in kindergarten is included which helps explain a large share of the variability in first grade. In fact, chronic absenteeism in kindergarten helps account for 10.6 percent of the variability in chronic absenteeism in first grade.

As children reach second grade, their health, approaches to learning, and racial/ethnic backgrounds continue to help explain variability. However, approaches to learning now accounts for a much larger share of variability relative to the share it explained in both kindergarten and first grades. In total, all child-level attributes explain roughly 13 percent of the total variability. Consistent with kindergarten and first grade results, both parental SES and employment status continue to explain variability in chronic absenteeism. In contrast to the results for a children's kindergarten and first-grade years, closeness with a teacher accounts for a larger (albeit still relatively small at 1 percent) share of the variability. The final model, which includes all relevant predictors, including school-level factors, explains about 16 percent of the variability; about 84 percent remains unexplained.

Though school-level predictors account for negligible amounts of total variability, they have the potential to explain larger proportions of between-school variability. Identifying which school-level predictors explain larger shares of between-school variability can be useful when thinking about factors that should be considered in the design of whole-school absenteeism interventions.

To gauge how much school predictors account for between-school variability in chronic absenteeism, I calculated proportion reduction in variance:[14]

$$\text{Proportion of variance explained} = \frac{\hat{\tau}_2^2 \text{ (null model)} - \hat{\tau}_2^2 \text{ with predictor)}}{\hat{\tau}_2^2 \text{ (null model)}}$$

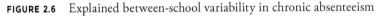

Figure 2.6 displays these results.[15] One noteworthy finding is the role of measures associated with a negative school climate; school-level theft, aggressive behaviors, and bullying together explain the highest proportion of between-school variability. School-level racial/ethnic concentration alongside poverty level also help explain variability, particularly in kindergarten. Finally, school-level predictors as a whole account for around 20 percent, 9 percent, and 10 percent of the between-school variability in kindergarten and first and second grades, respectively.

FIGURE 2.6 Explained between-school variability in chronic absenteeism

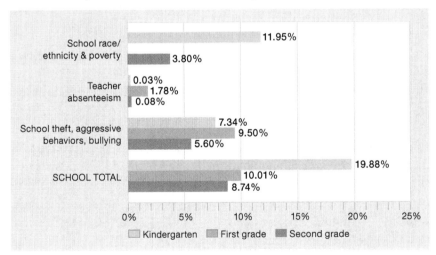

Discussion and Implications

There are several important takeaways from these analyses. First, variability in chronic absenteeism is largely attributable to individual differences relative to differences between classrooms or schools. Second, there is no one predictor or set of predictors that accounts for a large share of the variability in children's probabilities of being chronically absent. Of the proportion that I can explain (ranging from 12 percent in kindergarten to 20 percent in first grade), I am more successful in explaining total variability with individual-level predictors relative to classroom- or school-level predictors. Further, of the predictors, prior chronic absenteeism accounts for nearly half of total variability for first and second graders. Finally, while school-level factors account for a negligible amount of total variability, factors reflecting a negative school climate help explain between-school variability in chronic absenteeism.

Just as children's academic achievement varies more widely within schools versus between them, so does their propensity for being chronically absent.[16] Thus, addressing chronic absenteeism will require multitiered strategies that emphasize the individualized needs and challenges of children who struggle to attend school regularly.[17] Some of those needs are related to a child's health and learning strategies—both of which, as these results show, account for relatively larger shares of the variability in chronic absenteeism. Both are also within the purview of the educational system (learning more so versus health) and both are significantly predictive in ways that we expect: poorer health is linked to higher absenteeism, while higher approaches to learning are linked to lower absenteeism.

It's important also to keep in mind the role of parental attributes in explaining variability in absenteeism. Both parental socioeconomic status and employment help explain some, albeit a small proportion, of the variability.

The relatively large proportion of individual variability in absenteeism within schools also suggests that districtwide efforts at reducing absences at the school site level will require administrators to be attuned to individual differences within schools. If, for instance, a district wants schools to reduce their chronic absenteeism rate, they will need to look within their schools to identify key differences between children.

Finally, the strong predictive power of prior absenteeism and the substantial proportion that it explains relative to what can be explained overall suggests that efforts at reducing absenteeism in the earliest grades will be critical to prevent chronic absenteeism in future grades.

3

Attending to Attendance

Why Data Quality and Modeling Assumptions Matter When Using Attendance as an Outcome

SHAUN M. DOUGHERTY AND JOSHUA CHILDS

THE PREVALENCE OF attendance-based measures as outcomes when studying the effects of schooling has increased in recent years, with particular emphasis being placed on chronic absence.[1] However, there has been less focus on the relationship between specific measurement and modeling decisions concerning attendance and the resulting interest and inferences. With few exceptions, attendance outcomes are chosen and implemented without assessing the sensitivity of findings to the particular choice of measure or statistical model.[2] Focusing on how attendance is measured and modeled is particularly important because much of the research using attendance outcomes addresses critical issues of access and equity in social outcomes, demonstrating that absences are higher and educational outcomes are lower among lower-income students.[3] If attendance differs systematically by family income, it is critical that we understand how measurement and modeling decisions may impact the inferences we make regarding attendance and students experiencing disadvantage.

Research on absenteeism has not addressed concerns about the use of chronic absence as an outcome. Binary measures like being a "chronic absentee" rely on cutoffs in the attendance rate attendance behavior deemed to exceed a high level of concern. And there is considerable variability in the thresholds that states, let alone individual school districts, are using to define chronic absence. Since much of the focus on the importance of chronic absenteeism relates to its ability to predict other undesirable outcomes (e.g., the likelihood a student drops out), it is important to pin down how measuring absence might matter differently at various points in time in school (grade levels) as well as for a variety of student groups. In this chapter we point out the importance of acknowledging variation in what chronic absence might mean at various points in the educational process, and under different choices of measurement and modeling, and propose a way forward for research so that policy makers and practitioners can be better informed about how to interpret and use attendance-related research.

Why We Care About Attendance as an Outcome

Attendance is an important measure for policy makers, practitioners, and researchers. Schools use attendance as a way to capture evidence of potential challenges for families and children. In most elementary schools, attendance is tracked as a way to flag the need for outreach to families. In middle school and high school, attendance is a reliable predictor of student disengagement from school and, as such, is often used as a leading indicator for dropout. Increasingly, policy makers are also incorporating measures of attendance into accountability systems, including in many of the newly submitted and approved plans under the Every Student Succeeds Act (ESSA), the successor to No Child Left Behind.[4] In ESSA, chronic absenteeism fits within the law's requirement for indicators of school quality and student success (SQSS). The use of chronic absenteeism as a nonacademic indicator reflects ESSA's attempt to capture aspects of learning that are not often captured in traditional academic or testing methods. Given the variation across states in more traditional measures like academic standards, proficiency, and adequate yearly progress, it is not surprising that the operationalization of chronic absenteeism as a nonacademic indicator has resulted in states proposing a wide range of conceptions of chronic absenteeism. Indeed, the ways in which states would hold schools accountable for reducing chronic absenteeism, the variance of chronic absenteeism as an SQSS metric depending on type of school, and even the definition of chronic absenteeism differ by state.[5]

Plenty of research that evaluates the relationship between attendance and outcomes also bolsters the understanding that going to school is important. Evidence from early education– and elementary-focused studies show clear connections between school attendance and learning.[6] However, this association also extends to older children and includes promising, though limited, evidence that interventions to improve attendance can be effective.[7]

Research demonstrating that higher levels of attendance can lead to other bad outcomes has lead researchers and policy makers to seek out indicators of concerning attendance behavior so that the occurrence of such high levels can trigger interventions or other policy- and practice-based responses. In turn, this has led to the increased use of chronic absence as an outcome. Chronic absence is typically measured in a binary form; a student receives a value of 1 if they are absent above a defined threshold on absences (or below a threshold on attendance rate) and a 0 otherwise. Despite the generalized use of the term in research and policy conversations, there is no standardized definition of chronic absence in the research.[8] Ranges for what counts as "chronic" span from missing 10 school days to 18 days (10 percent of a 180-day school year). Opacity or inconsistency in the meaning of chronic absence is potentially problematic if the data include students who are mobile and who are enrolled only a small share of the total school year. However, these measures provide data that is more easily understood by parents and community members who can assist in curbing the impact of chronic absenteeism. Furthermore, it provides data points for where targeted interventions should be focused and on which student populations/subgroups.

Despite these potential benefits, the simplifying assumptions that using measures of chronic absence permit also invite potentially important technical flaws. Specifically, the increased focus on absence as an outcome of interest, particularly as part of state accountability plans, emphasizes the importance of understanding how decisions related to measurement and predictive modeling will influence the policy- and practice-related inferences that researchers, policy makers, and practitioners would like to make. For instance, the systematic differences in attendance patterns by grade in school and by family income suggest that any policy that ignores these dimensions of student experience may make bad decisions or interferences about their students.

Methods

Our study utilized a state longitudinal dataset covering the academic years 2002–2014. Analysis includes only students enrolled in grades 1 through 12 and includes more than 11 million student-by-year observations. We did not include students in kindergarten because not all schools have full-day kindergarten in this state, and research indicates that the length of the school day in kindergarten may impact attendance.[9]

The dataset includes basic demographic information on race, gender, ethnicity, and town of residence, as well as measures of what school a student is enrolled in, how many days they are enrolled in a given school year, and how many days they are recorded as being in attendance. Measures of whether students are identified as having a disability, eligible for free or reduced-price lunch, and/or eligible for English language learner services are also included.

We constructed the critical outcomes of interest from a handful of attendance-related measures maintained in the state longitudinal data system. Specifically, total days attended and total days enrolled were used to calculate days absent as well as a ratio measure of attendance rate. The attendance rate measure is then used to define binary measures of chronic absence. To demonstrate the sensitivity of inferences in the choice of cutoff defining chronic absenteeism, we use attendance rate thresholds that range from 85 percent to 95 percent. Importantly, this range overlaps with the cutoff of 10 percent most commonly adopted by policy makers or practitioners.

Findings from earlier work which demonstrates that attendance behavior and its relationship to learning differ by a student's family resources lead us to focus specifically on further understanding differences in attendance by family income.[10] Specifically, in our modeling approach, we focus on whether a student is eligible for free or reduced-price lunch to distinguish among families with more and less financial resources. We then focus on whether the way attendance is measured and modeled has differential meaning for higher- and lower-income students. To ensure that this coarse indicator for family income is not really picking up differences on some other important dimension, we also add additional control variables, including gender, race and ethnicity, disability status, English learner (EL) status, town of residence, school and district of enrollment, and total days enrolled, which improve precisions and reduce potential bias.

To understand average attendance outcomes, we provide basic summary statistics for all attendance and absence measures of interest for all students, disaggregating by grade in school and free or reduced-price lunch status to highlight important descriptive differences by grade and family income. These summary statistics also illustrate the ways in which attendance can differ depending on the outcome used. Knowing that descriptive differences may mask important and more complex relationships, we build on this descriptive evidence to prove how the modeling decisions that get made in predicting attendance outcomes depend on the measure of attendance and the model used to predict it. In particular, we demonstrate that how chronic absence is defined impacts key inferences of interest, particularly when trying to estimate differences in the incidence of chronic absence by grade in school or by family income. Given the highly skewed nature of the distribution of attendance measures, we show how modeling choices matter when trying to reproduce the underlying attendance phenomenon of interest.

Results

Overall, results from these analyses indicate substantial variation in patterns of attendance by grade level and eligibility for subsidized meals. These differences are evident for all attendance measures and persist even in regression-adjusted estimates that account for other student and community-specific factors that may influence attendance.

Differences Over Time

We find clear differences in the attendance behavior of students by grade and level of schooling, as well as by whether their families are ever eligible for subsidized meals. Not only do attendance outcomes differ along these key measures, but there is evidence of a clear, descriptive interaction. Specifically, rates of attendance fall in later grades, and, independent of grade, attendance is always lower among students who are eligible for the free or reduced-price lunch program. These differences in attendance by grade and family income exist regardless of which attendance measure is used.

We demonstrate the difference between attendance rates by family income and by grade in school in figure 3.1, which shows that rates are higher and subsequently increase in early grades and then fall off, with the largest drop occurring in high school. At all points there is a clear difference in attendance rate by family income, with children from less-resourced families attending school at lower rates. Also of note is that the income-based difference is largest in high school, where earlier evidence suggests this is also tied to differences in high school graduation rates.

Accounting for Measurement

How we model attendance rates may impact our ability to capture fully the underlying processes related to absences from school. Perhaps more importantly, the threshold used to define chronic absence alters the share of students who are identified as chronically absent, and the implications for this choice also affect how we understand differential patterns by family income.

We consider how cutoffs used to define chronic absence relate to estimates of the difference in chronic absence by subsidized meal eligibility. In figure 3.2

FIGURE 3.1   Average attendance rates by grade and eligibility for subsidized meals

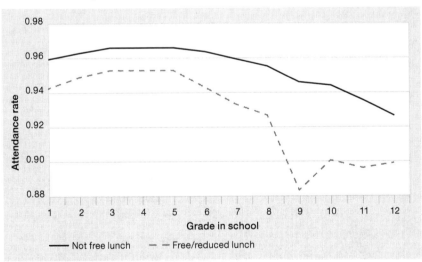

Source: Adapted from Shaun M. Dougherty, "How Data Quality and Modeling Assumptions Matter to Assess Dimensions of Inequality," *Journal of Education for Students Placed at Risk (JESPAR)* 23, nos. 1–2 (2018), doi:10.1080/10824669.2018.1438203.

FIGURE 3.2 Percentage of students identified as chronically absent under various definitions of chronic absence, by subsidized meal eligibility

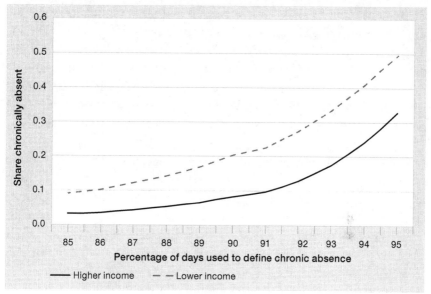

Percentage of days used to define chronic absence

—— Higher income   — — Lower income

we present the descriptive share of students who are identified as chronically absent using a range of attendance rates to denote chronic absence. The share of students identified as chronically absent is on the vertical axis, and the cutoff used to define chronic absence is on the horizontal axis. The two trends relate to students who are, and are not, eligible for subsidized meals. This visual evidence clearly demonstrates that the percentage of students who are identified as chronically absent differs substantially based on cutoff choice. Also clear is that the higher the threshold, the bigger the difference in the share of students who are chronically absent when measured by family income. In fact, when using a threshold of 90 percent attendance to define chronic absence, the difference in the share of students identified as chronic absence is 11 percentage points higher for students eligible for subsidized meals. However, at a cutoff of 95 percent, the difference is 16 percentage points. Thus, there are clear policy implications for this differential relationship between chronic absence, family income, and the cutoff used to define chronic absence.

Accounting for Modeling Strategy

To demonstrate the relative merit of using models whose assumptions better fit the underlying data, we include below a pair of figures that compare the distribution of predicted outcomes when using both the conventional ordinary least squares (OLS) approach and models that better capture important dimensions of the distribution of the outcomes of interest. In addition to the traditional OLS model, we employ Tobit and fractional logit models, both of which are designed to always predict within the bounds of 0 and 1 (natural bounds of attendance rates) and that better adapt to the skewed distribution of this outcome.

Figure 3.3 shows the distributions of attendance rate in raw form (panel A), predicted values using an OLS model (panel B), a two-way censored Tobit model (panel C), and a fractional logit model (panel D). What is immediately clear is that OLS fails to reproduce the skew of the underlying distribution for attendance rate, whereas the fractional logit model appears to best reproduce the actual raw data. Figure 3.4 presents an analogous set of figures using

FIGURE 3.3 Distribution of raw attendance rate and predicted rates using several statistical models

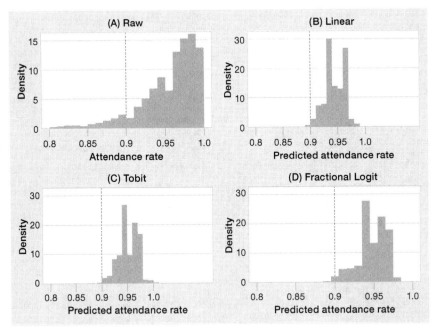

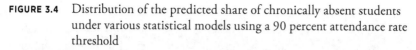

FIGURE 3.4 Distribution of the predicted share of chronically absent students under various statistical models using a 90 percent attendance rate threshold

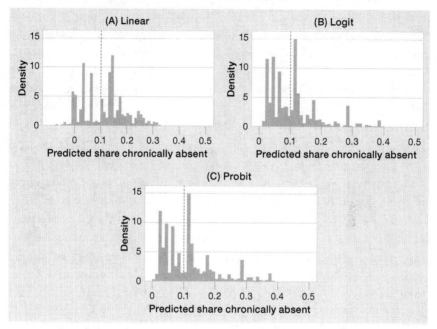

chronic absence as the outcome but fitting models that are better tailored to a binary outcome that occurs with relatively low frequency. Panel A displays the OLS estimates of the percentage of students who are chronically absent, panel B presents estimates under a logistic model, and panel C shows predictions from a probit model.

Consistent with what we demonstrated using attendance rate as the outcome, we again find that non-OLS approaches are better at reproducing the underlying data. For this binary measure, chronic absence, the most glaring evidence of problems with modeling is seen in the predicted negative values generated by OLS. Thus, while we did not rigorously compare multiple dimensions of model fit, we did provide compelling evidence that model choice does influence the extent to which predicted values reflect the underlying distribution of the outcome data. This fact alone has implications for how analyses are interpreted, especially for points in the distribution away from the mean. Specifically, in the linear model we systematically underpredict the occurrence of larger shares of students being chronically absent, including the average share of students to cross the threshold defining chronic absence. As a result, the specific choice used to define chronic absence can influence predicted absence behavior in the statistical models. The implications of this effect have further implications for whether, how, and for whom schools provide supports. Without recognizing how measurement choices impact statistical predictions, practitioners and policy makers will be blind to the fact that these particular choices dictate who does and does not receive appropriate attention.

Discussion

With our study, we aimed to demonstrate that attendance is not a monolithic outcome and that how we measure it, at what grade and for which students, has implications for the inferences we want to draw from the data. Our findings—that attendance is systematically better at lower grades and for higher-income students—have clear relevance to the policies that could and should be designed to identify and help address problematic levels of school absence. These findings highlight the importance of measurement decisions when defining a measure like chronic absenteeism and have import for researchers who employ such measures and for the policy makers and practitioners who use them as in many states' proposed ESSA plans. Especially salient is that these measurement decisions differentially affect inferences made from them depending on a student's eligibility for subsidized meals, a group that is known to already be more likely to bear other risk factors.

Our findings both corroborate and challenge previous evidence that was focused on answering similar questions using different data, and they also extend the related research in a few important ways. First, by following students across a large segment of their K–12 education, we were able to cover several levels of schooling and break the earlier, narrower focus on just single levels.[11] This longitudinal approach allowed us to reduce concerns that student-specific factors might drive attendance behavior at any one point in time. In addition, while not focused on learning outcomes, our focus on differences in attendance outcomes by socioeconomic status, school level, and measurement and modeling decisions adds important policy relevant information that has to this point been underexplored.

Beyond policy relevance, our findings also have import with respect to recent scholarship that has also focused on absences, especially studies including the use of cutoffs to define chronic absence. Our evidence corroborates several other recent studies which find that the chronic absence threshold does not actually predict important differences in outcomes. For instance, Gershenson and colleagues found that higher rates of absence are associated with lower academic achievement among elementary school students and that those effects on outcomes are larger for lower-income students.[12] However, that study did not find discontinuous effects around the threshold for chronic absence, suggesting that a binary measure of absenteeism has limited value in relating school attendance with learning outcomes. Our results are also similar to conclusions reached by Morrissey and colleagues, who demonstrated that more absences were associated with lower achievement but that there were no nonlinearities of effects to be captured using cutoff-based measures of absence.[13]

The best available estimate of the occurrence of chronic absence suggest that the national rate may be about 14 percent.[14] We argue that this single estimate of chronic absence masks important variation across school grade and student characteristics. In this state, about 12 percent of students would be identified as chronically absent using the 90 percent attendance rate threshold, yet this estimate differs considerably by school level. In high school 18 percent of students would be identified with absence rates of 11 percent and 7 percent in middle and elementary school, respectively, when using the 90 percent threshold. Thus, the threshold for chronic absence represents the twentieth percentile in high school, the tenth percentile in middle school, and below the tenth percentile in elementary school. Assuming a national graduation rate of about 80 percent, it might seem reasonable to identify the twentieth percentile of attendance as roughly corresponding to the group of students who would be less likely to finish high school.

It's hard to argue, however, that we should apply the same metric, in absolute terms, to much younger students without additional evidence that such a threshold is really predictive of other problematic short-term outcomes. Rather than simply relying on models of absence that were generated to identify high school dropouts and apply them to younger grades, we might be due for an update to the system that better incorporates longitudinal student data, differentiates models by school level or grade, and includes interaction effects among important student demographic characteristics (e.g., race/ethnicity, family income). For instance, the 2016 release of the US Department of Education's Office for Civil Rights data collection, which revealed that 13 percent of all US students were chronically absent in 2013–14, could provide new insights on chronic absence estimates and an understanding of the degree to which students are affected by missing multiple days of school.

As with differences by schooling level, the sensitivity of conclusions to cutoff choices and subsidized meal eligibility highlight another area of possible concern. Among students eligible for subsidized meals, the 90 percent attendance rate threshold for chronic absence represents the thirtieth, twentieth, and fifteenth percentiles for high, middle, and elementary schools, respectively. Thus, these cutoffs suggest that more conservative choices of attendance thresholds could be better when trying to understand the potential risks associated with absences among lower-income students.

Whether attendance-based policies are used for accountability or monitoring, more attention must be paid to acknowledging baseline differences in the typical attendance behavior based on a student's grade in school and eligibility for subsidized meals. With more than half of states using chronic absenteeism as a SQSS indicator in their ESSA plans, states are in a unique position to implement systems and accountability standards that are flexible to the types of differences in attendance indicated in this study. Furthermore, ESSA has given states the flexibility to use chronic absenteeism as a measure that could lead to innovation as it relates to reducing chronic absenteeism. With this information, schools and districts should be proactive in designing systems and implementing practices that account for these differences and appropriately focus on the different subgroups affected at a greater rate by being chronically absent from school. Also, schools and districts need reliable data that can assist them in reaching their state's goals in their ESSA plans while also instituting interventions that can improve student attendance and academic outcomes.

In addition, choices of threshold for chronic absence must be carefully selected in studies that attempt to understand differences among more and less economically privileged groups. While we point out only the importance of family income in understanding measurement and modeling decisions on policy outcomes, researchers should be aware that similarly heterogeneous implications may exist by race, gender, and identified disabilities.

Further, if chronic absence is to be used as a diagnostic measure in early warning systems, such systems need to account for the fact that patterns of attendance in earlier grades appear to operate differently than in later grades. Additionally, for students who are eligible for subsidized meals, differentiated thresholds should be used to diagnose patterns of potentially problematic behavior. Both of these recommendations relate directly to the fact that differences in the underlying distributions evaluated around the same threshold used to define a binary outcome result in systematically different conclusions depending on which distribution one is located.[15]

For policy makers looking to set attendance thresholds in accountability systems, it is also worth noting that while all measures are subject to distortion when they receive greater focus (Campbell's law), cutoff-based measures are more easily subject to manipulation. This particular point garners attention as at least thirty-seven states appear to have included chronic absenteeism in their accountability plans under ESSA, and it is not yet clear whether a common threshold for defining the outcome has been adopted or whether appropriate differentiation by grade-level or eligibility for subsidized lunch has been considered.[16]

Educators are expected to use data to improve teaching and learning, student outcomes, and promote successful matriculation to the next grade level or graduation. Educators are also expected to incorporate and use a variety of data to properly assess students and then relay that information to parents and relevant stakeholders. However, when it comes to data and data use, most educators interact with student achievement data that is rarely connected with attendance or nonacademic outcomes data. What complicates matters is that educators, while expecting to know student-, classroom-, school-, or district-level data, still struggle with using data in their day-to-day practice. Adding another data metric, such as chronic absenteeism, without proper training, could lead educators to misunderstand or misuse attendance data.[17] Our findings suggest a need for those states that have included chronic absenteeism in their accountability plans to focus on providing professional development that trains educators on how to make sense of chronic absenteeism data. Furthermore, educators should be trained on understanding the pattern of attendance over time during a student's K–12 schooling experience. This will give the educators an opportunity to see their role in curbing chronic absenteeism and understand how to incorporate relevant strategies and interventions into their practice. Data should inform educator practice and be incorporated into teaching and leadership routines that will lead to improved learning environments, school culture, and school policy so that chronically absent students are no longer "hidden in plain sight."[18]

Accountability systems that account for the differentiation in patterns of attendance could help spur the development of interventions and strategies that could lead to the improvement of student attendance. These interventions should hit multiple dimensions within a student's daily life and should consider the range of experiences students have, especially those that come from low-socioeconomic backgrounds.[19] Also, knowing that the pattern of attendance differs between earlier and later grades, policy makers and researchers should focus on making sure that interventions are grade-level and context relevant. Approaches might include messaging parents around the importance of enrolling their young children in preK and kindergarten or creating strategic partnerships that involve multiple stakeholders providing their expertise around addressing student attendance. In addition, states should begin to get at the root causes of why students miss school.[20] In doing so, states could develop improved protocols and metrics to capture absence reasons and provide another indicator for researchers and policy makers to better understand the students who are missing a significant number of school days.

The right measures and modeling could also lead to better data sharing agreements and cross-sector collaborations among schools, districts, and community organizations that are focused on improving student attendance. Clear data metrics could lead to more learning opportunities among various stakeholders, a more robust policy agenda that focuses on transforming educator practice, and specific policies and interventions that help to reduce chronic absence.

While education policy makers and practitioners have made important strides by more fully incorporating the importance of attendance and, in particular, high levels of absenteeism, there remains room for improvement in the way they approach this work. In particular, as we show in this chapter, the specific choices made about how to define problematic levels of absence also impact how we conceive of between-group differences in attendance behavior. Thus, as practice and policy advance, it is crucial that more nuance is incorporated into the measurement choices that are made and how those choices are further related local policy decisions.

4

The Distributional Impacts of Student Absences on Academic Achievement

SETH GERSHENSON, JESSICA RAE MCBEAN,
AND LONG TRAN

A SERIES OF RECENT rigorous academic studies document the harm that student absences inflict on student achievement.[1] Evidence of a causal relationship between absences and achievement has motivated educators, school administrators, and policy makers to reassess and create both proactive and reactive interventions that might lessen the consequences of student absences. It has also led policy makers to explicitly consider attendance as an indicator of school and student success. However, the extant research base that motivates such interventions and policies focuses exclusively on the average effects of student absences. While average effects conveniently reduce the relationship between absences and achievement to a single number that represents our best guess of how an absence (or chronic absence) would affect the test scores of a representative student, which undoubtedly adds to our understanding of how absences disrupt educational and developmental processes, they overlook potential variation across the achievement distribution in the relationship between absences and student achievement. The limitations of focusing solely on average effects has been discussed in the context of instructional time and school vouchers, but this nuance has yet to be considered in the case of student absences.[2] Understanding the extent to which the impact of absences varies across the achievement distribution has important implications for policy makers seeking to either close achievement gaps or improve the achievement of schools' lowest-performing students.

In this chapter we address this gap in knowledge by extending the methods used in past research to isolate the harmful *average* effects of student absences to instead examine how student absences shape the entire *distribution* of student achievement.[3] We do so using quantile regressions, which model conditional quantiles (percentiles) of the achievement distribution in a similar fashion to how linear regressions model the conditional mean of student achievement.[4] Specifically, we use student-level data on first and third graders who participated in the Tennessee STAR (Student Teacher Achievement Ratio) class size reduction experiment to estimate value-added quantile regressions that relate student absences to student achievement at each decile of the achievement distribution. Consistent with previous research, we first replicate the basic result that, on average, a one standard deviation (SD) increase in absences (6.3) reduces achievement by 0.03 to 0.04 test score SD.[5] Our novel contribution, though, is showing that the harmful effects of student absences are actually fairly constant across the achievement distribution. This means that the extant literature's focus on the average effects of student absences is appropriate and not missing significant nuances in the relationship between absences and achievement.

The Setting for Our Analysis

Tennessee's Project STAR was a seminal field experiment in education designed to identify the impact of class size on student achievement.[6] It began in 1985–86 by randomly assigning kindergarten students and teachers in participating schools to either small- or regular-sized classrooms. The experiment continued over the next three years, randomly assigning students from the 1986 kindergarten cohort to small- and regular-sized classrooms in grades 1–3 while also refreshing the analytic sample in each year with new entrants to participating schools. Small classes significantly improved student performance on standardized tests.[7] Subsequent analyses document long-run effects of random assignment to a small classroom on educational attainment.[8] Random assignment to a small class may have also reduced absences by about one per year in kindergarten and third grade.[9]

While Project STAR influenced debates over the efficacy of class size reduction, other researchers recognized that the random assignment of students and teachers to classrooms could be leveraged to study other questions. For example, scholars have leveraged the random classroom assignments generated by the STAR experiment to estimate the impacts on test scores of having a same-race teacher, the long-run effects of high-quality kindergarten classrooms on earnings, and peer effects.[10] Here we similarly use Project STAR data to address a question unrelated to class size, asking, "How do student absences affect the distribution of test scores?"

We do not directly exploit the random assignment of students and teachers to classrooms since student absences were not randomly assigned to students, and also because doing so would be both unethical and impossible. Nor is our goal to estimate the impact of classroom characteristics, which were randomly assigned, on student outcomes. Nonetheless, Project STAR's random assignment does alleviate some concerns common to research on student absences. First, random assignment mitigates the concern that students with past attendance issues are assigned to particularly effective teachers, as research shows that teachers affect student attendance.[11] Second, it addresses the concern that students prone to attendance issues are sorted into classrooms with students who have similar attendance (and related behavioral) issues, in which case the effect of absences might be confounded with classroom-level peer effects.[12] To our knowledge, the relationship between attendance and achievement has yet to be studied in the public-use Project STAR data. Thus, documenting the impact of absences on achievement in the Project STAR schools adds to the generalizability of extant evidence on the harmful effects of student absences and is a secondary contribution of this chapter.

Our empirical analysis focuses on the relationship between absences and achievement in grades 1 and 3. While the STAR experiment covered a single cohort of students as they progressed from kindergarten to third grade, attendance data was not collected in second grade, and thus the lag score value-added models (VAMs) cannot be estimated for the kindergarten year because there is no lagged measure of achievement. the average first- and third-grade

STAR student was absent about seven times, which is similar to the average absence rates observed in the nationally representative ECLS-K (Early Childhood Longitudinal Study: Kindergarten Cohort) survey and statewide administrative data from North Carolina.[13] The chronic absence rate among STAR students was about 6–7 percent, which is also similar to corresponding rates in the ECLS-K and North Carolina.[14] We define *chronically absent* as being absent eighteen or more days during the school year; this is the most commonly used definition of chronic absence and it corresponds to about 10 percent of school days. Figure 4.1 reports a histogram and kernel density estimate that show the distribution of student absences.

Figure 4.2 motivates the analysis by plotting the distribution of math scores separately for students who were and were not chronically absent.[15] Two points merit attention. First, the vertical bars show that the average score of chronically absent students is significantly lower than that of students who were not chronically absent. This is consistent with previous research documenting the achievement gap between more- and less-absent students. Second, the distribution of math scores for chronically absent students is

FIGURE 4.1   Distribution of total annual absences

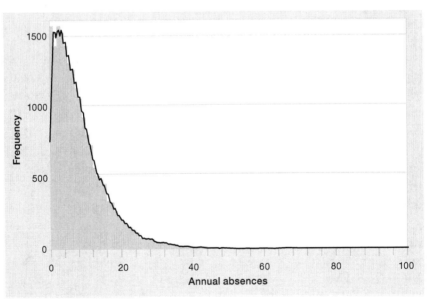

Notes: The bars represent histogram (one absence bins). The line is a kernel density plot.

FIGURE 4.2 Math score distributions of chronically absent and non-chronically absent students

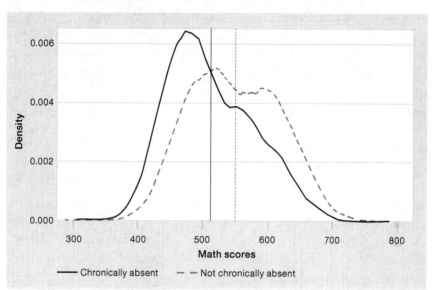

Notes: Distributions are kernel density plots. Vertical bars represent mean scores. Epanechnikov kernel with bandwidth of 13.1715.

decidedly to the left of the non–chronically absent distribution. However, the distributions have different shapes, suggesting that the effect of absences might vary at different points of the distribution.

How We Isolate the Impact of Student Absences

Following Gershenson and colleagues, we investigate the relationship between student absences and academic achievement by including absences as a contemporaneous input in VAMs of the education production function.[16] Intuitively, VAMs exploit longitudinal student data by using lagged test scores to proxy for the unobserved histories of educational and familial inputs received by each child. Accordingly, our baseline model of the spring test score (y) of student i in classroom j in grade g is

$$y_{ijg} = \alpha y_{i,g_{-1}} + f(A_{ig}) + \beta \mathbf{x}_{ig} + \eta_j + u_{ijg}$$

where **x** is a set of indicators for student characteristics such as race, gender, and free-lunch receipt, the latter of which can vary over time; η is a classroom fixed effect (FE); and u is a composite error term that contains student i's innate ability as well as unobserved, year-specific factors that affect achievement.[17] We let absences (A) enter the model linearly because Gershenson and colleagues show that the effect is approximately linear.[18] However, we also estimate specifications that replace A with a "chronically absent" indicator that equals 1 if the student was absent 18 or more times during the year, and 0 otherwise.

The year, grade, teacher, and school indicators commonly included in VAMs are subsumed by the classroom indicators, which are crucial to our identification strategy. Specifically, classroom FEs are indicator variables that control for the common factors experienced by all students in a given classroom; therefore, they control for nonrandom sorting of teachers across schools and classrooms, classroom-specific shocks that jointly influence both absences and achievement (e.g., a flu epidemic, a particularly effective teacher), and potential differences across classrooms in how absences are coded.[19] As a result, our estimates of absences' effects on performance rely on within-classroom variation in student absences, holding past achievement constant. Intuitively, this means that all estimates are generated by comparisons between the current outcomes of students who were in the same classroom and had the same test score in the previous year. Because students in the same classroom are exposed to the same peers, same teacher, same broader school climate, same grading standards, and same absence-recording procedures, this strategy effectively eliminates all potential school- and classroom-level confounders.

We begin by estimating the equation by ordinary least squares (OLS), essentially replicating past research using a different dataset. The OLS estimates of a linear model such as this equation provide evidence of absences' effects on the conditional mean of achievement; that is, *on average*, how does an additional absence affect achievement, net of prior achievement, student background, and so on? This is not say that all students are affected in the exact same way. Indeed, some individual students may be harmed more and some less by additional absences. But the OLS estimate tells us the average of these individual effects. Average effects are appealing for two main reasons. First, everyone is familiar with the concept of averages, so there is no new terminology to explain. Second, the average effect is a single parameter value that is easily reported and interpreted.

However, the simplicity and elegance of OLS estimation of average effects comes with two main costs, or limitations. First, OLS estimates (and averages in general) are susceptible to the influence of outlying (extreme) observations. Second, by assuming a constant average effect for every student in the sample, the OLS estimate necessarily ignores the possibility that student absences affect the entire distribution of student achievement, whether or not the mean of the distribution remains the same. Accordingly, we address these shortcomings by estimating quantile regressions that take the right side of equation as the linear index.

As the name suggests, quantile regressions estimate the effect of independent variables (e.g., student absences) on specific quantiles of the outcome distribution. This means that we no longer think about what, on average, will happen to a specific individual but, rather, about what will happen to the distribution of outcomes for individuals who receive the treatment. To fix ideas, consider the binary treatment of "chronic absence." In the linear regression case, the OLS estimate identifies the average difference in an outcome, say test scores, between students who were and were not chronically absent (treated). In the quantile regression case, for the fiftieth quantile (the median), the quantile regression coefficient estimate represents the difference between the median scores of those who were and were not chronically absent. We similarly estimated a unique coefficient (effect) for each quantile (percentile).

A simple thought experiment makes clear the difference between constant and distributional effects (figure 4.3). Suppose that a group of ten students are sent to the school gymnasium, where they are randomly sorted into two groups of five: the A Team and the B Team. Each group forms a line, where students' places in line relate to differences in performance. Because team assignment was randomly selected, we'd expect performance in the two groups to be similar. The result is two identical lines with similar spacing, start points, and end points (3A). Now suppose that all members of the B Team are forced to be absent and the effect of that absence is a constant, average effect (as estimated by OLS). The result is that each student in the line moves backward by the same number of steps (3B). Now entertain the possibility that in addition to moving students on the B Team backward, the absence also changed the spacing between the students. For example, suppose that students towards the end of the line moved farther backward than their peers in the front of the line, because it was more difficult for them to catch up following the absence (3C). Alternatively, it could be that absences

FIGURE 4.3 Visualizing distributional effects

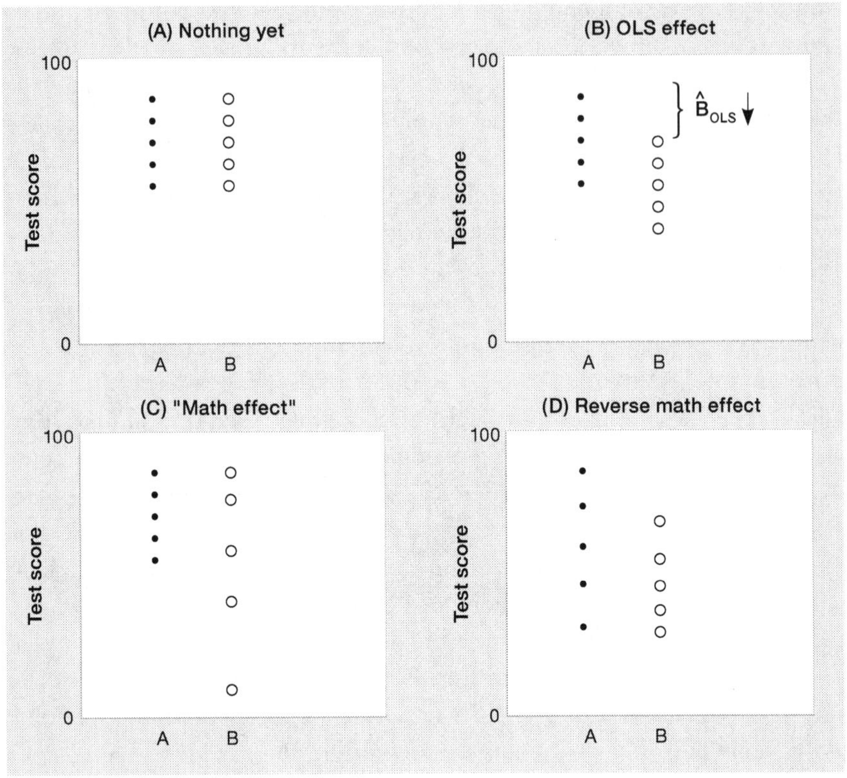

prevent students from attaining high levels of achievement while doing relatively little harm to low-achievers who would score about the same regardless of being absent (3D).

The scenarios presented in figure 4.3 highlight the misleading conclusions that might be reached by focusing only on constant, average effects of student absences. We address this gap in understanding by estimating the impact of student absences on each quintile of the achievement distribution.[20]

How Absences Affect the Distribution of Student Achievement

It is easiest to report, compare, and interpret quantile regression estimates visually. Accordingly, the OLS estimates (average effects) and quantile-regression estimates (distributional effects) of third-grade students' absences' effects at each decile of the third-grade math score distribution are reported in figure 4.4. Figure 4.5 does the same for the effect of being chronically absent. All estimates come from the linear- and quantile-regression versions of the equation. Patterns and magnitudes for the reading results and first-grade results are qualitatively similar and are therefore omitted in the interest of brevity.

The solid horizontal line in figure 4.4 represents the OLS estimate of the average harm associated with one additional absence in third grade on the standardized third-grade math test. The dashed horizontal lines represent the 95 percent confidence interval, which excludes 0, indicating that the estimated effect is statistically significantly different from 0 at the 0.05 level. The point estimate of -0.007 is identical to the corresponding point estimate in North Carolina reported in Gershenson et al., suggesting that the harmful effects of absences are approximately constant across time and locale.[21] Specifically,

FIGURE 4.4   Marginal effect of one absence on math scores in grade 3

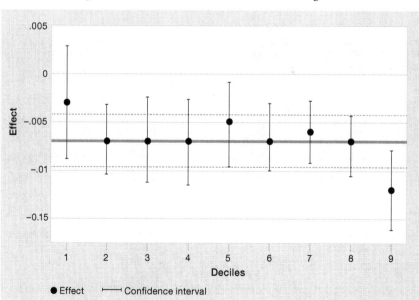

Notes: The solid line and the circles represent the OLS and quantile regression coefficient estimates, respectively. The dashed lines and the error bars represent the corresponding 95 percent confidence intervals.

FIGURE 4.5   Effect of chronic absence on math scores in grade 3

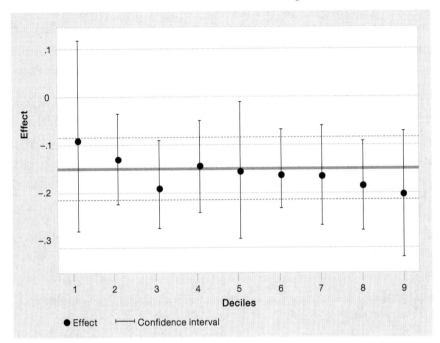

Notes: The solid line and the circles represent the OLS and quantile regression coefficient estimates, respectively. The dashed line and the error bars represent the corresponding 95 percent confidence intervals. The chronic absence indicator equals 1 if 18 or more absences, 0 otherwise.

the point estimate of 0.007 indicates that, on average, 10 additional absences reduce achievement by about 7 percent of a test score SD.

Here we also report quantile regression estimates that reflect the impact of absences on different parts of the achievement distribution. The dots in figure 4.4 represent the quantile regression estimate of the effect of an absence on each decile of the distribution. The associated error bars are 95 percent confidence intervals, which show the range of estimates that we'd expect to see in 95 percent of cases were the same analysis to be repeated hundreds of times on different samples. All but one of the error bars exclude zero, indicating that the quantile regression estimates are also statistically significant at traditional confidence levels. Interestingly, the nine quantile coefficients bounce around the OLS line in no discernible pattern, and seven lie within the OLS confidence interval. This suggests that the effect on each decile is approximately the same as the OLS (average) estimate. Overall, then, figure 4.4 provides no evidence that absences change the shape or spread of the achievement distribution and, instead, that they shift it to the left.

Two slight exceptions to this interpretation are observed in the tails of the distribution: the tenth and ninetieth percentiles. Regarding the former, there is no significant difference in the tenth percentile score of students who do and do not experience one additional absence. The effect is about half as large as the OLS estimate and statistically indistinguishable from zero. Regarding the former, the effect of a marginal absence on the ninetieth percentile is about twice as large as the OLS estimate and strongly statistically significant. Together, these results might suggest that high achievers are disproportionately harmed by absences, while low achievers are not. However, we caution against making too much of these results, as both estimates are relatively imprecise, and neither is significantly different from the OLS estimate.

Figure 4.5 presents the same set of estimates for a model that operationalized absences' role in the educational process as a binary indicator for chronic absence. The reason is that, although the average effect of absences is linear, it is possible that there are nonlinearities in the effect of absences across the achievement distribution.[22] Figure 4.5 makes clear that there are no such nonlinearities, as the quantile estimates all fall within the OLS confidence interval and bounce around the OLS point estimate. Moreover, these estimates are exactly what we would expect to see if the effects were additively linear: they are about twenty times the linear estimate, since being chronically absent means being absent about twenty times. Like the linear model reported in figure 4.4, figure 4.5 suggests that the harmful effects of student absences are approximately constant across the achievement distribution.

What We've Learned about the Distributional Impacts of Student Absences

The extant literature on the impact of absences on student achievement focuses entirely on average effects estimated via linear-in-parameters regression models. While this focus is a natural starting point for the study of any educational input, it necessarily overlooks the possibility that student absences alter the shape and spread of the achievement distribution in ways that linear estimators such as OLS miss. This chapter fills this gap in knowledge by estimating quantile regressions that examine whether the impact of absences on student achievement varies across the achievement distribution.

We find no evidence that student absences alter the shape or spread of the achievement distribution. Rather, student absences reduce achievement by simply shifting the achievement distribution to the left. Accordingly, at least in the case of the relationship between absences and student achievement, OLS estimates of the average effects of student absences adequately capture the policy-relevant relationship of interest.

Ruling out the presence of nuanced distributional impacts of student absences is useful for the policy discussions in this volume for two main reasons. First, it means that attendance advocates can focus on a simple, easy-to-interpret number: the average effect of chronic absence. This number can be used in cost-benefit analyses of interventions and in selling the importance of attendance, and associated interventions, to parents, students, schools, teachers, and policy makers. Second, that the effect is constant and shifts the entire achievement distribution to the left means that increasing attendance is good for everyone and is therefore an easy policy and intervention to rally behind. Attendance can be a bipartisan cause relevant to schools in all parts of the country and to schools serving students of all sociodemographic backgrounds.

The quantile regression analyses we present fill one of the few remaining holes in the research literature on the harmful effects of student attendance. Rigorous studies have now documented an arguably causal impact of student absences that is remarkably constant across schools, students, and geographic locales. Moreover, this effect is approximately linear in the number of absences and approximately constant across the achievement distribution. That the harm caused by student absences is fairly constant across schools and students of differing backgrounds and linearly additive in the number of absences suggests that the precise definition of chronic absence used in school accountability policies is relatively unimportant. A student who is absent 15, 18, or 20 times per year will score about 10–15 percent of a SD lower than an otherwise similar student who misses only a handful of days per year. These results suggest that educators' and policy makers' valuable but limited bandwidth can be focused on implementing interventions that boost attendance and help students catch up following an absence, rather than getting mired in technical debates about the exact threshold used to define chronic absence.

It also suggests that while all students would benefit from such interventions, targeted interventions provide an opportunity to close achievement gaps, as students of color and students from low-income households are absent more frequently than their white and more advantaged counterparts.

PART II

Policies, Programs, and Practices

5

Reinforcing Student Attendance

Shifting Mind-Sets and Implementing Data-Driven Improvement Strategies During School Transitions

STACY B. EHRLICH AND DAVID W. JOHNSON

BEING IN SCHOOL MATTERS. A lot. School attendance is one of the most consistent predictors of student's academic success, from pre-kindergarten through high school. Students with better school attendance have better learning outcomes, including earning higher grades, failing fewer classes, and having higher test scores.[1] This is not altogether surprising since students who attend school more often have more opportunities to learn. Given these strong relationships, attendance can serve as an early indicator of whether students are likely to struggle or succeed with academics in the future. In fact, students' attendance rates in the middle and high school grades are stronger predictors of their future educational attainments than are their test scores or demographic characteristics.[2]

While regular school attendance promotes learning, the opposite—being absent from school—results in lower learning outcomes.[3] Accordingly, the recent shift in federal education policy prompted by the Every Student Succeeds Act (ESSA) has helped raise the stakes for schools around student absences. Under ESSA, states determine which academic and nonacademic metrics are used to measure school performance. Driven by a greater amount of school-level data and a new wave of research over the last decade elevating the detriments of student absences, thirty-seven states included chronic absence as their nonacademic indicator in their ESSA plans as of September 2017.[4] The implications of this are important: schools will now be held accountable for their students' absences in a way this country has never before seen. Previous policies assumed that parents were primarily responsible for attendance and answerable to absences. Now state policy makers want to turn absenteeism into a problem that schools have to address.

Grappling with student absence is not new to schools, but the raised visibility presented by ESSA means this is a critical time to understand what schools can do to decrease student absences. We argue in this chapter that the first place to start would be to focus on major transition points along the educational spectrum. Transitions—such as into the school system (in pre-kindergarten or kindergarten) or from middle to high school—are often both developmentally challenging and chaotic for students and families, and this shows in the higher absence rates during these grades.[5] School transitions, therefore, are critical moments for schools to establish connections to students and families, creating a sense of belonging that encourages more regular student attendance and sets the stage for future success.

The Importance of Focusing on Attendance During School Transitions

School transitions cause disruption and present new challenges. In a national study of the kindergarten transition, when many students enter the school system, teachers reported that at least half of their students had specific challenges adjusting to kindergarten (following directions, negotiating differences in home and school culture, working as part of a group).[6] We know that students from low-income neighborhoods and those from many nondominant ethnic/racial backgrounds are significantly more likely to experience difficulties with the transition into kindergarten.[7] Research also shows that absenteeism in these early years, in pre-kindergarten and kindergarten, is the highest for the elementary years. The number of students who are chronically absent—who miss at least 10 percent of their enrolled days—is staggeringly high. In urban areas, which have been studied the most, anywhere between 20 percent and 45 percent of pre-kindergarten students are chronically absent, meaning they miss at least three weeks of school, and often more than that. In Chicago, more than 15 percent of pre-kindergarten students missed more than *six* weeks of school.[8] More importantly, we now know that absences, even in these earliest years of schooling, are closely related to children's cognitive and behavioral development, both during those early grades and in future years.[9]

Similarly, the transition into ninth grade, when students are in a new environment and often being given new responsibilities (e.g., switching classes on their own), appears to be jarring. Data from the early 2000s show that Chicago students' attendance sharply declined when transitioning from eighth grade to ninth grade.[10] Notably, these declines occurred across all subgroups of students (by race/ethnicity, gender, and prior academic achievement) and across all subjects.[11] The severity of the drop in attendance is particularly troubling because, for ninth-grade students, course absences are the primary factor affecting course grades and failures, which in turn are the best predictors of graduation.[12] Thus, ninth grade presents itself as another critical moment to support students, as a critical opportunity to ensure that students are set on a positive trajectory for high school.

Transitions hold promise as being particularly effective moments for engaging in outreach to students and families in support of better attendance. Initial entry into schools may be the time when students and families are most receptive to outreach, allowing for the early development of relationships. It is an opportunity to send a message that school staff are partners with families and students in identifying and removing barriers to regular attendance.[13] Once this is established, it can set the climate, relationships, and infrastructure for ongoing commitments to regular attendance in future years.

Schools Play a Role in Influencing Student Attendance

A number of studies have explored absences, identifying the individual (e.g., demographic, achievement), family (e.g., parental occupation and work status, family health), and sociocontextual (e.g., peers' academic, demographic, and behavioral characteristics) factors related to the likelihood of missing school.[14] However, only recently have studies begun to focus on the specific role schools play in both reducing student absences and encouraging better attendance. Those that do largely focus on the effectiveness of specific interventions for reducing absences.[15] But there are also schoolwide approaches that more generally support better attendance.

Data from Chicago show that schools serving similar student populations can exhibit vastly different student attendance patterns. For example, figure 5.1 shows school-by-school pre-kindergarten attendance rates after taking into consideration background characteristics of the students served.[16] The variation here indicates that while individual and family factors contribute to attendance, schools play an important role as well. Although schools cannot solve all the obstacles students and families may face within their communities (and society), they do have agency around how they approach attendance within the walls of their buildings. Previous research suggests that schools and early childhood education settings with better organizational climate (e.g., trust, collaboration) have pre-kindergarten students with better attendance (although this relationship is correlational and does not speak to directionality).[17] Evidence from high schools also shows strong relationships between school climate and students' attendance.[18] As these studies underscore, attendance is critical not only because it is strongly predictive of future outcomes but also because it is malleable and can be influenced by school practices.[19] This chapter shares our learnings from studying these two critical transition points, pre-kindergarten and ninth grade.[20] We focus on the ways in which schools in Chicago shape welcoming, caring, and supporting environments where students and families feel most engaged and regularly show up for learning opportunities.

Overview of Student Attendance in Chicago

We focus here on students enrolled in Chicago Public Schools (CPS). In 2017–18, almost 80 percent of the roughly 370,000 students were considered economically disadvantaged, and almost 90 percent are racial minorities.[21] Roughly 20,000 three- and four-year old pre-kindergarten students enrolled in a range of programs, including Head Start, state-funded Preschool for All, Child-Parent Centers, and tuition-based options in both charter and noncharter schools, most, but not all, of which are free. While pre-kindergarten is

FIGURE 5.1 Schools serving similar student populations exhibit different preK attendance rates

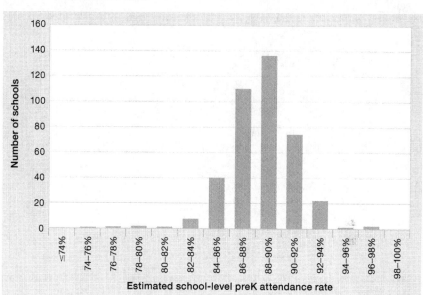

not compulsory, neither is kindergarten in Illinois. For high school, students enroll in charter, neighborhood, or selective-enrollment schools. Figure 5.2 shows the average attendance rates for students across all types of schools and programs during 2015–16, showcasing two points. First, pre-kindergarten students had lower attendance than students in any other early grade. Kindergarteners' attendance was 5.7 percentage points higher than pre-kindergarten students' by an additional 10 days per student, on average. Second, there was a steep drop in attendance between eighth grade and ninth grade. Though this graph represents different students in each grade, similar drop-offs happened for the same students over time. Students who moved from eighth grade in 2011–12 to ninth grade in 2012–13 missed almost twice as many days in ninth grade, from 8.5 days to 16.5 days of absences.[22]

Across the district, attendance has been increasing in recent years. Among pre-kindergarten students, attendance has improved two full percentage points over the last four years (figure 5.3). While this may seem minimal, when applied across all students in the district, it corresponds to many more days of instructional time. That means more opportunity for learning and

FIGURE 5.2 Attendance is lowest among preK and high school students

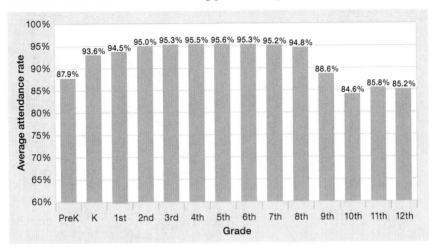

social engagement and less time teachers need to spend catching children up when they return to school after absences. Importantly, attendance has increased the most among students who traditionally have had the lowest attendance in Chicago: Black students and those living in high-poverty neighborhoods.[23]

Even steeper improvements are evident among high school students, where ninth-grade attendance saw a boost from 73.6 percent in 2007–08 to 88.6 percent in 2015–16 (see figure 5.4). Large improvements are evident for tenth-, eleventh-, and twelfth-grade students as well. The proportion of ninth graders in Chicago who are considered "on track" to graduate—a key indicator of students' progress toward an on-time high school graduation—also rose substantially over the same period, with attendance driving much of these observed improvements.[24]

Districtwide Efforts Set the Context for Improved Attendance

District efforts to make data available to educators in schools helped set the stage for improvements at both the pre-kindergarten and ninth-grade levels. In addition to messages about the importance of attendance, CPS has supported

FIGURE 5.3   PreK attendance steadily increased in CPS between 2013 and 2016

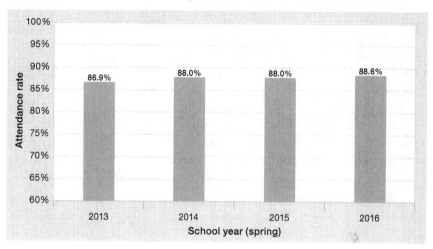

FIGURE 5.4   High school students' attendance increased more than 10 percentage points, 2008–16

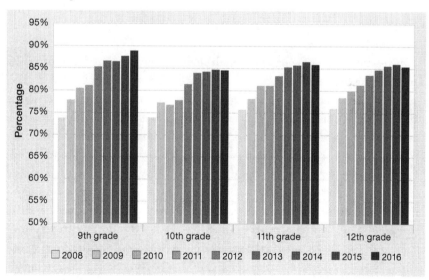

schools' attendance efforts with additional resources (e.g., attendance grants) and direct supports. The inclusion of attendance in K–12 school accountability metrics also evinces the value the district places on attendance. These efforts—coinciding with ground-up high school efforts to improve course performance and graduation—set the context for attendance improvement in Chicago.

Based on emerging research on the importance of pre-kindergarten attendance for student outcomes for 2012–13, CPS began investing substantial effort in their youngest students. Although pre-kindergarten attendance was not included in the district's schoolwide accountability metrics, CPS began supporting schools by elevating the visibility of pre-kindergarten attendance.[25] The district produced school-specific attendance data reports and parent-friendly fliers emphasizing the importance of attendance for students' learning. In addition, the Office of Attendance and Truancy, which had traditionally focused on grades K–12, increasingly included pre-kindergarten in its communications about attendance to elementary principals. In line with this shift, principals now have ready access to attendance data about their pre-kindergarten students on their data dashboard. While there is much more room for improvement, the awareness and focus on pre-kindergarten attendance from the central office down to the school level has been steadily increasing in recent years.

The focus on attendance at the high school level emerged differently. The development of a freshman on-track indicator helped propel school staff to closely examine ninth-grade students' course performance, with particular emphasis on the relationships between course failures and attendance.[26] However, this was not always the case. In the early 2000s, researchers at the University of Chicago's Consortium on School Research began seeing a pattern in who was likely to graduate high school in Chicago.[27] Using districtwide data, these researchers identified the factors that best predicted graduation: ninth-grade course performance, including grades and attendance, was far more predictive of high school graduation than test scores or background characteristics.[28] This was the basis for the freshman on-track indicator that would become adopted districtwide. In 2003, schools became accountable for on-track rates, but it wasn't until 2009, when CPS began providing monthly data reports, that they really began focusing on ninth-grade course performance and attendance. From then, there is a clear upward trend in on-track rates across the district.[29] The production of data and data reports are a common form of support the district has played at both the pre-kindergarten and ninth-grade levels.

Effective School Practices Supporting Improved Attendance

In order for schools—as whole organizations—to take on the task of supporting better student attendance, they must first acknowledge that students and their families do not bear full responsibility for attendance and that schools also influence attendance. Viewing attendance as an outcome of the school's policies and practices has tremendous importance for the approaches schools adopt to support and improve student attendance. Once there is common understanding within a school that it contributes to students' attendance and that it can also reduce absences, three key efforts can strongly support regular attendance. Across grade levels, these include creating a sense of collective responsibility, using data in transparent ways for improvement purposes, and building trust and supporting students and families (figure 5.5).

FIGURE 5.5   Conditions for schoolwide improvement efforts around student attendance

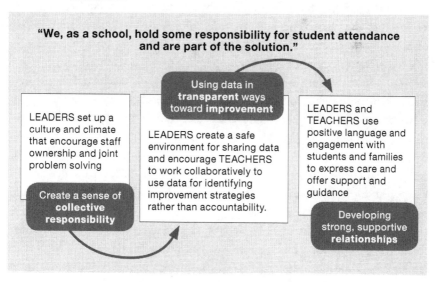

"We, as a school, hold some responsibility for student attendance and are part of the solution."

Using data in **transparent** ways toward **improvement**

LEADERS set up a culture and climate that encourage staff ownership and joint problem solving

Create a sense of **collective responsibility**

LEADERS create a safe environment for sharing data and encourage TEACHERS to work collaboratively to use data for identifying improvement strategies rather than accountability.

LEADERS and TEACHERS use positive language and engagement with students and families to express care and offer support and guidance

Developing strong, supportive **relationships**

Creating a Sense of Collective Responsibility

The most important lesson to emerge from Chicago has been the critical importance of creating and sustaining a strong sense of collective responsibility for improving students' attendance and grades. In practice, what this means is that teachers and staff share a belief that they are all responsible for helping support and improve attendance for all students in their school. When school staff collaboratively feel a sense of ownership over student attendance, joint problem solving can begin. We have seen this play out at both the pre-kindergarten and ninth-grade levels.

Through qualitative work in schools with improved versus stagnant pre-kindergarten attendance over a three-year period, we found that staff in schools with improved attendance were more likely to talk about how they worked together—across classrooms and with nonclassroom staff—to determine why students were absent and identify barriers families were facing.[30] Thus, teachers are not alone in responding to and engaging with families of children who are absent, many of whom are facing multiple, overlapping barriers to regular school attendance. In one CPS elementary school, a pre-kindergarten teacher described the close, collaborative, and supportive relationship she enjoyed with her school's counselor, who also served as the attendance coordinator: "I can just say, 'I'm having a problem with this parent—can you talk to them?' and then [the attendance coordinator] is another person that can talk to them." Importantly, this type of collaboration hinges on the intentional choices of elementary school leaders about whether and to what degree to integrate pre-kindergarten classrooms, teachers, parents, and families into the wider work of the school community. Teachers and staff who share ownership, who collaborate across grade levels to creatively problem-solve, develop and support teachers' capacity to identify and address barriers to regular attendance. This particular elementary school attendance coordinator (analogous in high schools to an on-track coordinator or ninth-grade teacher team leader) is an example of the kind of relational infrastructure that successful schools build in order to create and sustain a collective responsibility for and shared support around improving students' attendance.

A strong sense of collective responsibility for improving student outcomes, including attendance, plays a similarly critical role in the success of schools' efforts at the ninth-grade level. High schools, in a way that is often different from elementary schools, are frequently large, complex organizations, traditionally organized around content and departmental structures. This structure can isolate teachers of different subjects and grades and make students' experiences feel disjointed and alienating. However, high schools in which students report strong, trusting relationships with their teachers and in which teachers report a general sense of collective responsibility have stronger attendance.[31] Creating ninth-grade teacher teams, which allow teachers to discuss the same group of students across multiple contexts, and thus helping to break down existing department silos, can help foster strong relationships. In a number of Chicago high schools, teacher teams have implemented systems and structures for regularly reviewing students' course performance and attendance. Using discussion protocols to review student data, teachers develop deeper relationships with each other and build greater knowledge of students and their strengths. Similar to the collaborative problem solving that teams of teachers in some elementary schools do to support pre-kindergarten attendance, the shared sense of responsibility enables ninth-grade teacher teams to share insights and effective solutions and to collaboratively support each other. The students' experience reflects this wrap-around support from a team of committed and caring adults that motivates and sustains changed behaviors, including improved attendance.

Transparent, Improvement-Focused Use of Attendance Data

Schools that are effective in improving student attendance also support staff collaboration through systematic approaches to using attendance data, particularly in ways that focus on transparent improvement efforts. Moreover, the use of data in improvement-focused ways may prove to be especially useful during transition grades, when school staff and teachers are first getting to know the students who are likely to enroll in their school for the next several years. Largely speaking, data systems are intended to either inform changes in staff/students or hold schools and districts accountable for outcomes. Both are hypothesized to lead to change, but one does so through "building the knowledge and skills of teachers and principals so that they can be more effective in their professional work," while the other puts external pressure on schools to improve performance.[32] The former prepares teachers, leaders, and other school staff to identify solutions to attendance struggles. In contrast, using data for the latter often results in trying to use data to shame families and students into coming to school more—a strategy that does not work well.

Ongoing research in Chicago suggests the importance of not only regularly and closely examining pre-kindergarten attendance data at multiple levels but also ensuring that pre-kindergarten teachers have strong support for addressing absenteeism. In schools lacking strong, credible administrative commitment to using data for improvement, staff can often become engaged in what appears to be compliance behaviors: monitoring students' attendance but not acting on that data in a concerted, intentional way. As one pre-kindergarten teacher in Chicago explained, referring to a parent call log her principal asked teachers to keep, "I'll just make notations in my book" after each call home "because my principal always wants [us] to keep a call log, just in case the district comes in and says, 'Well, you know, your [attendance is low].'" By contrast, schools with both a strong sense of collective responsibility and commitment to using data for improvement frequently describe formalized structures for creating greater transparency of data and collaboration among staff. At one elementary school, attendance data were made transparent by publicly displaying class-by-class attendance every week on a bulletin board located in the main hallway. This way, "every class," including pre-kindergarten, "gets to know 'This is our [attendance] goal and this is where you [are] at. And this is where we are as a school.'" Teachers interpreted the attendance board as a motivational tool rather than a shaming mechanism toward compliance. One pre-kindergarten teacher explained that the attendance board was explicitly aimed at creating dialogue between classroom teachers and administrators about how to improve attendance and identifying what additional supports teachers needed to help families get their children to school.

The emphasis on creating transparent, systematic, and improvement-focused approaches to data use has been a critical element of successful efforts to increase attendance at the ninth-grade level as well. Successful high schools in Chicago developed a variety of systems and structures (e.g., ninth-grade teacher teams) to make regular, strategic use of student-level data, including attendance. Effective teams used data-driven conversations, often with the support of partner organizations, like the Network for College Success (NCS), to identify students struggling in their classes, often due to absences, and collectively explore reasons for and solutions to address absences and disengagement.[33] As noted by NCS, "Data-driven conversations require careful facilitation to ensure a safe and supportive environment wherein educators take ownership of their outcomes."[34] Similar to efforts to improve pre-kindergarten attendance in elementary schools, within these safe spaces and led by a leader who is empowered to drive the work by administration, high school teachers share data to illuminate patterns in course performance and attendance across classes.[35] In turn, this then facilitates teachers' ability to learn what other teachers know about students and enables joint problem solving. Using attendance data to identify which students needed more individualized outreach was an early success of many schools in Chicago. Regular data use among ninth-grade teacher teams also removed barriers to sharing information, undercutting the culture of private practice in many high schools and building trusting, collaborative relationships among ninth-grade teachers.[36]

Putting such teams in place at both the pre-kindergarten and the ninth-grade levels, creating a safe and trusting space for discussion, and protecting time for collaboration can provide teachers with key opportunities to share information, strategies, and insights about individual students' and families' strengths and needs. This can form the basis for targeted, timely outreach to struggling students.

Creating Strong, Supportive Relationships with Students and Families

Ultimately, a strong sense of collective responsibility and transparent, improvement-focused approaches to using attendance data lay the foundation for creating strong, supportive relationships between schools and students and families. When staff work together to support attendance, they often find that positive messages and engagement with families and students are most effective. One CPS elementary principal discussed how a shift from negative messaging to engagement with families resulted in better attendance: "We find that if you do the negative thing constantly . . . if we constantly berate parents about not attending and make them feel bad, we didn't solve the problem. There were still the chronic students, always absent. So, by trying to turn the tables and make it more exciting to be here and make them feel like they want to be a part of what we're doing here . . . our attendance this year is above last year's."

Ongoing research on pre-kindergarten attendance in Chicago, as well as recent work in Washington, DC, underscores the importance of both clear and regular communication between schools and families, as well as building intentional, collaborative relationships that clearly reflect the shared value placed by schools and families on students' learning and development.[37] These messages evince a fundamental humility and sensitivity in approaching parents and families with offers of support and assistance. Ultimately, they underscore schools' willingness to make common cause with parents and families in addressing the reasons pre-kindergarten students miss school.

In high school, relationships between teachers and ninth-grade students appear to have many of the same characteristics of pre-kindergarten teachers' relationships with parents and families. High school students have many of the same needs that parents respond to in the early years—feelings of belonging and trust and that the sense that someone is looking out for them. Interviews with students in the transition to high school reveal that many students begin to skip classes in ninth grade simply because they can.[38] Whereas teachers followed students from one class to the next in the middle grades, students are left to their own devices to show up for class in high school. As one student explained, "In [elementary school] . . . you still walk around in groups, you walk in a line. In [high school] you just walk. It's your choice to go to lunch or English or all those classes. In [elementary school] you gotta go to all those classes. You get a choice in [high school] . . . It's more free."[39]

Building on evidence that the quality of relationships and trust between students and teachers was associated with better student attendance, high school staff invested substantially in regularly monitoring grades and attendance, providing timely support for struggling ninth graders so as to not leave students "free to fail."[40] Teachers more clearly communicated shared expectations for high levels of student performance and demonstrated concern for students as individuals. Ninth-grade students reported that individualized teacher support made a big difference in their effort to attend class.[41]

Like pre-kindergarten teachers' successful relationships with parents and families, ninth-grade teachers' relationships with students emphasize a willingness to engage in ongoing problem-solving efforts with students, devote additional resources and supports, and develop shared approaches to addressing the barriers that keep ninth graders out of class and school. In schools where ninth grade teacher teams succeed in creating strong, collaborative outreach to students, the net effect can be a powerful demonstration of collective concern and commitment. Additionally, by focusing on the transition into high school, efforts can create positive, cascading effects on students as they progress through subsequent grade levels. In Chicago, improvements in freshman on-track rates were sustained across the district as cohorts of students moved through high school, despite the relatively narrow initial focus on the ninth-grade year in most schools. Subsequent studies have validated the link between rising freshman on-track rates and increases in high school graduation, strongly suggesting that schools' emphasis on building systems and structures to address students' attendance and course performance during the transition into a new environment pay both short- and long-term dividends for students and families.[42]

A School's Role in Supporting Student Attendance Under the Current Policy Movement

Evidence from Chicago and elsewhere increasingly suggests that absenteeism is far from the intractable problem many observers may be tempted to assume. Nationally, this growing recognition is underscored by changes to federal and state accountability policies. Under new ESSA guidelines, thirty-eight states and territories have adopted chronic absenteeism as an indicator of school quality or student success.[43] This shift represents an important opportunity as the national conversation moves from a focus on individual students' attendance to a more nuanced reflection on the role that school policies and practices play toward improving attendance. Real improvement in attendance is possible and attainable with a clear focus on shifting school-wide mind-sets about attendance, using data in improvement-focused ways, and intentionally investing in the quality of relationships between school staff and students and their families.

School-based efforts to improve attendance do not occur in a vacuum. Previous research highlights the scale and complexity of the challenges chronically absent children and their families face. However, barriers to regular attendance are not deterministic, and here we show that school leaders and staff play a vital role in shaping how students and families connect and engage with schools and, ultimately, whether or not they attend regularly. Evidence from Chicago suggests that taking ownership of and responsibility for improving attendance is a necessary condition for schools to be able to make intentional improvement. School leaders must set the expectation and conditions for staff to share a commitment and a sense of collective responsibility for addressing the needs of their chronically absent students and families. Transparent, improvement-focused data use routines are a critical lever within schools for connecting that principled commitment to concrete practice.

Efforts in Chicago to build the capacity of staff to explore, analyze, and act on data provide strong evidence that educators have not only the capacity but also a critical role to play in addressing chronic absenteeism in their schools. Intentional investments in protecting time and resources for them to do so pays significant dividends. Finally, findings from Chicago and from elsewhere underscore the ongoing importance of developing and sustaining strong, supportive relationships between school staff, on the one hand, and students and families, on the other. Strong, credible commitments to partnering with families to meet their needs, together with consistent and constructive uses of data, enable educators to provide students and families with the individualized supports they need to be successful.

As states, districts, and schools focus on addressing chronic absenteeism, evidence from Chicago—at both the pre-kindergarten and high school freshman years—strongly suggests the value of explicitly capitalizing on school transitions as key moments to improve attendance. Transitions are critical opportunities to ensure there is a culture of partnership with students and families. At a moment when students may be at substantially greater risk for adverse outcomes, students and parents alike, as they are just forming their own sense of belonging, may also be more open to learning new expectations that they can carry forward as students progress through school. Schools play a vital role in shaping how students and families experience these new expectations and can make deliberate, effective efforts to build quality relationships with the children and families they serve.

It is worth noting that these schoolwide efforts will not solve all attendance problems. Students with extremely high rates of absenteeism are likely to need a range of individual-focused (tier 3) supports. These interventions—such as assigned mentors, volunteers who text regularly with families, or incentives that are carefully designed to remove barriers for families—are complementary and can be incorporated into many of the schoolwide systems and structures we discuss. Additionally, as states move toward holding schools accountable for chronic absenteeism under ESSA, it is important to keep in mind the challenges associated with poorly implemented accountability policies. Efforts to anticipate, understand, and respond to the emergence of perverse incentives, efforts to game attendance metrics, and the tendency to superficially incorporate new measures into existing "business as usual" routines and practices will likely be key to the success of these and other related efforts to learn from Chicago's experience and to improve attendance at any level within schools.[44]

6

Schools as Sanctuaries?

Examining the Relationship Between Immigration Enforcement and Absenteeism Rates for Immigrant-Origin Children

CAROLYN SATTIN-BAJAJ AND
JACOB KIRKSEY

SCHOOLS ARE AT THE FOREFRONT of the current national immigration crisis. Estimates indicate that more than 11 million people, over half of whom are of Mexican origin, are living in the United States without formal legal status.[1] Three-quarters of a million children under the age of eighteen are included in this total. Moreover, approximately 5.5 million children, or 7.3 percent of all children enrolled in public and private K–12 schools, are living with at least one undocumented parent.[2] Immigration policies, including those that govern enforcement, exert widespread influence on the lives of millions of students in US schools.[3]

When nearly 2,000 students in Las Cruces, New Mexico, stopped going to school in the days following raids by Immigration and Customs Enforcement (ICE) agents in March 2017, a spotlight was shone on the ways in which immigration enforcement activities can directly impact students in schools, particularly through attendance.[4] While a growing body of literature has identified some of the educational and developmental challenges associated with being undocumented and/or living in mixed-status families, few studies have directly examined the relationship between immigration enforcement activities and students' educational outcomes.[5] The drastic shifts in federal approaches to immigration enforcement that have occurred since President Trump took office in January 2017 highlight the need for studies that empirically capture the educational impacts of different immigration enforcement policies.[6] The consequences of immigration enforcement actions can extend far beyond those people immediately at risk of removal. Using the framework of a pyramid of immigration enforcement effects, scholars have documented the ways in which children of immigrant parents can experience negative effects just by virtue of living in immigrant families, even if all family members are authorized. People living in communities where many families may be targeted by ICE or may have already experienced arrest, detention, and deportation have also demonstrated signs of increased stress, health, and mental health issues.[7] Immigration enforcement policies therefore stand to affect large numbers of US citizen children and noncitizen children and their families alike.[8]

Recent Policy Landscape in Immigration Enforcement

Immigration enforcement under the Obama administration was guided by "prosecutorial discretion," an approach intended to take into consideration family ties in the United States (including citizen children) and prioritize deportation of individuals who posed risks to national security or public safety.[9] At the same time, large increases in rates of deportation began under President Obama, whom critics disapprovingly nicknamed "Deporter in Chief." Between 2009 and 2016, nearly 5.3 million people were deported, over half a million of whom were parents of US-citizen children.[10] Part of this increase in deportations resulted from the Secure Communities policy that was in place between 2008 and 2013, which required local and state law enforcement agencies to automatically submit the fingerprints of arrested individuals to the Department of Homeland Security's Automated Biometric Identification System (IDENT) to identify people who were "unlawfully present in the United States or otherwise removable."[11] The Secure Communities policy was suspended in November 2014 and replaced by the 2014 Priorities Enforcement Program, which more narrowly targeted unauthorized immigrants who had been convicted of serious crimes and modified the local and state reporting requirements about people who had been detained.[12] Despite this change, the large numbers of deportations effectuated during the Obama presidency had serious implications for the well-being of individuals and families.[13]

Tougher immigration enforcement was a cornerstone of Donald Trump's campaign platform, and since his first days in office he has moved swiftly to fulfill these promises. Almost immediately, the Department of Homeland Security abandoned prosecutorial discretion and reinstated the Secure Communities policy. Both of these changes have resulted in a major increase in immigration arrests and heightened deportation fears among immigrants and their children.[14] In addition to repeated threats from the Justice Department to withhold federal funding to "sanctuary cities" that fail to release information about arrests to federal agents, ICE has ramped up the number of arrests of undocumented immigrant parents occurring near school grounds and other formerly "safe" spaces, such as hospitals and court houses.[15] This marks a stark reversal in tactics from those used in the previous administration.[16] It also raises important questions about whether schools were at one point protected spaces for undocumented students and their families and under what conditions families in situations of legal uncertainty believe schools to be safe.

Student absenteeism is a powerful measure of educational engagement.[17] It can also reveal families' perceptions of how safe it is for a student to travel to or remain in school. In this chapter we investigate the relationship between immigration enforcement activities and student absences in elementary grades during the height of the Obama administration's immigration enforcement efforts. Studying student absences represents the starting point of a larger research agenda needed to evaluate the impact of immigration enforcement actions on a range of students' educational outcomes and to examine the role schools can play in reducing the harmful effects of punitive immigration policies and removal strategies.[18]

Although many of the key Obama-era policies have since been changed, this chapter provides a first evidence base about the influence of immigration enforcement policies on student absences on which future studies using data from the current ICE regime can build. Even at the height of the deportation push, the overall approach to immigration enforcement during Obama's time in office is generally seen as more humane and family centered than the current system.[19] As such, an analysis of students' responses to immigration-related apprehensions during the Obama era can begin to identify the conditions under which schools may be more likely to function as sanctuaries for undocumented families, at least as measured by school attendance. This also provides a baseline for comparative analyses of the educational ramifications of distinct approaches to immigration enforcement. We explore how the number of apprehensions made by the ICE Enforcement and Removal Operations (ERO) relates to absenteeism in elementary grades and consider whether this association differs for first- and second-generation immigrant-origin students.

Absenteeism is a particularly useful measure to consider when examining the educational consequences of immigration enforcement because it can serve dual purposes. First, absenteeism rates may help explain any achievement disparities associated with being a child of unauthorized immigrants and therefore point to specific opportunities for targeted intervention.[20] Second, student absences, and specifically changes in absenteeism after immigration enforcement action, may be a strong indicator of parents' and students' perceptions of safety around traveling to and being in school during a time of increased legal uncertainty. On one hand, absences may rise with increased incidence of ICE apprehensions and deportations if parents are afraid they or their children will be detained en route to and from school or even on school grounds. On the other hand, parents may view schools as a protected space where they can have greater confidence that their child will not be in danger during school hours.

Unauthorized immigrants tend to be reluctant to engage with public institutions, particularly during times of heightened enforcement.[21] Less is known about how students and parents view schools when the number of arrests and deportations increases. Schools have typically been on the sidelines of discussions about the causes of student absenteeism, with absenteeism frequently attributed to factors beyond their control.[22] By studying changes in absenteeism over a period of intensified immigration enforcement, schools become a primary focus of our analysis, allowing us to consider the importance of schools in understanding patterns of absenteeism among immigrant-origin students, particularly in terms of their potential function as a respite from negative out-of-school climates. Our study offers a window into understanding the role schools can play in attenuating an environment of fear by providing a secure space for young people and families.

Examining Immigration Enforcement and Immigrant Student Absenteeism Using Nationally Representative Data

To examine the relationship between immigration enforcement activities and student absences in elementary grades, we used data from the US Department of Education's Early Childhood Longitudinal Study: Kindergarten Class of 2010–11 (ECLS-K:2011).[23] This dataset was produced by the National Center for Education Statistics (NCES), which surveyed and interviewed the families and schools of a nationally representative sample of kindergarteners in public and private schools in the country. These data are the most recently available gathered from a national cohort of elementary students. For our analysis, we utilize data from each wave made available by NCES, which include information on the children in the fall and spring of kindergarten, the fall and spring of first grade, the spring of second grade, and the spring of third grade.

Longitudinal studies such as ECLS-K:2011 often are missing information on the children, families, and schools because some information either was not provided by participants or was repressed by NCES. However, since such data are not considered missing at random, we used a statistical technique known as chained multiple imputation to fill in missing data for each child in the dataset based on other reported characteristics.[24] This technique maintains relationships among variables in the dataset and allows for each child to be included in our analyses.

Immigrant Students

After imputing missing information for children, we restricted our analysis to the sample of students who are considered first- or second-generation immigrants to the United States. First-generation immigrant students were born outside of the country; second-generation students are US-born and have at least one non–native born parent. To identify these students, we asked parents if their child was born in the US and whether one or both parents were born in the US. Our sample included approximately 330 first-generation immigrant students and approximately 4,790 second-generation students, totaling about 5,120 elementary students. Table 6.1 presents all the variables we used in our study.

School Absenteeism

Much of the research on school absenteeism evaluates whether students were chronically absent (missed 10 percent, or 18 days, of the school year). In our study, similar to most research using ECLS-K:2011 data, we examined each child's absences based on a range of days, not a count of absences.[25] This information was reported by teachers in the spring surveys in each year of data collection. Specifically, teachers indicated the number of days a child had missed up to that point in the school year from several ranges: 0, 1–4, 5–7, 8–10, 11–19, and 20 or more. We recoded these responses as category midpoints, except for the end categories, which took the mode value of 0 or 20.[26]

Immigration Enforcement Activities

The key variable of interest in this study was the number of apprehensions made by immigration-related enforcement offices throughout the US in 2010–13. ICE publishes annual data on the number of apprehensions made by their ERO program in the Yearbook of Immigration Statistics reported by jurisdiction and area of responsibility, including the city and state). We merged data on the number of apprehensions processed through each office into the ECLS-K:2011 dataset. Then, using the geocoding command *geodist* in STATA, we used the number of apprehensions processed through the nearest ERO office to a student's home zip code (reported in ECLS-K:2011) to predict student-level absences that year. This means that immigrant-origin students will have different apprehension statistics predicting their absences from school based on where they live in the country. Table 6.2 illustrates the locations of each ERO program, the number of apprehensions processed through each program, and the number of kindergarteners in the ECLS-K:2011 sample that fell under that jurisdiction based on location.

To avoid producing biased estimates that do not take into account various other factors that may relate to student absenteeism, we included a robust set of control variables in our analysis (see table 6.1).

Analysis Using Multilevel Modeling

We began our analysis with a two-level hierarchical linear model (HLM). This technique accounts for the fact that children and schools are nested within

TABLE 6.1

Descriptive statistics for main study variables

	1ST GENERATION		2ND GENERATION		ALL	
	Mean	SD	Mean	SD	Mean	SD
Absence outcome						
Number of absences	5.11	4.53	5.91	4.89	5.86	4.88
Immigration enforcement variables						
Apprehensions	13223	7860	15364	8146	15226	8144
Distance to nearest ERO office	169	256	178	217	178	220
Child demographic characteristics						
Male	0.45	0.50	0.52	0.50	0.52	0.50
Black	0.10	0.30	0.21	0.41	0.21	0.40
Hispanic	0.28	0.45	0.39	0.49	0.38	0.49
Asian	0.45	0.50	0.16	0.37	0.18	0.39
Other race	0.05	0.22	0.09	0.29	0.09	0.28
English learner	0.38	0.48	0.24	0.42	0.25	0.43
Kindergarten entry age (months)	65.80	5.01	65.62	4.65	65.63	4.68
Poorer health rating	1.71	0.83	1.73	0.87	1.73	0.87
Disability	0.13	0.34	0.18	0.38	0.18	0.38
Measured skills at kindergarten entry						
Math	32.19	11.23	29.89	11.43	30.03	11.43
Reading	47.69	12.54	45.69	11.73	45.82	11.79
Externalizing behavior problems	1.56	0.63	1.62	0.64	1.62	0.64
Interpersonal skills	2.96	0.62	2.93	0.65	2.93	0.65
Self-control	3.10	0.61	3.04	0.64	3.04	0.64
Approaches to learning	3.02	0.67	2.90	0.69	2.91	0.69
Internalizing behavior problems	1.41	0.43	1.47	0.51	1.46	0.51
Eager to attend school	1.18	0.46	1.20	0.48	1.20	0.47
Kindergarten and preK experiences						
Full-day kindergarten	0.81	0.39	0.84	0.37	0.84	0.37
Private school	0.15	0.36	0.10	0.30	0.10	0.30
Distance from school (miles)	4.78	2.22	4.45	2.55	4.47	2.54
Average minutes to school	12.20	7.55	11.61	7.26	11.65	7.28
Before-/Afterschool center care in kindergarten	0.18	0.39	0.19	0.40	0.19	0.40
Hours of before-/afterschool center care in kindergarten	2.36	6.49	2.38	6.06	2.38	6.09
Center-based preK care	0.66	0.47	0.64	0.48	0.64	0.48
Hours of center-based preK care	15.35	15.31	16.36	15.97	16.29	15.93
Out-of-home care prior to preK	0.76	0.43	0.79	0.41	0.79	0.41
Household characteristics						
Two-adult household	0.82	0.38	0.49	0.50	0.52	0.50
Number of siblings	1.33	1.18	1.40	1.16	1.40	1.16
Older sibling attends same school	0.42	0.49	0.49	0.50	0.49	0.50

(continued)

TABLE 6.1 (*continued*)

Descriptive statistics for main study variables

	1ST GENERATION		2ND GENERATION		ALL	
	Mean	SD	Mean	SD	Mean	SD
Household characteristics						
Age of mother at first birth	24.79	5.47	23.30	5.88	23.40	5.86
Two-adult household	0.82	0.38	0.49	0.50	0.52	0.50
Number of siblings	1.33	1.18	1.40	1.16	1.40	1.16
Older sibling attends same school	0.42	0.49	0.49	0.50	0.49	0.50
Age of mother at first birth	24.79	5.47	23.30	5.88	23.40	5.86
Number of children's books at home	56.65	87.87	59.66	115.50	59.47	113.90
Mother-reported depression	0.19	0.39	0.23	0.42	0.23	0.42
Mother's education						
Some college	0.18	0.40	0.30	0.46	0.29	0.46
College graduate or beyond	0.46	0.51	0.24	0.44	0.25	0.45
Father's education						
Some college	0.13	0.36	0.10	0.32	0.10	0.32
College graduate or beyond	0.45	0.50	0.17	0.39	0.19	0.41
Household income	6685	11936	9541	16093	9356	15873
Received government food assistance	0.23	0.41	0.39	0.48	0.38	0.48
Urban	0.46	0.50	0.42	0.49	0.42	0.49
Suburban	0.38	0.49	0.37	0.48	0.37	0.48
Problems with safety on school route	0.61	0.49	0.59	0.49	0.59	0.49
Safe to play outside	0.04	0.20	0.03	0.17	0.03	0.17
Takes bus to school	0.33	0.47	0.29	0.45	0.29	0.45
Maternal employment						
Full-time	0.35	0.47	0.43	0.50	0.42	0.49
Part-time	0.20	0.41	0.19	0.40	0.19	0.40
Paternal employment						
Full-time	0.68	0.46	0.45	0.49	0.46	0.49
Part-time	0.07	0.24	0.05	0.21	0.05	0.22
Regular bedtime	0.87	0.33	0.88	0.32	0.88	0.32
Number of breakfasts at regular time	5.37	1.75	5.18	1.84	5.19	1.83
Number of breakfasts together as family	3.70	2.52	3.47	2.37	3.49	2.38
Number of dinners at regular time	5.55	1.92	5.47	1.94	5.48	1.94
Number of dinners together as family	5.77	1.78	5.75	1.80	5.75	1.80
Observations	330		4790		5120	

TABLE 6.2

Enforcement and removal operations jurisdictions

ERO OFFICE LOCATION	2010 APPREHENSIONS	STUDENTS IN ECLS-K
Atlanta, GA	21,742	1,424
Baltimore, MD	2,973	63
Boston, MA	5,107	340
Buffalo, NY	1,169	235
Chicago, IL	19,272	1,473
Dallas, TX	16,548	988
Denver, CO	8,073	716
Detroit, MI	7,781	1,001
El Paso, TX	6,432	2
Houston, TX	19,052	388
Los Angeles, CA	27,748	1,017
Miami, FL	13,656	384
New Orleans, LA	12,179	305
New York, NY	9,346	634
Newark, NJ	5,585	372
Philadelphia, PA	5,358	567
Phoenix, AZ	17,558	362
Saint Paul, MN	7,371	981
Salt Lake City, UT	9,194	385
San Antonio, TX	24,337	229
San Diego, CA	10,608	724
San Francisco, CA	28,972	1,244
Seattle, WA	10,246	198
Washington, DC	5,069	1,168

counties and are likely to share countless characteristics that are not controlled for in simpler statistical approaches (e.g., OLS [ordinary least squares] regression). Additionally, we used a three-level HLM that controls for the issue of students being nested in schools, which are then nested within counties.

To understand why it is appropriate to use these two models, consider that students attending the same school share many characteristics. For example, Garfield Elementary in Oakland Unified School District was recently featured as a school that successfully reduced its chronic absenteeism rate by implementing a three-tiered system of support.[27] Moreover, every school in Oakland Unified is considered a "sanctuary school," where there is expressed support for immigrant-origin families and students and no cooperation with immigration enforcement agencies. For the purpose of our analysis, the added resources for students attending school as well as local support for immigrant-origin populations would have confounded our results by not accounting for these characteristics that extend beyond the relationship between enforcement activities and school attendance. And a simple statistical analysis would have shown that fewer enforcement activities leads to fewer absences, when absences may also be related the unobserved variable of the implementation three-tiered intervention.

Results

We ran our HLM specifications examining the relationship between apprehensions processed by the nearest ERO and absenteeism rates for students in their kindergarten, first-, second-, and third-grade years of elementary school (tables 6.3 and 6.4).

Kindergarten

The results from the two-level HLM model show an increase in the number of apprehensions made by a student's nearest ERO office is associated with a decrease in first-generation student absences with a moderate effect size of -0.21σ. Also, the number of apprehensions is also related to a decrease in absences for second-generation students with a small effect size of -0.08σ. The results for second-generation students are nearly identical to that of the combined sample, with the exception being that Hispanic students were no longer more likely to be absent.

The results from the three-level HLM specification, which accounts for the numerous variables that relate to student absenteeism and enforcement activities at the county and school levels, show results nearly identical to those produced in the two-level model. Note that for the kindergarten year, the

TABLE 6.3

Effect size estimates of enforcement activities and immigrant-origin students' attendance in kindergarten

	TWO-LEVEL MODEL			THREE-LEVEL MODEL		
	1st gen.	2nd gen.	All	1st gen.	2nd gen.	All
Intercept	-0.20	0.37***	0.32***	-0.21	0.38***	0.33***
	(0.37)	(0.10)	(0.10)	(0.36)	(0.10)	(0.10)
Immigration enforcement variables						
Apprehensions	-0.21*	-0.08**	-0.08**	-0.21*	-0.09**	-0.09***
	(0.11)	(0.03)	(0.03)	(0.10)	(0.03)	(0.03)
Distance to nearest ERO office	-0.29+	-0.05	-0.05	-0.29+	-0.07	-0.06
	(0.16)	(0.05)	(0.05)	(0.17)	(0.05)	(0.05)
Child demographic characteristics						
Male	0.22*	-0.04	-0.02	0.23*	-0.05+	-0.04
	(0.11)	(0.03)	(0.03)	(0.10)	(0.03)	(0.03)
Black	-0.03	-0.14*	-0.13*	0.03	-0.14**	-0.14**
	(0.20)	(0.05)	(0.05)	(0.22)	(0.05)	(0.05)
Hispanic	0.26+	-0.10*	-0.07	0.28+	-0.10+	-0.07
	(0.14)	(0.05)	(0.05)	(0.14)	(0.05)	(0.05)
Asian	0.22	0.01	0.01	0.24	0.01	0.02
	(0.15)	(0.05)	(0.04)	(0.15)	(0.05)	(0.04)
Other race	-0.29+	0.06	0.05	-0.32+	0.07	0.06
	(0.16)	(0.06)	(0.06)	(0.16)	(0.06)	(0.06)
English learner	-0.15	-0.17***	-0.18***	-0.17	-0.16***	-0.18***
	(0.15)	(0.04)	(0.04)	(0.15)	(0.04)	(0.04)
Kindergarten entry age (months)	0.01	-0.03+	-0.03+	0.02	-0.03	-0.03+
	(0.05)	(0.02)	(0.02)	(0.05)	(0.02)	(0.02)
Poorer health rating	0.04	0.05***	0.05***	0.03	0.06***	0.05***
	(0.06)	(0.01)	(0.01)	(0.06)	(0.01)	(0.01)
Disability	-0.14	0.10*	0.09*	-0.14	0.11**	0.10*
	(0.16)	(0.04)	(0.04)	(0.16)	(0.04)	(0.04)
Measured skills at kindergarten entry						
Math	0.05	-0.00	0.00	0.01	-0.00	0.00
	(0.09)	(0.03)	(0.02)	(0.09)	(0.03)	(0.03)
Reading	-0.09	-0.05	-0.05+	-0.07	-0.05+	-0.06*
	(0.06)	(0.03)	(0.03)	(0.06)	(0.03)	(0.03)
Externalizing behavior problems	0.05	-0.03	-0.03	0.04	-0.03	-0.03
	(0.07)	(0.02)	(0.02)	(0.07)	(0.02)	(0.02)
Interpersonal skills	0.04	0.04	0.04	0.03	0.04	0.04
	(0.11)	(0.03)	(0.03)	(0.11)	(0.02)	(0.03)
Self-control	0.06	0.00	0.01	0.04	-0.00	0.00
	(0.13)	(0.03)	(0.03)	(0.13)	(0.03)	(0.03)
Approaches to learning	-0.04	-0.06*	-0.06*	-0.02	-0.06*	-0.06*
	(0.12)	(0.03)	(0.03)	(0.11)	(0.03)	(0.03)
Internalizing behavior problems	0.08	0.04**	0.04**	0.08	0.04**	0.04**
	(0.07)	(0.01)	(0.01)	(0.07)	(0.01)	(0.01)
Eager to attend school	0.04	0.02	0.02	0.04	0.02	0.02
	(0.05)	(0.01)	(0.01)	(0.05)	(0.01)	(0.01)

(continued)

TABLE 6.3 *(continued)*

Effect size estimates of enforcement activities and immigrant-origin students' attendance in kindergarten

	TWO-LEVEL MODEL			THREE-LEVEL MODEL		
	1st gen.	2nd gen.	All	1st gen.	2nd gen.	All
Kindergarten and preK experiences						
Full-day kindergarten	0.22+	0.02	0.03	0.20+	0.01	0.01
	(0.12)	(0.05)	(0.05)	(0.12)	(0.06)	(0.05)
Private school	0.05	0.11+	0.11+	0.03	0.11+	0.09
	(0.16)	(0.06)	(0.06)	(0.16)	(0.06)	(0.06)
Distance from school (miles)	0.13	0.03	0.04	0.11	0.04	0.03
	(0.13)	(0.03)	(0.03)	(0.12)	(0.03)	(0.03)
Average minutes to school	-0.01	-0.01	-0.01	-0.01	-0.01	-0.01
	(0.06)	(0.02)	(0.02)	(0.06)	(0.02)	(0.02)
Before-/Afterschool center care in kindergarten year	-0.32	-0.16*	-0.17**	-0.28	-0.14*	-0.15**
	(0.20)	(0.06)	(0.06)	(0.20)	(0.06)	(0.06)
Hours of before-/afterschool center care in kindergarten	0.09	0.01	0.02	0.07	0.00	0.01
	(0.08)	(0.03)	(0.02)	(0.08)	(0.03)	(0.02)
Center-based preK care	-0.19	-0.06	-0.07	-0.23	-0.05	-0.06
	(0.15)	(0.06)	(0.05)	(0.15)	(0.06)	(0.05)
Hours of center-based preK care	0.00	-0.00	-0.00	0.00	-0.00	-0.00
	(0.00)	(0.00)	(0.00)	(0.00)	(0.00)	(0.00)
Out-of-home care prior to preK	0.04	0.04	0.04	0.06	0.05	0.05
	(0.12)	(0.04)	(0.04)	(0.12)	(0.04)	(0.04)
Household characteristics						
Two-adult household	0.17	-0.01	-0.00	0.15	-0.02	-0.01
	(0.17)	(0.05)	(0.05)	(0.17)	(0.05)	(0.05)
Number of siblings	-0.06	-0.01	-0.01	-0.06	-0.01	-0.01
	(0.06)	(0.02)	(0.02)	(0.06)	(0.02)	(0.02)
Older sibling attends same school	-0.01	-0.18***	-0.17***	-0.02	-0.17***	-0.16***
	(0.15)	(0.03)	(0.03)	(0.15)	(0.03)	(0.03)
Age of mother at first birth	-0.04	-0.10***	-0.09***	-0.05	-0.10***	-0.09***
	(0.07)	(0.02)	(0.02)	(0.06)	(0.02)	(0.02)
Number of children's books at home	0.05	0.02	0.02	0.04	0.02	0.03
	(0.09)	(0.02)	(0.02)	(0.09)	(0.02)	(0.02)
Mother-reported depression	-0.12	0.07+	0.06+	-0.09	0.07+	0.06+
	(0.14)	(0.04)	(0.04)	(0.14)	(0.04)	(0.03)
Mother's education						
Some college	0.23	-0.00	0.01	0.22	-0.00	0.01
	(0.19)	(0.04)	(0.04)	(0.18)	(0.04)	(0.04)
College graduate or beyond	0.04	0.05	0.04	0.05	0.04	0.03
	(0.16)	(0.06)	(0.05)	(0.15)	(0.06)	(0.05)
Father's education						
Some college	-0.07	0.05	0.03	-0.05	0.04	0.02
	(0.16)	(0.07)	(0.06)	(0.16)	(0.07)	(0.06)
College graduate or beyond	0.10	0.04	0.03	0.13	0.03	0.03
	(0.19)	(0.07)	(0.07)	(0.19)	(0.07)	(0.07)

(continued)

TABLE 6.3 (continued)

Effect size estimates of enforcement activities and immigrant-origin students' attendance in kindergarten

	TWO-LEVEL MODEL			THREE-LEVEL MODEL		
	1st gen.	2nd gen.	All	1st gen.	2nd gen.	All
Household characteristics (continued)						
Household income	0.02	0.01	0.01	0.02	0.01	0.01
	(0.08)	(0.01)	(0.01)	(0.07)	(0.01)	(0.01)
Received government food assistance	0.04	0.14***	0.14***	0.02	0.14***	0.14***
	(0.16)	(0.04)	(0.04)	(0.15)	(0.04)	(0.04)
Urban	-0.11	-0.10	-0.10	-0.12	-0.07	-0.07
	(0.19)	(0.06)	(0.06)	(0.19)	(0.06)	(0.06)
Suburban	-0.18	0.01	0.00	-0.19	0.02	0.01
	(0.16)	(0.08)	(0.07)	(0.17)	(0.06)	(0.06)
Problems with safety on school route	0.16	-0.01	0.00	0.15	-0.01	-0.00
	(0.13)	(0.03)	(0.03)	(0.13)	(0.03)	(0.03)
Safe to play outside	-0.04	0.19*	0.17*	-0.05	0.17+	0.15+
	(0.29)	(0.09)	(0.08)	(0.28)	(0.09)	(0.09)
Takes bus to school	-0.06	-0.05	-0.05	-0.06	-0.05	-0.05
	(0.15)	(0.05)	(0.05)	(0.15)	(0.04)	(0.04)
Maternal employment						
Full-time	-0.20	-0.15***	-0.15***	-0.24+	-0.14**	-0.14***
	(0.14)	(0.04)	(0.04)	(0.13)	(0.04)	(0.04)
Part-time	-0.16	-0.11*	-0.11*	-0.20	-0.11*	-0.12**
	(0.16)	(0.05)	(0.04)	(0.16)	(0.05)	(0.04)
Paternal employment						
Full-time	-0.40*	-0.07	-0.08+	-0.41*	-0.06	-0.07
	(0.19)	(0.05)	(0.04)	(0.19)	(0.05)	(0.04)
Part-time	-0.38	-0.10	-0.11	-0.39	-0.07	-0.08
	(0.25)	(0.08)	(0.07)	(0.24)	(0.07)	(0.07)
Regular bedtime	0.05	-0.11*	-0.09*	0.10	-0.12**	-0.10*
	(0.15)	(0.04)	(0.04)	(0.15)	(0.04)	(0.04)
Number of breakfasts at regular time	0.10*	-0.01	0.00	0.09	-0.00	0.00
	(0.05)	(0.02)	(0.02)	(0.06)	(0.02)	(0.01)
Number of breakfasts together as family	-0.04	-0.01	-0.02	-0.04	-0.01	-0.01
	(0.05)	(0.01)	(0.01)	(0.05)	(0.01)	(0.01)
Number of dinners at regular time	-0.07	-0.03	-0.03+	-0.07	-0.03+	-0.03+
	(0.05)	(0.02)	(0.02)	(0.06)	(0.02)	(0.02)
Number of dinners together as family	-0.10	0.02	0.01	-0.09	0.02	0.01
	(0.06)	(0.01)	(0.01)	(0.06)	(0.01)	(0.01)
Variance components						
Student-level variance (σ^2)	1.39	3.57	3.53	1.77	4.41	4.33
County-level variance (τ_π)	0.05	0.00	0.00	0.90	1.64	1.59
School-level variance (τ_β)			0.12	0.01	0.01	
Observations	330	4790	5120	330	4790	5120
Number of groups	62	77	78	62	77	78

Notes: Robust standard errors in parentheses; ***p<0.001; **p<0.01; *p<0.05; +p<0.10

TABLE 6.4

Effect-size estimates of enforcement activities and immigrant-origin students' attendance in elementary years

	TWO-LEVEL MODEL			THREE-LEVEL MODEL		
	1st gen.	2nd gen.	All	1st gen.	2nd gen.	All
Immigration enforcement variables in kindergarten						
Apprehensions in 2010	-0.21*	-0.08**	-0.08**	-0.21*	-0.09**	-0.09***
	(0.11)	(0.03)	(0.03)	(0.10)	(0.03)	(0.03)
Distance to nearest ERO office in 2010	-0.29+	-0.05	-0.05	-0.29+	-0.07	-0.06
	(0.16)	(0.05)	(0.05)	(0.17)	(0.05)	(0.05)
Enforcement activity in first grade						
Apprehensions in 2011	-0.29**	-0.09***	-0.11***	-0.28**	-0.10***	-0.10***
	(0.09)	(0.02)	(0.02)	(0.10)	(0.02)	(0.02)
Distance to nearest ERO office in 2011	-0.29	-0.06	-0.08	-0.28	-0.09+	-0.09*
	(0.20)	(0.05)	(0.05)	(0.20)	(0.05)	(0.04)
Enforcement activity in second grade						
Apprehensions in 2012	-0.20**	-0.11***	-0.13***	-0.20**	-0.10***	-0.12***
	(0.08)	(0.02)	(0.02)	(0.08)	(0.03)	(0.02)
Distance to nearest ERO office in 2012	-0.14	-0.17**	-0.17**	-0.14	-0.18**	-0.16**
	(0.16)	(0.05)	(0.06)	(0.16)	(0.06)	(0.06)
Enforcement activity in third grade						
Apprehensions in 2013	-0.11	-0.13***	-0.12***	-0.10	-0.12***	-0.11***
	(0.08)	(0.03)	(0.03)	(0.08)	(0.03)	(0.03)
Distance to nearest ERO office in 2013	-0.00	-0.11*	-0.10*	0.00	-0.12*	-0.10*
	(0.14)	(0.04)	(0.04)	(0.14)	(0.04)	(0.04)

Notes: Robust standard errors in parentheses; ***$p<0.001$; **$p<0.01$; *$p<0.05$; +$p<0.10$

distance between the nearest ERO office and a child's home (the other variable related to enforcement activities) was never statistically significant.

First, Second, and Third Grades

The same models used for the kindergarten wave were also used to analyze the later waves as children progressed through third grade (table 6.4). Note that the number of apprehensions by the student's nearest ERO office changed each year, so with each year immigrant-origin youth progressed through elementary school, the number of apprehensions predicting their absences changed to accurately reflect enforcement activities occurring at that time.

As students progressed from kindergarten to first and second grade, the relationship between the number of apprehensions and missing school remained the same in both the two- and three-level HLM specifications. This means that as the number of apprehensions conducted by students closest to an ERO office increased, students tended to be less absent from school. Results are notably stronger for first-generation students compared to second-generation students in these three grade levels. The table shows that first-generation students appear to have experienced the largest effect in the first grade. However, looking at the results of the students in their third-grade year, the results are no longer statistically significant for first-generation students. Yet, third grade is when the effect appears to be strongest for second-generation students.

Finally, the distance to the nearest ERO office, while statistically insignificant for the kindergarten year, appears to be statistically significant for the entire sample in the first-grade year in the three-level model. When considering both immigrant-origin samples collectively, students who lived further away from the nearest ERO office tended to have fewer absences. This variable remains statistically significant for second-generation students and for the entire sample for the second- and third-grade years of data, indicating that students who lived further away from the nearest ERO office were less likely to be absent in these years of elementary school.

Additional Analyses

Given the consistency in our results, we ran a series of tests on other academic and nonacademic outcomes for students in kindergarten, including the reading and math scaled-scores and the socioemotional skills assessed each year in the dataset. The socioemotional skills assessed included internalizing behavior problems, interpersonal skills, eagerness to learn, externalizing behavior problems, and self-control. These measures were validated by the NCES, and prior research has relied on these measures to examine various hypotheses related to schooling outcomes in elementary grades. Moreover, a recent study found that mothers' DACA eligibility significantly decreased diagnoses of adjustment and anxiety disorders among children, pointing to the potentially strong relationship between immigration status and children's mental health.[28] Interestingly, using the same three-level HLM specification illustrated in tables 6.2 and 6.3, we found no relationship between the number of apprehensions or the distance to the nearest ERO office on academic or socioemotional outcomes for kindergarteners. Results for first-generation immigrant-origin students in kindergarten are in the appendix.

As an additional test, we also compared how the relationship between immigration enforcement activities and attendance might differ for non-immigrant-origin children. Using the same models as presented for first- and second-generation immigrant-origin students, we found no statistically significant associations between enforcement activities and the other children included in the ECLS-K:2011 data.

Does This Relationship Hold When Examining ICE Activities and School Absenteeism in One California School District?

Immigration enforcement activities are likely to affect different schools in different geographic areas in different ways. To explore potential heterogeneity in the relationship between enforcement activities and school absenteeism, we examined whether the association we found using the ECLS-K:2011 data was consistent for a small, urban California school district during the 2013–17 school years. The administrative data contained daily logs of absences (an advantage over the ECLS data), but there were fewer control variables related to home and outside-of-school experiences for students (a limitation compared to the ECLS data). Additionally, we used local newspaper reports of ICE activities in the area as our indicator of immigration enforcement, which provides greater specificity around ICE activities near schools.

Using similar modeling techniques, we found that each documented ICE raid in the residential areas of the school district was associated with two additional days absent for every student in the district. The association was particularly pronounced for migrant students and Hispanic students and during the 2016–17 school year. This school year was the first year ICE operated under the Trump administration. We take these results to demonstrate that immigration enforcement is not a standardized phenomenon and will not be experienced identically. Moreover, the amplified effects of ICE raids after Trump's election further advance our claim about the necessity of comparative analyses of the impacts of different immigration enforcement regimes on children's education.

Discussion

Questions about how immigration enforcement policies impact students' educational engagement and outcomes have never been more relevant. With substantially higher numbers of arrests and removals of immigrants during the 2017 fiscal year compared to the previous year, and with the inclusion of many more people without prior criminal convictions among those arrested and deported, millions of families are living in fear and suffering severe consequences.[29] Unauthorized immigrants' already tenuous relationship with public institutions is often further weakened in times of increased enforcement or more stringent policy environments.[30] This pattern has borne out dramatically in the Trump era. In addition to dropping school attendance, reports of domestic violence and use of public health services, including enrollment in federally subsidized insurance plans, have declined substantially since January 2017.[31]

Although school attendance has generally stabilized in the weeks following immigration enforcement actions carried out by Trump's ICE agents, missing repeated days of school can have significant detrimental effects on students.[32] Evidence of the immigrant families' strong reactions to immigration enforcement point to the need for better empirical understanding of the policy and schooling contexts that minimize the educational risks for students. Moreover, the current national climate foregrounds questions about how, if at all, schools can function as a "protective factor" that positively supports students' adaptation in the face of harsh immigration enforcement policies and what school leaders can do to make all families—and especially undocumented immigrant families—feel welcome and safe in their buildings.[33]

Our analysis of student absenteeism in early elementary school grades during three years of the Obama administration's most intense immigration enforcement activity explores the relationship between school absences and immigration enforcement. Using absenteeism as a measure of students' and parents' school engagement, we established a baseline of evidence about the impact of increased apprehensions and proximity to the ICE office carrying out apprehensions on one key educational indicator: being physically present in school. We found that across all grades (kindergarten through third), a rise in the number of apprehensions was associated with lower rates of absenteeism. This pattern held for both groups of students in our sample: first-generation (immigrant) students and second-generation, US-born children of immigrant parents. Also, for all grades except kindergarten, living closer to the ERO office responsible for managing enforcement activities and apprehensions was associated with a decrease in absenteeism.

Tellingly, school absence was the only outcome measure we tested for in kindergarten students that was significantly related to the number of apprehensions and distance to ERO offices. None of the other academic and nonacademic outcomes we examined produced statistically significant results (see appendix). The strong link between apprehensions and student absences, and the inverse relationship between the two during this specific period of enforcement, brings schools to the center of the conversation about what might be done to counteract the negative impacts of immigration enforcement activities on students' health, developmental, and educational outcomes. Our results also raise questions about whether similar patterns have continued under the present immigration enforcement regime, which has been decidedly less family centered.

Immigration enforcement policies strongly influence the broader social and political climate in which immigrant families live and make decisions about their own and their children's safety, including security while going to school. Our results show that immigration enforcement influenced student absences in unexpected ways. Like many of the out-of-school factors that influence absenteeism, immigration enforcement operates outside of school personnel's realm of control. However, our data show that the when schools serve as safe havens for students, the educational costs of immigration enforcement may be lessened.

Immigration enforcement can wreak havoc on families through extended separations and deportation that cause severe hardship, including such educational consequences as lost learning time. When students and parents feel secure going/sending to school, immigrant-origin students may be shielded from at least some of the detrimental effects of immigration enforcement, since fewer missed days of school translate into fewer academic (and potentially social and health) consequences for students.[34] We therefore offer a counterpoint to traditionally held notions that schools are not well positioned to address the causes contributing to absenteeism with regard to immigration. Furthermore, we identify an important area in which schools, particularly those serving large numbers of immigrant-origin students, should develop capacity: creating a welcoming environment for students and families struggling with immigration-related challenges.

Researchers and practitioners have begun to investigate school-level responses to immigration enforcement. Studies have identified some of the policies and practices that yield the greatest benefits for immigrant-origin students and families in terms of providing necessary resources and protection from increasingly invasive enforcement attempts.[35] School leaders who are leading the way in this work are focusing on those factors within their control. They are investing in training school personnel about undocumented students' legal rights to education, working to ensure an inclusive and culturally responsive school climate, developing clear guidelines about how to respond to attempts by ICE agents to enter school grounds, and opening up their schools to serve as resource centers for families, connecting them with legal counsel and other services.[36] A number of these practices are consistent with some of the more successful initiatives to specifically address absenteeism and improve school attendance. Increased family contact, closer school-family relationships, and engaging multiple school and community resources to address barriers to attendance have all been shown to produce improvements in attendance rates.[37] Yet, we know very little about the extent to which the existing efforts to combat absenteeism are effective for immigrant students fearing deportation or whether school-level initiatives in response to the immigration enforcement context are geared toward reducing absenteeism.

The extant research on school-level responses to immigration enforcement activities has only scratched the surface of what educators and policy makers need to know about effective school-based strategies for engaging and supporting immigrant-origin families during these especially challenging times. More empirical research is needed to understand what schools and districts are doing in the face of rising hostility toward immigrant families—manifested through xenophobic acts and expanded immigration enforcement efforts by the federal government—and to measure the impact of school-led initiatives on youth and their families. Studies of what is working, for which students, and what resources and guidance school leaders and teachers require to successfully implement effective strategies are essential if schools are to offset some of the damaging impacts of immigration enforcement. Analyses of how current immigration enforcement approaches enacted under the Trump administration affect student absenteeism and other educational outcomes are necessary to determine the consequences of even less child-sensitive immigration enforcement policies than those implemented by the Obama administration. This evidence, including changes in patterns of student attendance, behavior, and academic performance in the post-Obama era, has implications for schools seeking to understand how to best support students in the face of intensified deportation fears and associated trauma.

In many ways, we introduce as many questions as we answer about whether and how schools can be sanctuaries for students during times of instability associated with immigration enforcement. We offer some evidence that immigration enforcement actions may not always been accompanied by a reduction in school attendance for those students most likely to be directly impacted. Yet our data cannot tell us what schools were doing during periods of increased apprehensions, nor can they identify the resources and supports that facilitate schools' being perceived as safe spaces by families under duress. We caution against interpreting these results to indicate that more apprehensions could be beneficial for young people in any way (for example, through less absenteeism); to the contrary, the evidence overwhelmingly points to the significant short- and long-term consequences of apprehensions and deportations for youth and their families.[38] Instead, we call for researchers, policy makers, and educational leaders to consider the role and responsibilities of schools to provide a refuge for all students and families in this highly polarized time, to investigate these questions empirically, and to work to eliminate the obstacles to schools fulfilling their potential as sanctuaries.

APPENDIX 6 TABLE
Effect-size estimates of enforcement activities and other outcomes in kindergarten

| | ACHIEVEMENT MEASURES | | SOCIOEMOTIONAL SKILLS | | | | |
	Reading	Math	Internalizing	Interpersonal	Eagerness	Externalizing	Self-control
Immigration enforcement variables in kindergarten							
Apprehensions in 2010	-0.02 (0.07)	-0.07 (0.11)	0.00 (0.03)	0.01 (0.02)	-0.07 (0.11)	0.08 (0.08)	-0.00 (0.06)
Distance to nearest ERO office in 2010	0.12 (0.10)	-0.05 (0.19)	-0.03 (0.03)	0.03 (0.03)	0.02 (0.18)	0.09 (0.13)	0.01 (0.10)
Observations	330	330	330	330	330	330	330

Notes: Robust standard errors in parentheses. ***p<0.001. **p<0.01. *p<0.05.

7

Can School Buses Drive Down (Chronic) Absenteeism?

SARAH A. CORDES, MICHELE LEARDO,
CHRISTOPHER RICK, AND AMY ELLEN SCHWARTZ

FOR MORE THAN TWENTY-FIVE MILLION US students, the school day begins on the school bus. The morning bus commute has the potential to affect students' tardiness, absenteeism, and academic outcomes as it shapes whether, and to what extent, they arrive at school on time and ready to learn. For that reason, school bus and transportation policies play an important role in the current education context. As school choice continues to expand, students select from a widening array of charter, magnet, and traditional public schools over a larger geographic area and therefore face potential concomitant increases in commute distances and increased reliance on the school bus to attend these "choice" schools. Understanding whether, and how, school buses help or hinder student performance is critical for policy makers looking to leverage school transportation policy to improve student outcomes.

Recent research by Michael Gottfried provides compelling descriptive evidence that school buses may reduce absenteeism.[1] Surprisingly, this is the only published direct examination of the relationship between the school bus and academic outcomes. Unfortunately, the Early Childhood Longitudinal Study: Kindergarten Class of 2010–11 (ECLS-K:2011) data used for the study constrains the analysis and limits generalizability in two key ways. First, the transportation data are parent reported and limited in scope. Second, the sample includes only kindergarten students. In this chapter we use new administrative data on pupil transportation for students in grades K–6 to explore the generalizability and robustness of these results. More specifically, we use rich student-level administrative data on the census of students attending New York City Department of Education (NYCDOE) schools, including information on pupil transportation and attendance to examine the relationship between the school bus and (chronic) absenteeism among elementary school students. We address four key questions: Are students who take the bus less likely to miss school than other students—is there a "bus gap" in absenteeism? How much of the bus gap among eligible students reflects differences in student characteristics? How much is explained by differences in where students go to school? And how do these disparities differ across racial/ethnic groups?

We find that, on average, bus riders are absent about 0.66 percentage points less than nonriders (approximately one day) and are 3.99 percentage points less likely to be chronically absent. Roughly 40 percent of the bus gap in absenteeism is explained by differences between the characteristics of students who ride the bus and those who do not. Further, more than three-fourths of the remaining gap is explained by differences in the schools bus riders attend, such that the within-school disparity between students who take the bus and those that do not is relatively small. Thus, school buses may matter because of their effect on the school the student attends. Although our descriptive evidence does not support a causal interpretation, the finding is intriguing, suggesting that school buses may reduce absenteeism because students who ride the bus attend better schools. While much additional research needs to be done to understand whether this is because better schools are more likely to offer the bus, or because students *use* the bus to attend better schools, these findings highlight the potential importance of school buses in making school choice work by allowing students to attend schools that better suit them.

Previous research offers limited insight into the role of the school bus in reducing student absenteeism. Rather, it tends to focus on safety concerns, such as seat belts or bus driver training, bullying and managing disruptive behavior, or the consequences of busing in the context of desegregation efforts.[2] Other work examines the school bus in the context of rural school district consolidation.[3] Theoretically, the relationship between the school bus and student absenteeism is ambiguous. On one hand, the school bus might *increase* absenteeism if students miss school because of missed morning pick-ups, unpleasant experiences on the bus (e.g., due to long rides or bullying), or the spread of illness among students sharing the bus.[4] On the other hand, taking the school bus might *decrease* absenteeism by lowering the time and/or monetary cost of getting to school.[5]

Closest to our study, Gottfried's study explores the association between absenteeism and bus riding.[6] Using a nationally representative sample of kindergarten students in the ECLS-K:2011, he estimates the disparity in attendance between students taking the bus and similar students who do not take the bus. He draws on data from parent and teacher surveys, including questions on how students travel to school and student absenteeism, and accounts for a wide array of factors, including child demographic character-istics, measured skills at kindergarten entry, kindergarten experiences (e.g., full-day, public, categorical measure of distance to kindergarten), and house-hold characteristics (e.g., income, parental education, number of siblings, number of books at home). Gottfried also estimates disparities between bus riders and nonriders attending schools in the same district and any disparities between riders and nonriders in the same school. He finds that kindergart-ners taking the bus are absent about 0.4 fewer days per year, a statistically significant difference that may have small but potentially meaningful effects on academic outcomes. As Gottfried notes, data limitations constrained the research design, leaving important questions unanswered about robustness and generalizability. We address a number of these in this study.

First, rather than focusing on kindergarten students, our sample includes students in kindergarten through sixth grade, allowing us to examine the relationship between the bus and absenteeism for both younger and older students. Moreover, the kindergarteners in our sample are likely to be rep-resentative of students in other grades, as kindergarten in New York City was mandatory during our study period. In contrast, since kindergarten is currently mandatory in only a handful of states, families that place a high value on education (and perhaps attendance) and choose to send their chil-dren to kindergarten are likely overrepresented in the ECSL-K:2011 data. Second, rather than using survey data, we use administrative data from the

NYCDOE Office of Pupil Transportation (OPT) on individual bus assignment for the universe of public school students and administrative records from the NYCDOE on student daily attendance. These data are collected and used for effective delivery of service for the largest pupil transportation operation in the country and are therefore not subject to the same concerns over misreporting bias or missing data, particularly the concern that nonresponse or reporting errors may be related to bus use, as in survey data. We also use NYCDOE administrative data that includes the exact number of days absent for the entire school year, allowing us to construct richer and more precise measures of absenteeism.

The New York City Bus Context

With a fleet of 9,500 school buses serving more than 100,000 students in 1,500-plus schools, NYCDOE oversees the largest pupil transportation operation in the country. While New York City includes neighborhoods characterized by skyscrapers and a high population density, it also includes lower-density neighborhoods with single-family homes. The student population is large (more than 1.1 million students enrolled each year) and demographically diverse, as are the schools that serve them. This heterogeneity in students and schools, combined with uniquely detailed data on individual student absenteeism and bus services, makes New York an ideal context to examine the role of the school bus for reducing absenteeism in an urban setting.

Within the NYCDOE, the OPT sets broad policy and provides school bus infrastructure (e.g., contracting with vendors, developing computer systems, school bus routing), giving school-level administrators considerable discretion over bus services. This discretion includes deciding whether the school will offer *any* bus services to general education students; it is individual school, not district, administrators who decide whether a school bus is available to an eligible student.[7] In 2015, only 57 percent of elementary and middle school principals chose to provide buses, so nearly 20 percent of students who were eligible for the bus under OPT guidelines attended a school that did not offer bus service.

In schools that offer buses, principals are responsible for identifying students who may be eligible for bus service based on where they live and the feasibility of accommodating them on a bus route. Principals use student home addresses to provide initial identification of students who may be eligible for transportation based on grade and distance from school. Students in grades K–2/3–6 must live more than 0.5/1 miles from school to be eligible for the bus. Principals suggest location of bus stops (again, following OPT guidelines), and OPT verifies individual student eligibility for transportation and creates bus routes following these rules: (1) routes to a given school may not exceed five miles (as driven through the streets); (2) there must be eleven eligible students *at the time of creation* to establish a route; and (3) routes may not cross borough boundaries.[8] Eligible students who cannot be accommodated on a bus route or who decline the offered service are given Metrocards allowing them free service on public transportation (city buses and subways).

The implication of these transportation policies is that differences in bus utilization will reflect differences between students attending different schools (say, because some schools offer buses and others do not) and differences between students attending the same school. These within-school differences will be driven by eligibility due to a student's grade and proximity to school, the ability (or not) of OPT to accommodate a student on a viable bus route, and, potentially, student or family preferences. We leverage this variation to examine the relationship between the bus and student absenteeism.

New York City Student-Level Data and Sample

This study draws on multiple sources of administrative data on public school students provided by the New York City Department of Education. Our key data set is student-level transportation data from the Office of Public Transportation for the academic year 2014–15. The transportation variables include student eligibility for the bus; categorical measures of distance between home and school grouped into one of four categories (less than 0.5 miles, 0.5–1 mile, 1–1.5 miles, or at least 1.5 miles); and assigned bus route.

We matched the pupil transportation data to student sociodemographic variables, including gender, race/ethnicity (black, white, Hispanic, Asian, other), eligibility for free or reduced-price meals, and, importantly, the number of days absent and the total number of school days registered. In addition, these data contain the school attended and the location of home residence (latitude and longitude, census tract, and borough). Finally, we obtained school-level location data (address, latitude and longitude) from the Common Core of Data. Thus, we are able to calculate the distance between a student's residential address and school.

Our sample includes all New York City public school students in grades K–6 in the 2014–15 academic year (hereafter 2015).[9] We exclude students missing critical transportation, demographic, or attendance data.[10] We also exclude full-time special education students for whom bus services are markedly different than for general education students.[11] Our final sample includes approximately 86 percent of all K–6 students attending NYC public schools in 2015.

Measures and Methods

Our analyses use two distinct measures of absenteeism. The first, *absenteeism*, is the percentage of days a student is absent from school. The second, *chronic absenteeism*, is an indicator equal to 1 if a student is absent for 10 percent or more days (roughly 18 days in a 185-day school year). While there is little empirical research identifying a specific, appropriate threshold distinguishing chronic absenteeism, 10 percent is consistent with thresholds used in both prior research and in practice by the NYCDOE. Our key transportation variable is an indicator, BUS, which is equal to 1 if a student is assigned to receive bus services.

We begin with a simple comparison of absenteeism between students who ride the bus (riders) and those who do not (nonriders). This yields a naïve measure of the bus gap, which will reflect both differences between those who live close to school (and are not eligible for busing) and those who live far enough away to be eligible. If proximity to school is correlated with the importance families place on education, then this measure will conflate those preferences and confound the effort to learn about bus use. For example, students who live within the walk zone may place a higher value on education and tend to have lower absenteeism regardless of bus service, in which case raw comparisons will understate the bus gap that might exist between otherwise similar students. Conversely, it may be that students within the walk zone place a lower value on education (since they are less willing to travel) and tend to have higher absenteeism regardless of bus service, in which case raw comparisons will overstate the bus gap between otherwise similar students. In both cases, students ineligible for the bus likely serve as a poor comparison group for bus riders. Thus, we proceed by limiting our analysis to those students living far enough from school to be eligible for the bus and control for differences in grade in the following regression model:

$$Yisg = \alpha + \gamma BUSis + \eta \textbf{GRADE}g + \varepsilon isg$$

where Y is a measure of absenteeism (or chronic absenteeism) for student i in school s in grade g; BUS is an indicator taking a value of 1 if the student is a bus rider and 0 otherwise; and **GRADE** are grade effects. Here, γ captures the average difference in absenteeism (or chronic absenteeism) between riders and nonriders in the same grade who live far enough from school to be eligible for the school bus. We estimate this model separately for students in grades K–2 and 3–6 because of the differences in eligibility criteria described above. We then expand the model to control for a set of student characteristics, including race/ethnicity, eligibility for free or reduced-price lunch. In this model, γ captures the difference between observationally equivalent bus riders and nonriders (again, those living far enough away to be eligible). Finally, we estimate a set of models that includes school fixed effects, in which γ captures the difference in absenteeism (or chronic absenteeism) between observationally equivalent riders and nonriders attending the same school. We then reestimate our models separately by racial/ethnic group to explore whether and to what extent the bus gap differs for minority students as compared to their white peers.

Results

Who Rides the Bus?

In 2015, more than fifty thousand of New York City's K–6 students rode the school bus. As shown in table 7.1, these riders differ markedly from nonriders on a variety of dimensions that may be important for attendance. A much smaller share of riders is eligible for free or reduced-price lunch (70.9 percent versus 82.7 percent).[12] Riders are disproportionately white and Asian (26.83 percent and 27.05 percent), while nonriders are disproportionately black (22.25 percent) and Hispanic (42.65 percent).

Bus riders are disproportionately enrolled in early grades, which is consistent with differences in eligibility criteria. While almost one-quarter of students in grades K–2 are riders, a much smaller proportion of older students are riders (approximately 7 percent of students in grades 3–5). Interestingly, bus ridership increases to about 14 percent in sixth grade, which is when many students begin to attend middle schools that may be farther from home. We also see significant differences in ridership by borough, which may

TABLE 7.1

Descriptive statistics for grades K–6 bus riders and nonriders

(percentages)	(1) ALL	(2) BUS	(3) NO BUS
Female	50.16	50.31	50.15
Ever poor	81.39	70.90	82.66
Limited English proficiency	16.72	13.77	17.07
Race/Ethnicity			
Black	21.67	16.80	22.25
Hispanic	41.21	29.27	42.65
Asian	19.91	27.05	19.05
White	17.18	26.83	16.02
Grade			
Kindergarten	14.92	24.88	13.72
1	15.26	19.55	14.75
2	15.19	19.49	14.67
3	14.33	7.62	15.14
4	14.04	7.64	14.81
5	13.29	7.03	14.05
6	12.97	13.78	12.87
Borough			
Manhattan	11.42	5.38	12.15
Bronx	22.28	11.89	23.53
Brooklyn	29.54	20.28	30.66
Queens	30.26	42.05	28.83
Staten Island	6.30	20.26	4.61
Distance zone			
<0.5 miles	56.90	0.64	63.69
0.5–1.0 miles	23.32	43.77	20.85
1.0–1.5 miles	6.33	21.47	4.50
>1.5 miles	13.46	34.12	10.97
Distance: Home to school miles (average)	0.73	1.16	0.67
Absenteeism rate	5.92	5.34	6.00
Chronic absenteeism (absent at least 10% of days)	17.42	13.95	17.84
Students	472,731	50,926	421,805
(percentage)	100.00	10.77	89.23

Notes: Sample includes K–6 students with transportation data; sample excludes students in charter schools or in full-time special education schools. *Ever poor* takes a value of 1 if the student is eligible for free or reduced-price lunch in any year they are observed. Except for gender, all differences in means are statistically significant at the 0.01 level.

reflect differences in neighborhood density. Students in the less dense boroughs of Queens and Staten Island are overrepresented among riders, while students in the denser boroughs of Manhattan, the Bronx, and Brooklyn are underrepresented.

Finally, bus riders tend to live further from school: 43 percent live .5 to 1 mile from school (versus 21 percent of nonriders), 21 percent live 1–1.5 miles from school (versus about 5 percent of nonriders), and 34 percent live more than 1.5 miles from school (versus 11 percent of nonriders). Conversely, the majority of nonriders (over two-thirds) live within .5 mile of school. This is also reflected in the average distance between home and school: the average rider attends school 1.16 miles from home, while the average nonrider lives only 0.67 miles from school.

Is There a Bus Gap in Absenteeism?

On average, absenteeism among bus riders is more than a half percentage point *lower* than it is among nonriders, implying a bus gap of approximately one additional day of school per year. There is a similar bus gap in chronic absenteeism (13.95 percent versus 17.84 percent). To some extent, these disparities reflect differences between students living near and farther away from school.

Results are more striking among students living far enough away from school to be eligible for bus service (albeit not required to take the offer). Bus riders have absenteeism rates about 1.9 percentage points lower than eligible nonriders. The magnitude of this disparity is significant compared to the 6.65 percent average absenteeism rate for this group of bus eligible students.

Adjusting for sociodemographic characteristics yields considerably smaller estimates of the bus gap in absenteeism: 1.17 percentage points among K–2 students and 1.07 percentage points in grades 3–6. Thus, roughly 40 percent of the disparity in absenteeism reflects differences in the characteristics of students taking the bus.

Finally, we explore how much of the bus gap is due to differences between schools, including, but not limited to, differences between schools offering buses and those not offering buses. We do so by introducing school effects in the regression model, estimating a "within-school bus gap," which captures the average disparities in absenteeism between riders and nonriders attending *the same school*. Doing so shrinks the differences in absenteeism substantially—by nearly 75 percent—to 0.25 percentage points in both grades K–2 and 3–6 (both statistically significant). This translates into riders attending approximately 0.42 more days of school than otherwise similar nonriders at the same school. This large drop in magnitude is intriguing and suggests that bus riders attend better schools. Notice, however, that this difference in school quality is consistent with two underlying mechanisms. First, the bus gap may reflect differences between schools offering the bus and those that do not. If, for example, schools that offer the bus have more administrative capacity, that may allow them to both oversee bus service and promote student attendance. Second, bus riders may use the bus to attend schools that better match their needs. For example, they may attend choice schools or magnet schools that are more effective at encouraging attendance. In this case, school buses effectively reduce absenteeism by allowing students to attend schools that are a better match.

Are Bus Riders Less Likely to Be Chronically Absent?

Since the average absenteeism rate in our sample is low (about 6 percent), a 0.25–1.17 percentage point reduction may not necessarily translate into meaningful differences in other outcomes (figure 7.1). Chronic absenteeism, however, may be a more critical measure of educational disadvantage, with larger negative consequences for a variety of student outcomes, including performance, attainment, and high school choice. As shown in figure 7.2, the results for chronic absenteeism mirror our previous findings. On average, bus riders are 9.6 percentage points less likely to be chronically absent in grades K–2 and 9.2 percentage points less likely in grades 3–6. Adjusting for student characteristics reduces the disparity by almost half such that riders in K–2/3–6 are 5.5/5.8 percentage points less likely to be chronically absent. Finally, our school fixed models indicate that much of the disparity is between schools rather than within schools: K–2/3–6 riders are 1.1/1.2 percentage points less likely to be chronically absent than nonriders in the same school. This is a modest reduction compared to the 20 percent rate of chronic absenteeism in this sample.

How Does the Bus Gap Vary by Race and Ethnicity?

We reestimate our models stratifying the sample by race/ethnicity. As shown in figures 7.3 and 7.4, the differences are striking, particularly among students in grades 3–6. Among black and Hispanic students in grades 3–6, the bus gap is 3–4 times larger than the estimated gap among Asian students and

FIGURE 7.1   Regression-adjusted mean differences in absenteeism for distance-eligible K–6 students

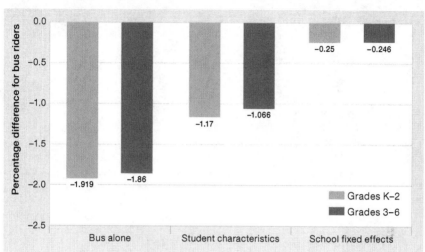

Notes: Each model includes all controls from previous estimations. For example, the second bar shows the regression-adjusted mean difference between bus and absenteeism when also controlling for student characteristics (race, gender, limited English proficiency status, free and reduced-price lunch status). The third bar shows the regression-adjusted mean difference when controlling for bus, student characteristics, and school fixed effects. Grades K–2/3–6 students are generally eligible for bus service if they live at least 0.5/1.0 miles from school. Students are excluded from the sample if they are missing transportation or biographical data or are in full-time special education. All mean differences are significant at the 1 percent level.

20–25 times larger than the gap among white students. Controlling for other student characteristics (namely, gender and poverty) has little impact on the estimated disparity. In contrast, the pattern of within-school gaps by race is reversed. Compared to students of the same race in the same school, the estimated bus gaps are *smaller* for blacks and Hispanics than for Asians and whites. Thus, it may be that the school bus plays a particularly important role for blacks and Hispanics in facilitating access to better schools.

Policy Implications

Overall, our descriptive findings indicate that the gap in attendance between bus riders and nonriders is both statistically and substantively important in both the early grades (K–2) and the later years (grades 3–6). Perhaps most

FIGURE 7.2   Regression-adjusted mean differences in chronic absenteeism for distance-eligible K–6 students

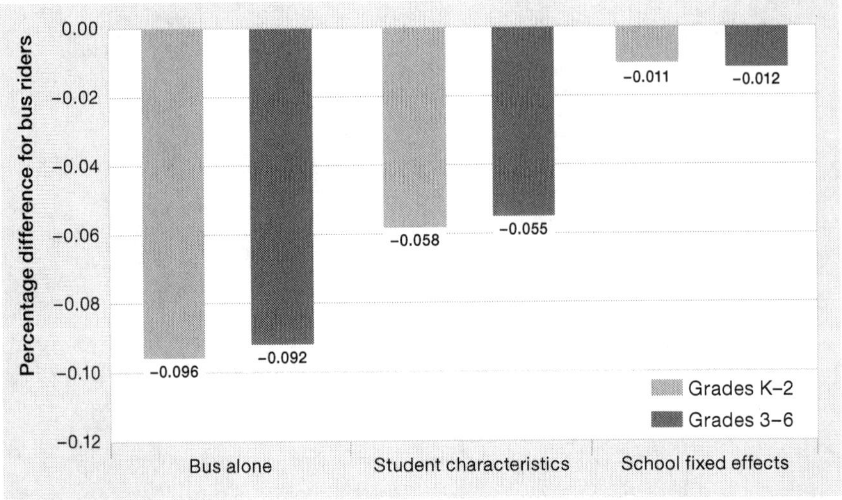

Notes: Each model includes all controls from previous estimations. For example, the second bar shows the regression-adjusted mean difference between bus and absenteeism when also controlling for student characteristics (race, gender, limited English proficiency status, free and reduced-price lunch status). The third bar shows the regression-adjusted mean difference when controlling for bus, student characteristics, and school fixed effects. Grades K–2/3–6 students are generally eligible for bus service if they live at least 0.5/1.0 miles from school. Students are excluded from the sample if they are missing transportation or biographical data or are in full-time special education. All mean differences are significant at the 1 percent level.

intriguing, however, is that much of the difference in absenteeism is driven by differences between schools rather than within schools, between bus riders who go to different schools rather than between riders and nonriders attending the same school.

This finding differs from Gottfried's study, which finds that bus gaps are virtually identical whether comparing riders and nonriders in the same school or riders and nonriders who attend different schools in the same district.[13] Specifically, his estimate that kindergarten bus riders miss 0.28 days less than their nonriding peers in the same district is nearly a tenth the size of our estimates of 1.919/1.860 days for grade K–2/3–6 students, and his estimate for chronic absenteeism is less than half the size of ours. This suggests that the school bus may play a more important role in facilitating school choice in New York City, or in allowing students to attend schools that better match

FIGURE 7.3   Regression-adjusted mean differences in absenteeism for distance-eligible K–2 students by race

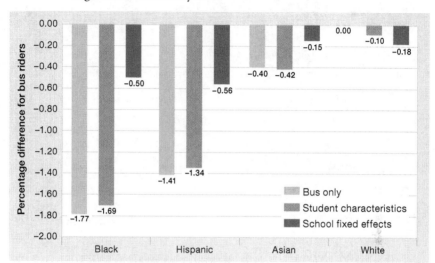

Notes: Each model includes all controls from previous estimations. For example, the second bar shows the regression-adjusted mean difference between bus and absenteeism when also controlling for student characteristics (gender, limited English proficiency status, free and reduced-price lunch status). The third bar shows the regression-adjusted mean difference when controlling for bus, student characteristics, and school fixed effects. Grades K–2/3–6 students are generally eligible for bus service if they live at least 0.5/1.0 miles from school. Students are excluded from the sample if they are missing transportation or biographical data or are in full-time special education. All mean differences are significant at the 1 percent level except results for white students.

their needs, than it does in the suburban and rural districts where the majority of ECLS-K:2011 bus riders attend school. Given this, one solution to chronic absenteeism in urban districts might be to expand school bus service to more schools.

Yet, while this may appear to be a straightforward proposition, expanding service and understanding the implications for absenteeism may be more complex for a number of reasons. First, we find that more than two-fifths of schools in New York City do not offer school bus transportation. Such schools may lack the administrative capacity to schedule, organize, and manage bus service, so adding bus service to these schools might only improve attendance if additional resources are available to support bus service. Districts could potentially support these schools by developing policies to help more schools offer bus service or to help build school-level capacity.

FIGURE 7.4   Regression-adjusted mean differences in absenteeism for distance-eligible grades 3–6 students by race

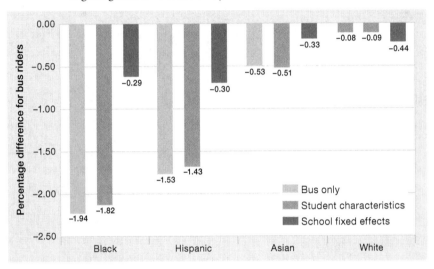

Notes: Each model includes all controls from previous estimations. For example, the second bar shows the regression-adjusted mean difference between bus and absenteeism when also controlling for student characteristics (gender, limited English proficiency status, free and reduced-price lunch status). The third bar shows the regression-adjusted mean difference when controlling for bus, student characteristics, and school fixed effects. Grades K–2/3–6 students are generally eligible for bus service if they live at least 0.5/1.0 miles from school. Students are excluded from the sample if they are missing transportation or biographical data or are in full-time special education. All mean differences are significant at the 1 percent level except results for white students.

However, expanding service to more schools could cause longer bus routes, and longer commute times, if a limited supply of buses were deployed to serve more schools, bus stops, or students. Some students may need to be picked up earlier in the morning and/or dropped off later in the afternoon, which could have unintended consequences for attendance and student performance more generally. For example, early pick-up times may make students more likely to miss the bus and be absent from school. Even for those students who make their morning pickup, earlier pickup times may mean less sleep and thus hindered performance, as prior literature shows that both early school start times and lack of sleep are related to students' lower academic outcomes and attendance.[14] Therefore, improved attendance may come at the cost of overall academic performance. In the same vein, recent research from Brazilian schools finds strong evidence that longer commutes have a negative effect on academic achievement.[15] Further, long bus rides and late-afternoon drop-offs may reduce participation in afterschool activities both at school (if students have to leave to catch the bus) or in the neighborhoods where students live (if they do not get home in time to attend neighborhood-based programs). Therefore, districts must balance the potential positive effects of expanding bus service against potential deleterious effects of early pickup or longer rides. Districts should also be mindful of how bus scheduling affects the availability of extracurricular activities.

Also, literature suggests that the bus ride can be unpleasant for a number of reasons, including illness and bullying. Bullying may be of particular concern when students from a wide range of grades share one bus, a practice that may become more common if bus service is expanded to more schools. Many buses also lack a bus monitor who is tasked with student supervision, so students may begin to avoid school because of unpleasant bus rides.

Finally, our results suggest that expanding service to more schools may be particularly beneficial for black and Hispanic students. Yet, we also find that even accounting for eligibility, black and Hispanic students are less likely to receive bus service than their white and Asian peers are. Thus, if service is expanded without special consideration for targeting these students, there is a potential for the school bus to exacerbate already large and persistent racial gaps in attendance and academic performance.

So, while expanding bus service to more schools has the potential to increase school choice and drive down absenteeism gaps, much additional investigation is warranted to inform policy makers about the possible benefits and drawbacks of expanding school bus service, including studies designed to isolate the causal effect of the bus or school choice from the effects of other potential differences in school environment.[16]

8

The Ills of Absenteeism

Can School-Based Health Centers Provide the Cure?

JENNIFER GRAVES, SARIT WEISBURD,
AND CHRISTOPHER SALEM

MOST OF US can recall taking the occasional sick day, staying home from school due to a stomachache or a sore throat. For others, however, their health status potentially contributes to chronic absenteeism from school with detrimental effects on their human capital accumulation and long-run outcomes. This chapter explores the relationship between health and absenteeism and whether, for these students, a school-based health center (SBHC) could provide a cure to the problem.

Parents cite health as the biggest factor in why they let their child stay home, stating it as the reason for absences 60 percent of the time.[1] Additionally, a 2014 study by the advocacy group Attendance Works found that high school students themselves cited illness as the most common reason they missed school.[2] Student health and access to health care have been a part of school culture and infrastructure in the United States since the Progressive Era, when nurses were first a regular presence on school campuses.[3] And while student health has never been a prime consideration in how schools are structured in this country, a number of school-based policies have been implemented to address student health. For example, physical education is considered a common subject in schools across the United States, the free and reduced-priced meals program has been in place since 1946, and in recent decades there has been an increased focus on nutrition standards for all foods available in schools.[4]

Given the potential importance of health as a driver of absenteeism and the demonstrated importance of attendance for academic success, addressing students' health in a more direct manner may rightly fall within the scope of schools' concerns. Additionally, policy makers are looking for *school-based* strategies and techniques to improve general outcomes for students. This chapter outlines one strategy that was initially developed to affect general student health and wellness outcomes but that may also prove valuable in addressing chronic absenteeism: school-based health centers.

An SBHC—also called a wellness center, an adolescent health center, a mobile clinic, or a health resource center—is a primary care clinic typically located on the campus of a primary or secondary school that provides a variety of services to students during their school day. The School-Based Health Alliance, a leading advocacy organization for the SBHC model, describes the goal of these centers as "giv[ing] students meaningful access to care in a location that is safe and convenient," as providing services that go beyond what a typical school nurse can provide in the areas of primary, mental, oral, and vision care for students at the school, as well as potentially serving family and community members.[5] SBHCs are usually funded through a mix of sources, local or state funds, reimbursements from health insurance companies, and/or grants among the most common. These clinics have existed in the US since the 1990s, and currently forty-nine states have at least one SBHC.[6]

In theory, SBHCs have the potential to reduce student absences in a variety of ways. To the extent that they provide health-care access to students who otherwise do not have such access, they may reduce absences through improvements in health and/or management of symptoms or chronic medical conditions. Treating illness and medical conditions can make kids healthier, and if kids are healthy they are more likely to attend school. Subsequently, both being healthier and attending school can improve learning. Also, SBHCs reduce the need to miss school to obtain needed medical care, since the child can visit the clinic and see a medical professional during a time that least disrupts the school day. Not having to travel to another location can also cut down on total instructional time missed to address medical needs.

Yet, despite such possible benefits of SBHCs as means to reduce absenteeism by incorporating health care for students into the school context, there is limited empirical evidence to support this effect. From a policy perspective, this is concerning considering the use of SBHCs in nearly all US states. After all, giving kids more access to health care in their schools certainly sounds like a good thing. But given the limited amount of money available to implement any services in schools, is it the best use of scarce funds? Demonstrating the impacts SBHCs have on both health and attendance is key to answering this important question. Thus, the purpose of this chapter is to review what is known about SBHCs and how that might relate to attendance. We focus on answering the following questions: How have SBHCs been implemented in the US? What does the existing empirical literature say about the links between SBHCs, student health, and attendance? What can be done to uncover the causal relationship between SBHCs and student attendance and determine the specific characteristics of SBHCs that are crucial for improving student health?

School-Based Health Centers in the US Context

The distinguishing feature of an SBHC is that it serves as a health-care access point on campus so that students can seek care without missing school or receive medical attention for issues they might have otherwise ignored. Because time in school accounts for a large portion of a student's day, and because their presence is generally required, an SBHC's physical location *on* a school campus allows students to easily and conveniently access medical care. From a health-care perspective, traditional medical facilities and delivery points, which have less convenient hours of operation and require transportation, cannot compete in terms of location and convenience.

In general, SBHCs can provide on-campus services in two main areas: medical care and assistance in accessing care. In the first area, medical professionals provide on-site care to students and sometimes even community members. These models can vary. An SBHC might have a full-time nurse practitioner, pediatrician, or another medical professional who can diagnose, treat, and prescribe as needed.[7] There may also be a dentist, eye doctor, or licensed therapist who provides services at the SBHC on certain days of the week or month. The combination of care varies based on needs, availability, and funding. In terms of aiding in accessing care, an SBHC will typically have a health liaison who is well-versed in the various health insurance, access, and assistance programs in the school's community and assists families in navigating them.[8] Table 8.1 compares services offered by a traditional school (e.g., school nurse) with those offered by a school with an SBHC.

SBHCs can and have been implemented in a variety of ways. US schools began employing health professionals in the early twentieth century, originally in New York, and they focused mainly on screening and identifying health problems among high school students.[9] The concern was that adolescents were not given enough access to quality health services.[10] In the 1960s, a few places (e.g., Cambridge, Massachusetts; Dallas, Texas; and St. Paul, Minnesota) expanded medical services beyond screenings and preventative care to also include treatment services by nurse practitioners, physicians, even social workers and nutritionists for poor children on school campuses. These were the first SBHCs.[11] SBHCs experienced significant growth in the late 1990s and early 2000s.[12] Some states, such as Delaware, prioritized the their development and provided the funding and guidance necessary to make them more widespread as part of a coordinated effort at the state level. Today, every Delaware high school has an SBHC, and the majority of their funding comes from the state.[13] In other places, significant interest in SBHCs has resulted in organizations dedicated to the development of SBHCs in a certain city or region. For example, the Los Angeles Trust for Children's Health is a non-profit organization devoted to opening and maintaining SBHCs mostly in LA Unified schools. Since 1991, it has worked in partnership with the district and county agencies to open wellness programs across the county, including thirty-five SBHCs and fifteen Wellness Centers, which are an update to their original SBHC model.[14]

Even as our understanding of the relationship between health and education continues to evolve, the implementation of SHBCs remains sporadic and inconsistent in the United States. Currently, at the federal level, there is no official definition for what constitutes an SBHC or any detailed guidance on how to open an SBHC in a school or district. The Centers for Disease Control (CDC) does advocate for building relationships between communities and schools to achieve a variety of health-related goals, which they promote

TABLE 8.1

Comparison of services provided by a school nurse and an SBHC

	SCHOOL NURSE	SBHC
ADMINISTERING CARE		
Assess student health issues and refer for treatment and/or prescription	✔	✔
Provide care on-site, particularly primary and behavioral care but can also provide vision, dental, and other	X	✔
EMERGENCY CARE		
Create emergency plans for students with life-threatening allergies or emergency prescriptions (e.g., epi-pen or emergency seizure medication)	✔	✔
Administer advanced emergency care	X	✔
MEDICATIONS		
Obtain orders to administer medications at school	✔	✔
Issue orders to administer medications at school	X	✔
HEALTH INSURANCE ACCESS		
Provide a health liaison to facilitate insurance and other program sign-ups	X	✔
LOCATION OF CARE		
Provide medical, dental, vision, and therapy appointments on-site	X	✔
Refer to outside providers as needed	✔	✔
SCHEDULING OF CARE		
Schedule primary care appointments around a student's school day	X	✔
SPECIAL EDUCATION AND HEALTH		
Advocate for students to have appropriate interventions and services on an IEP	✔	✔
HEALTH OUTREACH		
Implement schoolwide health initiatives	✔	✔
FAMILY OUTREACH		
Help families understand health information about their children	✔	✔

through their Whole School, Whole Communty, Whole Child model.[15] This model aligns with the purpose of an SBHC on philosophical and practical levels but does not use the term directly or provide details on how an SBHC might be implemented in practice.[16] The model is, however, a part of the School Health Index (SHI), a recognized measurement tool that schools and districts can use to qualify for some federal and private grants.[17] Additionally, a few states (e.g., Florida and New York) provide their own frameworks for establishing an SBHC, but they are not required or widely used. For example, Florida has specified requirements for "Full Service Schools" (its name for full SBHCs), and these 382 schools (in the 2016–17 school year) serve approximately 11 percent of Florida K–12 students.[18] New York has 255 SBHCs that are state approved (in the 2016–17 school year), serving approximately 10 percent of the state's student population.[19]

SBHCs also have a varied history of funding. When they were first being introduced, much of the funding came from states' general funds or block grants, sourced as either state or federal funding.[20] But since the 1990s, the funding model has shifted toward reimbursement for services from insurance companies and securing funding through grants. In recent years, some federal grants have become available again, but not consistently. For example, from 2011 to 2013, approximately $150 million in federal grant money was awarded to applicants in forty-six states for the opening of SBHCs through the Affordable Care Act. However, the grant program was discontinued after that, and 2019 are at a pared-down level of $10 million.[21] Some SBHCs use a partnership approach, where a community-based agency, a university, or another government agency partners with the school or district to manage the SBHC on school property.[22] What constitutes an SBHC can vary widely from state to state, city to city, and even within the same district. Some schools and districts may provide only a few more medical services than what the school nurse can provide, while others have support from district, city, and community funds to provide new facilities and an expanded menu of services and care. Some of this variation originates from the varied funding mechanisms.

Implementation also varies greatly by geography. As figure 8.1 shows, a greater concentration of SBHCs is in urban and metro areas. For instance, Wisconsin is home to 5.7 million people and has seven SBHCs, six of which are located in Milwaukee. And Florida's SBHCs, the most of any state, are nearly all clustered in the four largest metro areas (accounting for over 50

FIGURE 8.1   Map of SBHCs from the National School-Based Health Alliance 2013–14 census

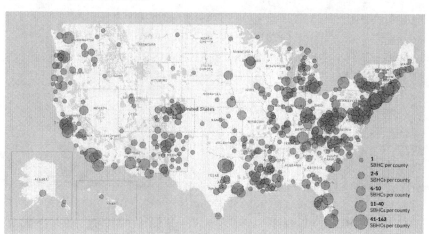

percent of the state population): Miami, Tampa–St. Petersburg, Orlando, and Jacksonville.[23] The reasons for this distribution are likely varied, and more research is needed to bear out if the concentration of SBHCs in urban areas is due to the availability of funding, proximity to populations in need, or even availability of trained health professionals who can provide services.

Evidence on the Links Between SBHCs, Student Health, and Attendance

To better understand what the existing empirical research says about the potential of SBHCs to impact student health and attendance, we studied the literature related to SBHCs in the United States. While there is literature on SBHCs internationally, such articles have limited applicability to those in the US, largely due to differences in health-care systems. Though the evidence connecting health to school absences is clearer (being a rather direct connection), the reliable empirical evidence regarding the role that SBHCs can play in reducing health-related absences has not yet led to many clear conclusions or policy prescriptions. The existing studies on SBHCs document interesting correlations but tell us very little about the *effects* of SBHCs on students. While some studies reviewed SBHCs' role in administering health services, more relate student health to different measures of student academic performance, such as dropout rates, suspension rates, and/or academic achievement.

The data indicate that recorded student absences are primarily due to health reasons, whether they are reported by parents, schools, or students.[24] An important distinction when considering the predicted connections to attendance is whether this refers to acute or chronic illness. Acute illnesses are temporary in nature, such as a cold, the flu, or an ear infection. The CDC states that children have more than three colds per year, and the average length of a cold is seven days.[25] Chronic illnesses or conditions require ongoing medical care for a longer time frame, possibly even a person's entire life. The University of Michigan Medical School found in one study that up to 18 percent of US children are living with chronic illnesses, the most common being asthma, diabetes, sickle cell anemia, cystic fibrosis, and cancer, and a separate study found that the rate of children living with multiple chronic conditions has been rising since 2010.[26] Furthermore, in 2012 nearly 10 million US children had a health problem for which they were prescribed medication for at least three months. So while both acute and chronic illness can impact attendance, chronic conditions play a larger role and therefore warrant particular research attention.

Though mostly suggestive in nature, there is some evidence that SBHCs may help students with asthma. In a literature review of school health programs (generally defined), researchers conclude that there are positive impacts for asthmatic children.[27] However, the study also finds limited and inconclusive evidence for other health interventions. And while most of the studies are quite small in scale, they do seem to support the finding that SBHCs potentially reduce not only absences but emergency visits and hospitalizations for children suffering from this chronic condition.[28]

A recent study also found that SBHCs in high schools reduce teen pregnancies.[29] While this study does provide reliable empirical evidence on the impacts of SBHCs, it does not directly study absenteeism. Nonetheless, to the extent that pregnancy itself presents absenteeism and/or dropout concerns, the study suggests another potential channel through which SBHCs could impact students by keeping them in school. Likewise, another study finds that on-site school mental health services reduce teacher-reported behavioral disruptions to learning.[30] Again, this study does not try to draw any links to absenteeism. However, considering mental health to be a concerning potentially chronic condition that can affect student attendance, it is promising that research finds positive impacts from school-provided mental health services. The availability and use of SBHCs has also been shown to be related to a wide variety of other student outcomes, including reduced drop-out rates, less risky teen behavior, and fewer disciplinary problems, course failures, and absences.[31] The assumed mechanisms behind these relationships are the physical and mental health services provided by an SBHC.

While it is fully possible that the use of SBHCs could result in such student outcomes, this literature mostly documents correlations. In some cases, the limitations of these studies are due to very small sample sizes or to a narrow focus of a specific intervention. However, even in larger-scale studies, the extent to which the findings only reflect the types of schools opting to have an SBHC or the types of students who use the SBHC is unclear, thus making any policy recommendations based on these results risky. Since SBHCs are not randomly allocated, there could be certain unobserved characteristics of schools that make them more likely to be selected to host an SBHC (e.g., very active parents, known health concerns). Similarly, it may be that only certain types of students elect to take advantage of an SBHC's services (e.g., those who are more health conscious). Since proving a causal link between SBHCs and student outcomes has so far proved largely elusive, there is a need for further research establishing causal effects of SBHCs as the movement continues to gain attention from districts around the country. The biggest hurdle facing future research is adequately controlling for selection concerns regarding the types of schools and students with access to SBHCs.

A Role for SBHCs?

Considering the lack of research evidence on SBHCs in general and, more specifically, in relation to student attendance, is there any reason to expect that SBHCs might play a role in reducing chronic absenteeism? To address this question, it is helpful to revisit the primary hypothesized mechanisms through which SBHCs may impact student attendance. First, by providing health-care services to students who would not otherwise have them, SBHCs could potentially increase student attendance through improvements in health and management of symptoms and chronic conditions. However, this link is not unique to SBHCs; other improvements in health-care access outside of the school context could also produce this result. Yet, an SBHC is uniquely positioned to provide students with more advanced care in a location they are more likely to access because they are already present. SBHCs' potential to reduce the need to miss school to obtain needed medical care is a direct result of care being provided *on-site* at school.

This unique aspect of SBHCs has been descriptively explored in a few studies. One study compares two school settings—one with a school nurse and another with an SBHC—and finds that the SBHC was associated with fewer student "early dismissals," or fewer students taking part of a day off from school.[32] Additionally, a study matching students on observable characteristics finds a correlation between using the mental health services at an SBHC (serving grades 9 and higher) and increased attendance and academic improvements.[33] Furthermore, several small-scale studies on students with asthma have found that the advanced services provided through an SBHC can potentially reduce asthma attacks and even decrease the number of emergency room visits for students with this chronic illness.[34] While far from conclusive, these studies are consistent with the hypothesis that SBHCs could reduce some of the inconveniences of receiving medical attention off-site that cause students to miss additional instructional time.

On-campus access to health care eases logistic problems for students and families. When considering single-parent families, two-working-parent families, or parents/caregivers who do not speak English, the disruption of having to obtain medical care at another location may be especially challenging. When care is provided through an SBHC, the disruption is minimized. Additionally, SBHCs are set up in a variety of different ways, with some even providing services to members of the community beyond enrolled students, such as to family members. Considering the potential role of convenience in the effective use of health services, such access for family members (a sibling or a parent) could also help manage logistical considerations that stand in the way of regular student attendance. Attending to medical needs and ensuring regular school attendance may be more than just a question of convenience, since such logistical issues can contribute to added stress in the household. This role of SBHCs, in the context of family logistics, has yet to be explored in the literature.

And while some of SHBC interventions relate to the treatment of chronic conditions, others focus on reducing contagion (e.g., head lice, conjunctivitis, immunizations). So another possible benefit of on-site care for students relative to care provided outside of the school is the potential to more effectively prevent, rapidly respond to, and control the spread of such conditions or diseases. As suggested in a literature review, "SBHCs deliver services such as immunizations, asthma care, treatment of head lice, ringworm and conjunctivitis that might result in fewer student absences," though "effects on academic indicators are more likely to be found for students who are being treated for chronic conditions that contribute to high rates of absenteeism, including asthma, depression or ADHD."[35]

Access to health care in the United States means having both health-care services and health insurance. Thus, having a doctor in the same school building but no way to pay for her services does not necessarily translate into more and better health care. Children without insurance are more likely not to have had contact with a doctor in two or more years.[36] Fortunately, results from other interventions provide promise: SBHCs may have the potential to provide the benefits of known health interventions in a format that is readily available for the school community. For example, an expansion of the federal State Children's Health Insurance Program (SCHIP) was found to increase daily attendance in schools for students who gained health insurance coverage. Also, an SBHC's health liaison's role is to guide families through accessing insurance and other health coverage available in the local area, thus ensuring that students who need care can afford it.[37]

While concrete evidence is still lacking to support these hypothesized benefits of SBHCs, the predicted channels through which SBHCs may impact student attendance provide direction for future research to better inform the larger conversation on whether there could be a beneficial role in providing health-care centers within the school context.

Moving Forward: Measuring the Effectiveness of SBHCs

Clearly, additional research is needed regarding the potential benefits of providing health services to students through a targeted SBHC model. While advocates of SBHCs tout the benefits of increased attendance, the existing frameworks for how they are implemented do not include many measures specifically designed to counter absenteeism.[38] Without reliable empirical evidence to support the case for SBHCs, it remains a promising but unproven school policy.

One of the main hurdles in establishing a causal relationship between SBHCs and attendance is that such policies are not implemented in a random nature. Therefore, the first factor that must be addressed is why certain schools have access to an SBHC while others do not and how the availability of health services is determined. If, for example, schools with SBHCs are more organized, have higher levels of community support to push for their implementation, and have lower observed rates of chronic absenteeism, compared to schools without SBHCs, they may simply reflect different family and community characteristics that directly relate to lower problems of absenteeism, regardless of any SBHC impact. But if SBHCs are more often implemented in schools or districts that are facing large family challenges, then there may be an observable negative relationship between SBHCs and school measures, such as student attendance, thus making SBHCs appear ineffective even if their effects on students were positive. These are important distinctions, since policy implementation based on such (lack of) evidence is not without cost, and the implementation of SBHCs requires funds that could potentially be put to better use. Ideally, an analysis would study absenteeism over time at schools with similar attendance concerns that received different treatment due to the existence (or lack) of an SBHC.

Future research into the effects of SBHCs may also benefit from exploring heterogeneous effects across different types of SBHCs and across SBHCs serving different types of communities. While SBHCs may not improve attendance for all student populations, those with chronic conditions or more family limitations around access to health insurance and care are predicted to have the largest potential impacts, as they would currently face the largest hurdles in overcoming issues of chronic absenteeism.

SBHCs could provide a promising solution to schools' chronic absenteeism problem. What's more, a wide range of benefits to students beyond improvements in attendance have been suggested in the literature. It is important to encourage more research that takes into account the endogenous relationship between SBHCs and the students they serve and focuses on the characteristics of SBHCs that can improve student outcomes.

Can SBHCs impact chronic absenteeism? Only future research will tell.

9

Tackling Truancy

Findings from a State-Level Policy Banning Suspensions for Truancy

KAITLIN ANDERSON, ANNA J. EGALITE,
AND JONATHAN N. MILLS

CHRONIC ABSENTEEISM AND TRUANCY have shot to the forefront of national attention in recent years in part because of growing awareness of their relationship to serious negative academic and economic outcomes. In this chapter we focus in particular on student truancy, on the unexcused and unlawful absences from school that occur without parental consent or knowledge and during which students typically spend time away from home and often engage in risky behaviors.[1] Both the legal definition of truancy and policy responses to this behavior vary widely across states and localities. Some states set a minimum number of days a student must be absent before being referred to legal authorities, but these minimum thresholds can range from three to twenty-one days.[2] Seven states, including Arkansas, have no state-defined threshold, leaving it up to each local school district to determine its own rule for who is truant and who is not. Even in states with an official state definition of truancy, school leaders may, in practice, use a variety of unofficial definitions.[3]

While policy makers and school leaders have a number of tools at their disposal to tackle truancy, there is little evidence about the effectiveness of various approaches. Some school districts, for example, respond by assigning an out-of-school suspension (OSS) as punishment. But in recent years, attitudes toward this response have changed, as it seems counterintuitive to punish truant students by further removing them from the school environment. An Ohio lawmaker supporting a ban on suspensions for truancy in his state reportedly compared suspending truant students to "punishing a child who won't eat broccoli by agreeing to never again make broccoli."[4]

In this chapter we focus on an attempt by Arkansas legislators in 2013 to take on this counterintuitive policy response by banning the use of OSS as a disciplinary response to truancy. Although the motivation for this policy change is straightforward—further removing truant students from school results in an even greater loss of instructional time for affected students—statewide bans are rare, making this an ideal case study to inform other states as they consider solutions to reduce chronic absenteeism and truancy.

Although we might expect that banning OSS for truancy would promote school engagement by increasing the amount of time students spend in the classroom, it is unclear if this goal will be achieved in practice. If school districts do not receive information about alternative approaches to discipline or additional state support to offset the costs involved with taking a new approach to schoolwide discipline reform—such as a multitiered system of support—administrators might feel unprepared and under-resourced to respond to a statewide directive. It is also possible that schools could attempt to retain decision-making power over this issue by strategically reclassifying student behavior away from the affected category. Finally, it is unclear how student engagement will be affected by a broad-based ban that is not accompanied by support for alternative approaches to transforming school discipline.

Our analysis of student-level data from Arkansas public schools sheds doubt on the efficacy of this particular policy response. We find, first, that compliance with the policy was low, particularly among the very schools for whom the policy was designed to target. Second, trends in the consequences for truancy changed after the policy went into effect. There was a slight decline in

OSS and a slight increase in the "other" category of consequences, suggesting that schools may have been responding to the policy by assigning alternative consequences that may still be exclusionary in nature. Finally, we find little evidence of improved student engagement after the policy went into effect, suggesting the logic model underlying the policy change was incomplete or must have overlooked important details, such as implementation support for alternative discipline policies. These clearly unintended consequences raise red flags about the efficacy of this particular state-level policy response to student truancy.

Background on Suspensions and Student Discipline Policy Reforms

Even as many school districts and states seek ways to reengage students in the school environment, some schools issue exclusionary discipline responses for student misbehavior, including truancy.[5] The counterintuitive response of suspending a truant student further removes the student from the learning environment, which could reinforce the undesirable behavior.[6] Imagine if a teacher's solution to students never turning in homework was to require them to not complete future homework assignments.

There are also equity concerns with assigning OSS as a response to student truancy, as data collected by the US Department of Education's Office for Civil Rights (OCR) have documented. Black students are more than 3.5 times as likely to be suspended and twice as likely to be expelled from school without educational services compared to white students.[7] It is unsurprising, therefore, that the US Department of Education and truancy prevention groups have denounced the use of exclusionary discipline as a response to truancy.[8]

In recent years, many states have addressed this issue by passing laws that focus on reducing suspensions for students in early grades, limiting the length of suspensions, or limiting the type of eligible infractions.[9] As of March 2017, twenty-seven states plus the District of Columbia had reformed laws to reduce the use of student suspensions, expulsions, and referrals to law enforcement authorities. Unfortunately, the research exploring whether suspension-reducing policies help improve student engagement is relatively thin.

Lauren Sartain and colleagues examined the impact of a similar policy change in the Chicago Public Schools just prior to the 2012–13 school year that reduced the length of suspensions for serious offenses. This reduction negatively impacted student and teacher reports of school climate, but attendance improved slightly. Test scores were unaffected.[10] Max Eden analyzed changes in school climate data in America's largest school district, New York City Public Schools, from 2012 through 2016 following two waves of reforms, one in 2012–13 under Mayor Michael Bloomberg and the other in 2014–15 under Mayor Bill de Blasio. Although Eden noted little changes in school climate under the Bloomberg-era discipline reforms, which were mild in scope (e.g., prohibiting the use of suspensions for first-time, low-level offenses), changes were more noticeable under de Blasio's more stringent discipline reforms. Eden reported notable declines in climate corresponding with a de Blasio–era reform requiring principals to obtain written permission to suspend a student for "uncooperative/noncompliant" or "disorderly" behavior. For example, a greater percentage of teachers reported that order and discipline were not maintained, and a greater percentage of students reported physical violence, frequent drug use or gang activity, and peers not respecting each other. In addition, schools with high concentrations of nonwhite students experienced the worst declines in school climate.[11]

Matthew Steinberg and Johanna Lacoe studied similar policy changes in the Philadelphia school district during the 2012–13 school year and reported disappointing results. The district banned OSS for low-level "conduct" offenses and reduced the length of OSS for more serious infractions. They found that most schools did not comply with the ban on low-level conduct suspensions and that the most economically and academically disadvantaged schools were the least likely to comply. Although previously suspended students were less likely to be suspended and had better attendance after the policy change, they experienced no change in test scores, and the initial decline in conduct suspensions did not persist. Findings for never-suspended students also were not encouraging, with those in the most economically and academically disadvantaged schools experiencing large declines in both math and English language arts (ELA) test scores.[12]

Other states, including Rhode Island and Ohio, have banned the use of out-of-school suspension for truancy, but there is no rigorous evidence on the effectiveness of these bans.[13] The language of these laws differs from that of Arkansas, and implementation likely does as well. In Rhode Island, "no school shall use a student's truancy or absenteeism as the *sole* basis for using an out-of-school suspension as a disciplinary action," which indicates that attendance may still be one of multiple factors used as justification for a suspension. Ohio's law, which prohibits a school from "suspending, expelling, or removing a student based solely on absences without legitimate excuse," similarly leaves ample room for interpretation. California's legal code includes even vaguer statements, such as, "It is the intent of the Legislature that alternatives to suspension or expulsion be imposed against a pupil who is truant, tardy, or otherwise absent."[14]

In contrast, Arkansas' policy change stands out for explicitly banning OSS as punishment for truancy. In this chapter we discuss what happened following the passage in March 2013 of Act 1329, an Arkansas law banning the use of OSS as punishment for student truancy, and the rationale for such a clear-cut policy decision, outlining its expected impact and testing for evidence of possible effects. After documenting disappointing findings regarding implementation fidelity, we discuss alternative policies that might be more efficacious and a number of key lessons for policy makers and practitioners.

What Can Be Learned from a Case Study About Arkansas?

Arkansas has a student population that is smaller and a bit less diverse than the country as a whole, with more white students (65 percent relative to the US average of 52 percent), more black students (21 percent versus 16 percent), and fewer Hispanic students (10 percent versus 24 percent).[15] While findings from a southern, largely rural state may not generalize well to urban centers, almost all of the existing evidence on suspension-reducing policies currently comes from places like New York, Philadelphia, and Chicago. Very little is known about what happens when state-level discipline policies are implemented in a rural state such as Arkansas. This is particularly important given that southern states dole out a large number of suspensions and expel students of color at disproportionately high rates.

One report, for example, indicates that 55 percent of all suspensions in the United States in 2011–12 occurred in just thirteen southern states: Alabama, Arkansas, Florida, Georgia, Kentucky, Louisiana, Mississippi, North Carolina, South Carolina, Tennessee, Texas, Virginia, and West Virginia. Moreover, black students in these districts were suspended and expelled at disproportionately high rates.[16] Thus, a state like Arkansas having a legal mandate to reduce suspensions serves as a unique opportunity to study the potential effects of these types of policies.

What Might Result from an Elimination of Suspensions for Truancy?

Arkansas' move to ban OSS for truancy was enacted at a time when many policy makers and practitioners in the state were working to reduce suspensions and move toward alternative responses to student misbehavior, such as restorative justice, culturally responsive teaching, and schoolwide tiered supports. The language in Act 1329 reinforces concerns about the use of suspensions generally, not just as a response to truancy, noting that "discipline that keeps students engaged in the learning process and in the school community is more effective than discipline that interrupts the learning process and separates the student from the school community" and that "the excessive use of out-of-school suspension . . . is harmful to the educational process."[17]

These statements reveal the policy makers' intent to improve student outcomes by maximizing instructional time for troubled students and hopefully avoiding the harmful negative outcomes associated with suspension. This rationale rests on a major assumption that schools are well-positioned to successfully reengage the students they would have otherwise suspended. If, however, a school continues to assign OSS or simply replaces OSS with an in-school suspension (ISS) or other punishment that still closely resembles OSS, this approach will likely fail to address the underlying causes for the truant behavior, and student outcomes are not likely to improve.

Truancy in Arkansas Public Schools

This analysis is based on student-level data for all K–12 Arkansas public schools between 2008–09 and 2015–16. These data include information on student achievement on state assessments, demographic characteristics, attendance, and disciplinary outcomes.[18] Truancy was not a particularly common student infraction over this time period, representing just 6.4 percent of all infractions. Instead, the most frequently reported infraction types during the study period were disorderly conduct (28.8 percent), "other" infractions (27 percent), and insubordination (24 percent).[19] Violent or potentially violent offenses, such as student or staff assault, fighting, bullying, and bringing weapons to school, were uncommon, representing only about 11 percent of all infractions during the study period. Similarly, drug-, tobacco-, and alcohol-related offenses were rare, representing only about 2 percent of all offenses.

In terms of school responses to student misbehavior, the most common consequences for any type of infraction in Arkansas schools during the study period were ISS (38.3 percent), "other" consequences (24.9 percent), OSS (22.2 percent), and corporal punishment (13.3 percent). As with the "other" infractions, the "other" consequences were those that did not fit neatly into a state-designated reporting category. This could include Saturday school or morning, lunch, or afterschool detentions. Expulsions (0.10 percent), referrals to alternative learning environments (0.31 percent), and no action (0.85 percent) were particularly rare.

The longitudinal nature of this dataset allowed us to examine the distribution of consequences for truancy over time (figure 9.1). Although we expected to see a sharp break in the assignment of OSS starting in 2013–14, that is not what we observed. As expected, in the years before the passage of Act 1329, the majority of truancy cases resulted in either an ISS, OSS, or "other

FIGURE 9.1   Consequences for truancy, 2008–09 to 2015–16

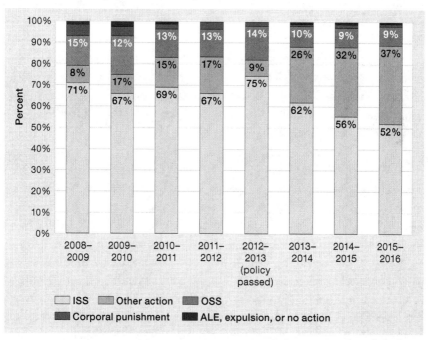

Notes: Rates for corporal punishment, no action, referrals to alternative learning environment (ALE), and expulsion are not labeled to improve graph clarity. ISS is in-school suspension; OSS is out-of-school suspension.

consequence."[20] Following the policy change, there was a decline in, but not a full elimination of, the use of OSS in response to truancy. Specifically, during the 2012–13 school year, 13.8 percent of truancy cases resulted in OSS, and by 2015–16 this figure had decreased to 8.7 percent. This indicates that a nontrivial number of schools simply failed to comply with the law.

Even though the new law only banned OSS as a consequence for truancy, the data in figure 9.1 reveal reductions in both OSS *and* ISS, suggesting that compliant schools shifted away from suspensions of any kind after the law's passage. The critical question is what disciplinary responses schools assigned instead. Schools may have followed the recommendations provided in Act 1329, which encouraged them to seek alternative, evidence-based approaches that "keep students engaged in the learning process," such as "positive behavior interventions and support systems" and "restorative justice." Such approaches require a wholesale change in school culture, however, and schools may not have had the bandwidth to implement these approaches with fidelity or the resources to send approximately ten staff members for a two-to-three-day training.[21] It is also possible that schools shifted to alternative consequences that were already available to them, such as before-school detention, lunchtime detention, and other consequences traditionally captured in the "other" category. Revealingly, the data show an expansion in the use of "other" consequences for truancy infractions at the same time as the decline in the use of OSS and ISS after 2011–12. While these data are suggestive, further investigation of a qualitative nature is needed to better reveal what happened on the ground after the passage of Act 1329.

Who Was Affected by This Policy Change?

To better understand who was affected by this policy change, we compared the characteristics of truant students to their nontruant peers, as well as to disciplined students generally and to nondisciplined students (table 9.1). We focused on comparing these groups in the year prior to the implementation of Act 1329 in case the passage of the policy changed how truant students were identified. The results indicate that truant students in the state tended to be disadvantaged in a number of ways. For example, truant students were less likely to be white, more likely to be receiving special education services, and more likely to have lower test scores, on average, than their nontruant, nondisciplined counterparts. There are also clear differences in attendance and discipline measures. Truant students have the largest number of days

TABLE 9.1

Characteristics of students in grades 7–12 by student type, 2012–13

	TRUANT	NOT TRUANT	DISCIPLINED (INCLUDES TRUANT)	DISCIPLINED BUT NOT TRUANT	NOT DISCIPLINED
Demographic characteristics					
Male	60.6%	50.6%	63.9%	64.6%	48.3%
Free or reduced-price lunch eligible	44.3%	48.4%	53.2%	55.1%	47.3%
Limited English proficiency	8.7%	5.6%	5.2%	4.5%	5.7%
Special education	15.7%	10.6%	15.6%	15.6%	9.8%
White	51.3%	65.5%	49.2%	48.8%	68.3%
Black	31.1%	20.9%	39.1%	40.8%	17.6%
Hispanic	13.2%	9.3%	8.3%	7.3%	9.7%
Other minority	4.3%	4.3%	3.3%	3.1%	4.4%
Average grade level	9.6	9.0	9.0	8.9	9.0
Academic measures					
Average math Z-score	-0.51	0.02	-0.46	-0.45	0.12
Average ELA Z-score	-0.52	0.02	-0.50	-0.50	0.11
Attendance measures					
Chronically absent	31%	12%	24%	23%	10%
Average days absent	14.77	8.56	12.76	12.33	7.71
Average percentage of days absent	9%	5%	7%	7%	5%
Discipline measures					
Average truancy infractions	1.4	-	0.2	-	-
Average total infractions	3.6	0.3	2.5	2.3	-
Total N	6,408	207,900	36,244	29,836	178,064

Note: Total N indicates the sample in each group, but certain measures (e.g., test scores, attendance data) were only available for a subsample of these groups. Math and ELA Z-scores are in standard deviations and were created by standardizing test scores by grade level, academic year, and testing group (with or without accommodations) to have a mean of 0 and standard deviation of 1.

absent (almost fifteen days per school year on average relative to nontruant peers) and the highest rate of total infractions (3.6 infractions per year on average).

We were also interested in learning more about the types of schools that were affected by this policy change. Among those schools using OSS for truancy in 2012–13, we found that schools with higher prior truancy rates and higher prior use of OSS in general were less likely to comply with the policy than other schools. In addition, schools with relatively disadvantaged student populations, such as those with lower ELA performance and with larger percentages of minority students, were less likely to comply. In sum, contrary to policy makers' presumed intentions, those schools that were targeted by the policy and schools serving relatively disadvantaged students were actually the least likely to comply.

How Did Act 1329 Affect Students?

The logic behind Act 1329 is straightforward: punishing truant students by suspending them from school is counterintuitive. Instead of taking a punitive approach, the new policy aims to improve truant students' engagement by increasing time spent in school and improving the overall school climate. That is, the legislation proposes that schools could adopt alternative policies, such as positive behavioral interventions and supports, that would hopefully improve the general school climate. The extent to which this logic model holds, however, is an empirical question that we test here by operationalizing "student engagement" as attendance.

Specifically, we tested to see if Act 1329 led to any changes in school engagement for truant students by comparing changes in absenteeism rates between truant and nontruant students over time, where absenteeism included all excused and unexcused absences. Our goal was to identify any noticeable jumps in absenteeism among truant students following the passage of Act 1329. We focused on two school years—the year before the policy was implemented and one outcome year—and used the year-to-year growth in absenteeism for nontruant students as a reference point against which to compare the year-to-year growth in absenteeism for truant students. By focusing on the *change* in absenteeism, we effectively controlled for preexisting differences between the two groups of students as well as general changes in student absenteeism over time.

Our analysis focused on students in grades 7–12 because 96 percent of truancy incidents in the outcome year occurred in these grade levels. Our estimation approach accounted for a variety of factors associated with absenteeism, including grade-level and demographic characteristics. We accounted for differences in district discipline policies and culture in schools by comparing different cohorts of students within the same district or school over time, respectively.

Our preferred approach identified "truant" students based on whether they were truant in the prior year instead of current year, as the prior year was not affected by the reform itself but still indicated a student's propensity for truancy. As a robustness check, we also repeated the analysis using a current-year truancy measure and found little change in the results.[22] Given the variation in policy compliance, we also tested for differential impacts based on whether or not a school complied with the policy.

Table 9.2 presents the results of our analysis. Odd-numbered columns indicate the overall effect on students, whereas even-numbered columns go one step further, estimating how results differ in policy-compliant versus noncompliant schools. The variable *post* captures underlying differences in student absenteeism between the policy year and post-policy year. The variable *truant in prior year* captures underlying differences between truant students and nontruant students; the coefficient indicates that, as expected, truant students were much more likely to be absent in the prior year than nontruant students. The key variable of interest in table 9.2, however, is *post X truant in prior year*, which is the combined, or "interaction," effect of both the post-policy and the truant-in-the-prior-year variables. This interaction effect identifies if there was any change in absenteeism among truant students after the passage of Act 1329; this is the variable that answers our research question.

Across multiple model specifications, the coefficient on *post X truant in prior year* reveals a null impact on absenteeism, which means that the policy reform had no effect on truant students' engagement. That is, truant students had zero change in their school engagement (as measured by absences) after the Act 1329 went into law. The reader should note that one model specification, presented in the fourth column, reports a statistically significant *increase* in absences of 0.65 percentage points (or about 1.2 days based on a 180-day school calendar), but this adverse outcome is only present in noncompliant schools and disappears in models that account for district-specific characteristics rather than school-specific characteristics. Overall, the bulk of the evidence points to a null impact on student engagement.

TABLE 9.2
Difference-in-difference estimation of policy impact on percentage of days absent (units = percentage points)

	(1)	(2)	(3)	(4)
Truant in prior year	0.0353 *** (0.0031)	0.0344 *** (0.0034)	0.0343 *** (0.0029)	0.0333 *** (0.0032)
Post	0.0010 (0.0011)	0.0006 (0.0014)	0.0008 (0.0011)	0.0002 (0.0015)
Post X truant in prior year	**0.0052 (0.0036)**	**0.0067 (0.0042)**	**0.0050 (0.0034)**	**0.0065 * (0.0039)**
Post X truant in prior year X compliant		**-0.0075 (0.0063)**		**-0.0072 (0.0059)**
Compliant		-0.0030 (0.0022)		
Post X compliant		0.0012 (0.0019)		0.0016 (0.0019)
Truant in prior year X compliant		0.0037 (0.0046)		0.0047 (0.0048)
Male	-0.0011 * (0.0006)	-0.0011 * (0.0006)	-0.0015 *** (0.0004)	-0.0015 *** (0.0004)
Black	-0.0091 *** (0.0020)	-0.0092 *** (0.0020)	-0.0111 *** (0.0011)	-0.0111 *** (0.0011)
Hispanic	-0.0116 *** (0.0020)	-0.0116 *** (0.0020)	-0.0112 *** (0.0019)	-0.0112 *** (0.0019)
Other race/ethnicity	-0.0070 *** (0.0014)	-0.0070 *** (0.0014)	-0.0061 *** (0.0011)	-0.0061 *** (0.0011)
Limited English proficiency	-0.0046 *** (0.0016)	-0.0047 *** (0.0017)	-0.0059 *** (0.0017)	-0.0059 *** (0.0017)
Special education	0.0087 *** (0.0006)	0.0087 *** (0.0006)	0.0085 *** (0.0007)	0.0085 *** (0.0007)
Free or reduced-price lunch eligible	0.0192 *** (0.0011)	0.0192 *** (0.0011)	0.0183 *** (0.0007)	0.0183 *** (0.0007)
Constant	0.0401 *** (0.0015)	0.0416 *** (0.0016)	0.0407 *** (0.0011)	0.0407 *** (0.0011)
Grade-level FE	Y	Y	Y	Y
District FE	Y	Y		
School FE			Y	Y
Observations	335,383	335,383	335,383	335,383
Adjusted R-squared	0.100	0.100	0.151	0.151
Total "effect" in compliant schools		**-0.0007 (0.0045)**		**-0.0007 (0.0045)**

Notes: Sample is restricted to students in grades 7–12. Standard errors in parentheses account for clustering of students within districts. *** p<0.01. ** p<0.05. * p<0.1.

Lessons from Top-Down Reform

Arkansas' Act 1329 banned the use of out-of-school suspension as a response to truancy. Unfortunately, the evidence we present here points to variation in compliance which suggests that this policy change did not effectively reach the students it was intended to help. Relatively disadvantaged schools were less likely to comply with the new policy, which meant that their students continued to receive OSS as punishment for truancy. This was similar to Philadelphia's experience with a ban on low-level "conduct" suspensions.[23]

We also assessed the impact of this policy change on truant students' engagement with school, as measured by attendance. The language in Act 1329 suggests that this ban on OSS for truancy was part of a larger effort to keep students engaged in the learning process by way of positive behavior interventions and supports. Despite this well-intended effort, we saw no evidence that student engagement improved. Using a difference-in-differences approach that compares students within the same district or school over time, we found that truant students experienced no change in their absenteeism rates relative to their nontruant peers. We also uncovered some evidence of adverse consequences that were concentrated within noncompliant schools, but these effects are small and not consistently observed across model specifications.

Where do we go from here?

A number of lessons can be gleaned from this experiment. First, state legislators would do well to recognize that clear communication with local communities is key to building buy-in and ensuring the successful interpretation and implementation of a new school discipline mandate. Indeed, there are many challenges to be overcome. Some argue that a state-level ban is unlikely to ever be as effective as local efforts to reform school discipline policies. Steinberg and Lacoe contend that "the biggest lesson from Philadelphia's experience is that 'discipline reform'—however defined or conceptualized—is best initiated at the school level rather than the district level, where the law of unintended consequences is more apt to prevail."[24] Aggregate up to the state level, and it seems even more likely that we should expect implementation challenges associated with a top-down discipline reform such as this one.

Another important consideration for policy makers pursuing a state-level ban such as the one we describe is whether or not the state can offer the resources, training, and personnel required to ensure that schools are equipped for full compliance. Positive behavioral interventions and support systems aim to address the root causes of conflict, to develop students' social-emotional skills, and to train staff to deescalate conflict, but they require extensive training prior to implementation that may prove cost prohibitive to schools and districts. Financial support for the costs and personnel hours necessary to pull this off is essential.

Something for states to keep in mind when promoting alternative approaches to maintaining student discipline is the strength of the research base on which such practices rest. A recent review suggests that the research supporting alternative discipline practices, such as Positive Behavioral Interventions and Supports and restorative justice, is relatively new and can offer only a weak foundation for the effectiveness of what may turn out to be a sweeping policy change.[25] A third recommendation for those considering such a policy change, therefore, is to think about ways to build knowledge and add to a weak research base by partnering with an external organization to rigorously evaluate the impact of any proposed changes.

There is still a lot to be learned about which interventions, programs, or policies can improve attendance and student engagement with school. A systematic and meta-analytic review of five experimental and eleven quasi-experimental studies on truancy interventions concluded that there is a "paucity" of research in this area and a strong need to further develop the evidence base.[26] Our findings add to this knowledge base by demonstrating that blanket bans on suspensions may not work in the absence of other supports. However, these results certainly do not indicate that OSS for truancy "works." Rather, they imply that even when the need for a policy change seems intuitive, successful implementation likely relies on a variety of additional factors, such as communication about the change, training and resource support for school personnel, and knowledge of effective alternatives to suspension.

PART III

Interventions

10

Ready . . . Set . . . Text!

Reducing School Absenteeism
Through Parent-School
Two-Way Text Messaging

KEN SMYTHE-LEISTICO AND LINDSAY C. PAGE

AS THE FLEETING DAYS of summer turn toward fall, as the leaves begin to fall, an annual rite of passage transpires. Each year, nearly four million misty-eyed five- and six-year-olds shuffle toward kindergarten.[1] For many, this marks the beginning of their formal education experience. Although this transition typically is celebrated, it is not without some fear and anxiety. Indeed, nearly half of all students struggle with the kindergarten transition.[2] This is especially so for students from low-income backgrounds whose early school experiences are more likely to include school failures, behavioral issues, low parental engagement, and a growing gap between their academic performance and that of their peers.[3] Encouragingly, proactive efforts to engage families and children from the beginning can be effective in improving academic and key behavioral outcomes for students cross the socioeconomic spectrum.[4] For both children and their families, the first experiences with schooling can set the stage for future expectations, successes, and challenges.

If first impressions matter, however, many schools are missing an important opportunity. Most commonly, schools engage in efforts to acclimate incoming children and families only after the school year has already begun. For example, back-to-school open houses, the most common formal transition event, are scheduled days or even weeks into the school year.[5] This is the equivalent of a workplace orientation long after beginning a new job. More concerning, many low-income parents report punitive phone calls as their typical first encounter with teachers, which creates a hostile dynamic that can have repercussions throughout the school year.[6]

In contrast, there are low-cost efforts that schools can implement to ease the transition and make it more positive for children and their families, setting the stage for stronger engagement and participation. Consider the experience of one parent, Ashley, who provided permission for her son Devonte's school to communicate with her via text message when she registered him for kindergarten.[7] At the beginning of the school year, Ashley received the following text message:

> Dear Ashley: This is Ken and Jessie from Bridges Elementary. This year, we'll be working with Ms. Johnson to do all that we can to help Devonte have a great kindergarten year. Save this number to text us any time with questions!

On receiving this message, Ashley breathed a sigh of relief and quickly texted back:

> Thank you so much! It's his first year in school because he didn't go to preschool. I feel lost and have so many questions.

So began a year-long text conversation between Devonte's school and parents through which we aimed to increase regular communication with families, provide guidance and supports to families (as needed), and promote regular school attendance among kindergarteners. We set our sights on reducing chronic absenteeism, which is defined as missing more than 10 percent of the school days in a given year through a combination of excused and unexcused absences. The need for this focus was clear to us. In the years leading up to our intervention, nearly one-third of kindergarten students enrolled in Bridges Elementary had been chronically absent.

Addressing absenteeism requires first understanding the factors that cause students to miss school. Attendance Works identifies three categories of reasons why students are absent in the early years of schooling: myths, barriers, and aversion.[8] Myths are the common misperceptions that parents hold about attendance, including the belief that problematic absences are limited to unexcused, consecutive days or those missed only by older children. Findings from the Ad Council revealed that many parents perceive the elementary years as a time primarily for social development with a focus on academic skills and content coming later.[9] Parents may also have an inaccurate understanding of the extent to which their child is actually absent.[10]

Students can also face legitimate barriers to strong school attendance. These may include poor health, unreliable daily transportation, and unsafe neighborhood pathways to school. Numerous studies reveal socioeconomic status to be a correlate of the experience of these barriers.[11] Students and families also may hold or develop an aversion to school based on prior negative experiences with the educational system or early experiences of academic struggle, poor school climate or ineffective discipline. These various drivers of absenteeism were evident in the text conversations captured through our messaging intervention.

Importance of Early Attendance

Helping students and families through the transition to kindergarten is far from the only challenge involved in giving the youngest students a successful start in school. Kindergarteners exhibit the poorest rates of attendance among all elementary school children.[12] Yet a strong kindergarten year may be critical for setting habits of mind and practice that serve students throughout their educational trajectories. Student attendance, even in the earliest years of schooling, is predictive of subsequent educational outcomes. Students with high rates of absence in kindergarten perform less well in core academic areas such as reading and mathematics, and they exhibit weaker social skills and executive function.[13] Such early school behaviors are particularly troubling given that of children who are chronically absent in the early years, only 17 percent read at grade level in third grade.[14]

Collectively, this evidence provides a strong case for focusing on student attendance in the earliest years—both to foster strong habits of daily school attendance from the beginning of formal schooling and to ensure that students have consistent exposure to foundational content and skills developed in these grades. Parents may also be most open to interventions involving supports and expectation setting as they adjust to the new routines associated with their child transitioning to school.

Encouragingly, interventions can be effective in increasing student attendance.[15] For example, in New York City, high school students with a Success Mentor—a staff member or volunteer assigned to meet one-on-one with identified students to provide encouragement, detect reasons for absenteeism, and assist with problem-solving strategies—were 15 percent less likely to be chronically absent and attended an average of two additional weeks of school.[16] And Todd Rogers and Avi Feller illustrate how providing parents with low-cost, written feedback by mail about how many days their child had missed school led to a 10 percent decrease in chronic absences.[17]

Between high-touch, personalized efforts and low-touch outreach, technology has a potential role to play in communicating with families about the importance of school attendance and connecting them with the supports and resources they may need to meaningfully reduce the number of school days their child misses. Outreach via text messaging is particularly promising. Cell phone ownership is nearly universal in the United States, even among adults in low-income settings and with low educational attainment.[18] In contrast to these high rates of cell phone ownership (and access to text messaging), we anticipate rates of internet (and email) access to be lower, especially among parents with phones that have only basic functionality (not smartphones). For all of these reasons, researchers have found that parents are much more likely to read correspondence sent via text rather than email.[19]

Although text messaging is beginning to become a more routine mode by which school systems communicate with families, educational practitioners may have questions about whether to invest staff and other resources in such strategies.[20] We contend that, done well, the expanded use of texting to deliver personalized and timely information to families could lead to improvements in daily attendance as well as downstream outcomes, such as educational achievement and attainment and parental engagement more broadly.

Text messaging is increasingly used in a variety of policy arenas, and growing evidence reveals text-based communication as a useful tool for improving

student outcomes. For example, numerous studies find that text-based outreach and support can facilitate the on-time transition to and progress through
college.[21] Messaging to parents about their children's educational progress
has also shown promise. For example, Benjamin York, Susanna Loeb, and
Christopher Doss investigated the impact of text-based outreach to suggest preliteracy activities, and Peter Bergman experimented with personalized outreach to parents about assignments that their school-aged children
needed to complete. In both interventions, the text-based outreach led to
improved outcomes at a low per-child cost.[22] Benjamin York and colleagues,
for example, reported that the cost of sending text messages was less than $1
per family and further note that the fixed expenses of program development
and administration will go to zero as their program reaches more families.
Matthew Kraft and Todd Rogers focused on the framing of information sent
to parents and found that emphasizing what students need to improve rather
than where they are excelling leads to heightened parental involvement and
improved student performance.[23]

This collective research base serves as motivation for Connect-Text, our
text-based strategy to improve daily attendance and reduce chronic absenteeism among elementary school children.

The Intervention

Ashley was one of the first and most active participants in Connect-Text.
Throughout the school year, she exchanged more than one hundred messages
with a school staff member on a variety of topics. She sought advice about
how sick is "too sick" to attend school. She requested district services for
transportation. She asked scheduling questions, like when picture day would
be held. And she provided explanations for why Devonte missed certain days
of school.

During the 2015–16 academic year, we provided all kindergarten families with the opportunity to enroll in Connect-Text. The program involved
a two-way text messaging system through which the school sent parents
preprogrammed, personalized messages approximately once each week. We
designed these messages with several purposes in mind, including increasing
parental awareness of the importance of strong school attendance, diagnos-
ing barriers to attendance, helping families know about and access available
resources as needs arose, and improving kindergarten attendance.

We designed Connect-Text in the mold of the successful Ready4K! model, which increased early child literacy skills by sending families several different types of messages aligned with the categories of utility, individualization, and support.[24] Our utility messages provided families with important school information and related family/child opportunities, such as out-of-school-time offerings:

> Reminder Parent-Teacher Conference Week: No Classes Thursday (10/15–10/16). Message me to reserve a slot with your teacher.

Individualization messages provided families with feedback on their child's attendance and motivation on why regular school attendance is critical to their child's educational success:

> Hi Ashley, we really missed Devonte today. Hope he feels better tomorrow. The field trip to the zoo will be great.

And support messages focused on positive affirmations regarding the importance of the current school year and tips for developmental opportunities to strengthen learning:

> Reading Rocks! Does your child have a favorite book? Text back and we'll share your fav with your teacher.

Most messages fell into the categories of event/activity sharing (utility) and resource provision (support). Individually targeted messages related to student attendance were sent only when children missed school. These messages were always positive in tone, expressing concern and offering assistance.

In designing the program, we sought to embed it into the core function of the school while also making it replicable. When implementing an effort such as this, a key question is whose job it will be to staff the text communication. The answer to this question is not trivial, however, given that school staff members often are stretched thin already. Connect-Text employed an AmeriCorps position to test the ability to connect with parents using a low-cost alternative to a new staff position. In addition to working on the texting initiative, Jessie, the AmeriCorps member, regularly spent time in the children's classrooms, took part in lunch duties, and assisted with dismissal to connect with faculty, staff, parents, and students. These efforts earned her the respect of school faculty peers while allowing her to forge relationships with the children and families.

Messages included prompts for families to respond with questions, concerns or additional information they wanted to share with the school. Jessie monitored the text-based communication from families via a web-based portal that allowed her to respond to families' text messages and engage in text-based dialog from a computer rather than from her personal cell phone.[25] She called on partnerships with community-based education, social service, and health service providers to refer families to appropriate supports as needs arose.[26] The most common referrals were to before-/afterschool programs. Commonly, parents reported difficulty matching childcare coverage for their longer work day (eight to twelve hours) with the shorter duration of the school day (seven hours).

Setting and Implementation

We launched the texting system as a pilot with the kindergarten classrooms of one elementary school in the Pittsburgh Public Schools system. We selected Bridges Elementary based on its recent history of high chronic absenteeism. In the year prior to the pilot, nearly one in three Bridges kindergarten students was chronically absent. The school serves a student population in which the large majority of students qualifies for free or reduced-price lunch and one in five students is classified as an English language learner.

We launched the text outreach in September 2015. Consenting parents had the opportunity to receive messages in either English or Spanish, and, importantly, our AmeriCorps member was bilingual and able to engage with parents in either language. The school invited parents to participate via a letter sent home, face-to-face recruitment at pick-up and drop-off times, and by phone.[27] The initial response to the Connect-Text opportunity was strong. Nearly all (90 percent) of the parents took the opportunity to receive the text message outreach, and of those participating, nearly three-quarters engaged actively by responding to one or more of the messages they received.

Many of the outgoing messages were prepared and scheduled in advance to be delivered on specific days throughout the month. Most of the messages, however, were individual exchanges with parents with specific questions or concerns. Surprisingly, Jessie reported needing less than thirty minutes to manage and respond to parent messages during a typical week. Most messages were questions around school schedules or requests to share information with teachers.

Tracking Attendance

During the school year, Jessie monitored and responded to attendance patterns in twenty-day cycles rather than responding to every missed day (with some exceptions). This was due to challenges associated with getting accurate "real time" daily attendance rates by child from the school. She assembled attendance records and created reports that assessed each child's attendance record within two categories: "year-to-date" and "previous twenty days." She then coded individual attendance records into one of three categories: good attendance (absent less than 5 percent of days); at-risk attendance (absent 6–9 percent of days); and chronically absent (absent more than 10 percent of days). Tracking the "previous twenty days" allowed us to be responsive to changes in attendance patterns, while "year-to-date" helped us monitor the larger picture. Jessie used these records to reach out to families to celebrate good and improved attendance, raise awareness of declining attendance, and offer more intensive supports to chronically absent students. Over the course of the year, teachers improved their communication with Jessie and notified her when there was a marked change or consecutive days missed.

Connecting Families to Needed Resources

The ongoing monitoring of attendance allowed for quick and targeted outreach to families. Prior to implementation, we established a formal referral process between the school and social service providers that ensured a rapid response for families facing a variety of issues.

For example, Devonte's attendance was sporadic throughout the school year but most problematic at the beginning of the year as Ashley struggled to establish a new school routine for him and manage the school-related anxiety he experienced. This all came to light through the following text exchange:

> Hi Ashley. I noticed Devonte has missed 3 days this week. Is there anything I can do to help?

Ashley's response illustrates her struggle to separate anxiety from physical illness:

> He will NOT miss anymore school unless he's deathly sick lol . . . Just hard sending him when he's crying curled in a ball and says his stomach hurts. He even went to the bathroom on himself. It was bad! My poor baby L ☹

This message prompted more intensive support for both Ashley and Devonte. Jessie worked with school staff to provide a more supportive environment for Devonte to help reduce his anxiety. This included providing positive encouragement and affirmation when he arrived in the morning and "check-ins" throughout the day. In addition, Jessie conducted home visits with Ashley to provide her with reassurance, discuss ways to reduce Devonte's anxiety, and demonstrate the commitment the school had to ensuring that her son felt welcomed at school.

After this, Devonte's attendance fluctuated between near-perfect for months followed by a rash of missed days. Jessie responded to the missed days with encouragement and support. In most cases, Ashley simply needed assistance with solving dilemmas that families commonly face. One particular challenge related to arranging transportation for Devonte after nights when she worked late. On these nights, Devonte stayed with his grandmother, and Ashley would pick him up and bring him home in the middle of the night, often waking him during transport. This disruption to Devonte's sleep may have been a contributor to his anxiety. Jessie helped Ashley identify a bus stop near Devonte's grandmother's home so that he could sleep uninterrupted and use an alternate route to school on the nights he stayed over. Ashley expressed her deep appreciation for Jessie's support:

> Jessie, I can't thank you enough for helping to rework on the bus arrangement. It helps to not wake D in the middle of the night to take him home.

Ashley was not the only parent to benefit from additional communication with and help from Jessie. The experience of Jasmine and her twins, Michael and Shavonne, demonstrates how Jessie's mediating role was able to improve the relationship between the family and the school. Early in the school year, the twins' teacher expressed frustration that both children would miss school when only one was sick. Their teacher requested that Jessie reach out to Jasmine. Her response was indicative of the misguided devaluing of kindergarten:

> Sorry they both missed. I guess I didn't realize how important kindergarten is. It's hard to get one on the bus when the other is sick.

This simple exchange led to a change in behavior. Jasmine worked to ensure that only the sick child missed school. And the next time Jasmine met a formidable barrier, she proactively reached out to Jessie for guidance:

> Hey Jessie, I need a list of before school programs. I got my job it starts tomorrow 7a to 3p.

Jessie first congratulated Jasmine on her new job and then scrambled to suggest resources. Through ongoing dialogue, a neighbor was recruited to watch the twins and place them on the bus until before-school care could be established.

Often the timing of requests was not convenient, but by responding quickly and reliably, Jessie became a trusted resource as families navigated challenges. We contend that the relative anonymity of the text-based service reduced the stigma of reaching out for services while still being able to access and benefit from a personal connection.

Of course, not all crises are created equal, as illustrated by Maura and her daughter Brynn facing their worst day. Maura wrote to Jessie:

> Please help, Ima get evicted today and we don't have no place to go.

This was Maura's first text message to Jessie, but it signified that Jessie's repeated offers of help to parents whenever and however needed didn't go unnoticed. Although Jessie did not have the means to fix the problem on her own, the established partners did. Jessie connected with a community agency to find both temporary housing and ten-day bus passes to transport Brynn to school while the school transportation system worked to accommodate the change in address. Not only did Maura and Brynn lose their apartment, but most of Brynn's clothes were discarded or lost as they were forced to move immediately. Again, Maura wrote to Jessie:

> Hey, so I guess I am going to need two more bus cards to get her to school Monday. Yea, some uniforms for her, maybe sock and underwear. We don't got much.

Later, Jessie arranged bus passes again for Maura and Brynn when they moved to a more permanent location. Encouragingly, Brynn maintained perfect attendance during this month of turmoil.

Maura's experiences illustrate the in-the-moment help that families sometimes need. For other families, needs are less acute but challenging nonetheless. So was the case of Manuel and Allegra. Manuel worked two jobs to make ends meet. From the beginning of the school year, his daughter Allegra was flourishing in the school's English language learner program. However, when this strong student with exemplary attendance missed three days, it did not go unnoticed. Allegra's teacher asked Jessie to reach out to Manuel in Spanish. This was indicative of teachers becoming more proactive in their response to absenteeism as the year progressed. Manuel responded immediately (translation below) to the offer of assistance:

> Our washing machine broke and I've not able to get her clothes clean at the laundromat because I work late. She will be there Monday after I wash her clothes this weekend.

Working families can be sent into turmoil when cars or household appliances unexpectedly fail. Fortunately, Jessie was able to provide support in response to this need. She provided a referral for the family to a local foundation that was able to provide one-time emergency support in response. She also orchestrated translation services for the community family support center charged with monitoring and dispersing crisis funds. The program provided Manuel with a voucher for a washing machine that was delivered to the family before the weekend. Jessie additionally arranged donated uniforms from the school clothing closet to ensure that Allegra didn't have to miss school before the washing machine was installed. Allegra finished the year demonstrating proficiency in her academic subjects while maintaining strong attendance.

Assessing the Impact of Connect-Text

The primary goal of piloting Connect-Text in Bridges Elementary was to reduce the high rate of chronic absenteeism among the school's youngest students. Ideally, to shed light on a question of impact such as this, we would conduct a randomized trial, essentially flipping a coin to assign only some eligible families to receive Connect-Text and comparing rates of chronic absence for the children whose families did and did not receive the outreach. Such an experimental study was not possible because of funding limitations and district research policies; so instead we offered the opportunity to all kindergarten families in the pilot school.

We used a case study method to investigate Connect-Text's impact. Just as in an experimental study, our goal was to compare chronic absenteeism among Bridges kindergarteners to kindergarteners in a suitably chosen comparison setting that did not implement the messaging intervention. We took a data-drive approach to constructing a suitable comparison in which we built a single "synthetic" control school that is a weighted average of other Pittsburgh Public Schools. We calculated weights such that the synthetic control school looked maximally like Bridges Elementary in terms of prior trends in chronic absenteeism and other student characteristics at the beginning of the intervention year.[28]

Our primary outcome of interest was the rate of chronic absenteeism among kindergarten students in the 2015–16 academic year. For the purpose of building our synthetic control, we used the absenteeism measures from the three years prior to intervention and the aggregated student characteristics from the intervention year and constructed a composite counterfactual that looked as similar as possible to the Bridges school on these preintervention characteristics.[29]

Figure 10.1 compares trends in chronic absenteeism for Bridges and the synthetic control school. Here we observe trends prior to the intervention year that are essentially equivalent. In the intervention year, both Bridges and the synthetic control exhibit improvements in chronic absenteeism. The improvement in the synthetic control school may be explained by a co-occurring districtwide "Be There" campaign sponsored by the United Way to raise awareness about school absenteeism. Compared to the improved rate in the synthetic control school, however, the improvement at Bridges is substantially greater. By the end of the intervention year, 13.3 percent of

FIGURE 10.1   Comparison in absence rates between Bridges Elementary and synthetic control school

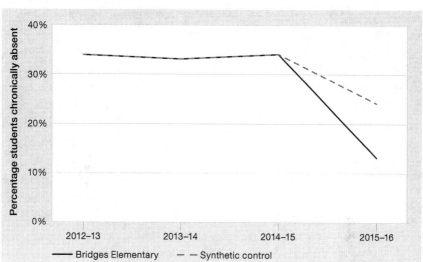

kindergarteners were chronically absent, compared to a rate of 24.4 percent for the synthetic comparison. This result is significant at the p < 0.10 level. In short, we conclude that the Connect-Text intervention contributed to a significant reduction in chronic absenteeism over the rate we would have otherwise expected.

Finally, a parent focus group data revealed that after texting had begun, participating parents rated the school-parent communication at a 10 (out of 10), compared to a baseline of parents sampled prior to the texting program who rated it as a 5. The highest praise for the program came from Latino families, who offered that the provision of messages in Spanish helped them feel included in and valued by the school.

Implications for Tracking and Combating Chronic Absenteeism

In 2015, when the Every Student Succeeds Act was signed into law to replace No Child Left Behind, it came with changes to the way school performance would be measured.[30] These changes included increasing a state's rights to tailor their education policies but at the same time required expanded data collection.[31] Diane Whitmore Schanzenbach and colleagues suggest that states should consider making chronic absence their self-selected indicator, given the research linking this measure to academic outcomes.[32] Indeed, a decade of research indicating chronic absence as a meaningful marker of student performance gave rise to a host of interventions to reduce chronic absence.

Efforts to reduce early chronic absence have, to date, focused more on comprehensive and systemic issues. Generally, younger children are not seen to be purposely truant; instead, their absence is viewed as the result of school, family, and community factors. Early prevention programs have thus tended to center on transportation, health, and community issues that hinder high rates of attendance.[33]

The intervention we report on here, Connect-Text, focuses instead on parents as a valuable source for support and a resource for their children. The goals are to communicate with parents on an ongoing basis; to provide specific feedback on their child's attendance; to reinforce the importance of kindergarten as a foundation for early school success and the notion that each day of schooling will drive later school success; and to connect families to needed supports when threats to strong attendance arise.

Although previous programs have attempted to foster this awareness through face-to-face interactions or phone calls, Connect-Text used text messaging, which Bridges parents indicated was their preferred method of communication.[34] The messaging focused on providing information about key school activities while engaging parents in two-way dialogue to address specific barriers to children attending school each day. The program also provided rapid outreach to assist the families of students whose attendance patterns revealed signs of risk. Indeed, given the formal referral process established among the school, social service providers, and community organizations prior to the start of the intervention, the project's AmeriCorps member was able to respond quickly to needs, such as transportation, temporary housing, and even a washing machine. The use of text messaging as a less intrusive communication strategy resonated with families. We believe that the anonymity of the text-based service reduced the stigma of reaching out and provided a "psychologically safe" space for families to present potentially sensitive challenges and seek guidance and support.[35]

When considering an intervention such as this, cost is a key component. The primary expenses in our implementation included the licensing of the Signal Vine platform and the AmeriCorps staffer's salary. The staffer devoted approximately one-quarter of her time to the Bridges kindergarten students and families; therefore, we estimate implementation costs of approximately $9,000, or $200 per kindergarten student in this pilot (supervisory and support staff were not included in this cost estimate). Because the technology could have been used to reach more students, we would anticipate a much lower per-student cost when scaling up to reach more students and families.

Although we do not expect that text messaging alone will solve the problem of chronic absenteeism, our results suggest that increased positive communication between families and schools can help. Qualitatively, school staff reported that the text-based communication facilitated their ability to assist parents with tasks and issues ranging from signing up for parent-teacher conferences to discussing when a child should stay home due to sickness and even accessing resources to avoid homelessness. Quantitatively, our results from comparing the intervention school to a synthetically constructed comparison suggest the potential of text-based communication to encourage attendance and surface and respond to real barriers families face.

Of course, we underscore that we report here on a pilot-level intervention implemented within one school and with close oversight by our project team. Many efforts to scale promising interventions yield results that are often disappointing, especially in the case of social interventions that rely heavily on human inputs, as the quality of human input can be highly variable.[36] Indeed, in addition to heavy involvement from our team, the AmeriCorps staffer was excellent at her job and over time became quite well-liked by the school's kindergarten community, teachers and families alike. Still, the intervention itself is relatively straightforward and reliant on a ubiquitous form of communication. So taken together, these promising results are worthy of further investigation to understand whether such a system of communication and support can be used successfully to improve school-family relationships and reduce chronic absenteeism at scale.

11

Keeping Families Front and Center

Leveraging Our Best Ally for Ninth-Grade Attendance

MARTHA ABELE MAC IVER AND
STEVEN B. SHELDON

IT IS COMMON KNOWLEDGE that the best leading indicators of college-ready high school graduation rates are ninth grade course passing rates, which are highly correlated with ninth-grade attendance. We know that attendance takes a significant hit as students move from eighth grade into ninth grade, just at the developmental stage when students want to declare more independence.[1] Yet, research also shows that just as students are making this critical transition from middle to high school, family involvement in their education declines precipitously.[2]

This chapter examines a continuous improvement initiative within the Seattle Public Schools to systematically engage more families as students are making the transition from middle school to high school. School efforts to help families understand the implications of absence before it is too late to undo its ramifications, and to equip them with strategies for promoting good attendance, are expected to help improve ninth-grade outcomes. At the core of this work is the assumption that all families are an asset to their children and to educators working to prepare students for college or careers after high school.

Chronic Absence, Student Achievement, and the Role of School, Family, and Community Partnerships

The causes of student chronic absenteeism are numerous and stem from every context, including schools, families, and communities. According to a recent report, factors related to absenteeism can be categorized as student-specific, family-specific, school-specific, and community-specific, though many reasons for students missing school fit in two or more of these categories.[3] Because the sources of school absenteeism include student characteristics, within-school factors, and out-of-school factors, any approach to helping reduce absenteeism should mobilize support from educators, families, and the community. These approaches cannot ignore the fact that students' lives intersect multiple contexts, and so they require collaboration with and partnerships among adults.

Increasingly, evidence is emerging that shows how educators' efforts to work with and engage students' families has a positive impact on a range of educational outcomes. In addition to evidence that schools' outreach to families is associated with higher academic achievement, other research suggests that schools can impact student attendance by developing stronger, more positive relationships with families.[4] Joyce Epstein and Steven Sheldon, for example, have found that daily student attendance levels are higher in schools with stronger, more comprehensive programs of school, family, and community partnerships.[5] Similarly, in a quasi-experimental study of partnership programs, Sheldon found that elementary schools with partnership programs showed, over time, higher levels of student attendance than a matched comparison group of schools and that the effects on student attendance were attributable to the schools' outreach to help families overcome factors that limit engagement with their children's teachers and schools (e.g., promoting two-way communication, translating communication, collaborating with community partners).[6] These studies provide a foundation of evidence showing the benefits of using family engagement as a strategy for improving student attendance.

Practices that strengthen the relationships between students' families and their teachers, such as home visits, have been shown to promote more regular school attendance. In a study of elementary and middle school students in an urban school district, Sheldon and Sol Bee Jung found that those whose families participated in home visits had higher rates of school attendance, even after controlling for prior rates of attendance and numerous family and student background variables.[7] In other studies, home visits conducted by teachers and other school staff have been associated with changes in how teachers and families view and communicate with one another.[8] Implementing practices that help families and educators develop more trusting and supportive relationships can be one way educators work to reduce absenteeism.

Communication between families and educators is an important aspect of the school-home relationship and a factor related to student attendance at school. Too often parents are told little about their child's academic progress. According to Peter Bergman and Eric Chen's study conducted in middle schools and high schools, about 50 percent of parents surveyed reported that they hear from the school about their child's academic progress less than once every three months.[9] Given the infrequent school-home communication, it is not surprising that parents tend to hold inaccurate beliefs about their children's schooling. In the same study, 50 percent of middle and high school parents reported that their children were missing no assignments, when in fact only 20 percent were actually missing assignments. Without frequent information from educators about their children, parents tend to underestimate the extent to which their child needs additional support and monitoring of their academic engagement.

Parents also underestimate how school attendance affects school achievement.[10] The Bergman and Chen study also found that although 86 percent of middle school and high school parents understood that attendance plays a significant role in their child's likelihood of graduating, about half (49 percent) thought it was okay for their child to miss three or more days of school each month. These findings suggest a substantial percentage of parents do not fully understand how daily absences add up to chronical absenteeism.

Helping more families stay accurately informed about their children's academic standing and progress may be one way schools can better position families to help improve student attendance. Using regularly scheduled text messaging to families of students grades 5–11 about their children's school performance, Bergman and Chen found that students of families receiving these messages were less likely to fail a course and had higher rates of school attendance, compared to those from families who did not receive the additional communications from the school. These strategies provide a new and effective way for schools to inform and mobilize families.

Strong, effective communication efforts are not necessarily limited to new technologies like texting. Carly Rogers and colleagues have reported on several randomized studies using traditional mail-based methods to communicate with elementary school (K–5) families and found that these mailings meaningfully reduced student absenteeism.[11] Not only did they find that student attendance improved for those students in the treatment group, but their analyses showed that the treatment effect was stronger with families whose children had lower rates of attendance and for those from socioeconomically disadvantaged households.

In total, the evidence suggests that when schools operate in a way that views families as assets, they can promote student attendance and engagement by strengthening communication and partnerships with families. However, numerous studies have shown that family engagement declines precipitously as students transition to middle school and particularly high school.[12] High schools have often not prioritized family engagement, and studies show that families of high school students often feel unwelcome and report insufficient communication about requirements and their students' progress.[13] According to one study using nationally representative data, most families are not experiencing outreach from both the middle and high schools as their student transitions to high school, and nearly one in five families receive no communication from schools at all.[14] Even middle and high schools that have committed themselves to pursuing family engagement focused on improving student outcomes as members of the National Network of Partnership Schools perceive themselves as needing improvement in how they help families negotiate the transition and how they monitor their students' progress.[15] Given that many of the interventions seeking to connect with families to address chronic absenteeism are focused at the elementary level, systematic efforts to help middle schools and high schools focus on how they can leverage their best allies for improving student outcomes—the students' families—are critically needed.

Design and Implementation of the Initiative

More systematic attention to engaging families and equipping them with information and strategies for supporting their students' attendance is a promising approach to improving course performance in ninth grade, a key predictor of high school success. Even in districts that are committed to family engagement and improving student achievement, there is generally little systematic capacity building to help *secondary* school leaders understand the importance of ninth-grade attendance and course passing as leading indicators of high school success and how more effective family engagement practices could help equip families to support their students in these areas. Guided by the following theory of change, we designed an initiative to help districts and their K–8, middle, and high schools improve their family engagement activities as students transition from eighth grade to ninth grade.[16] The theory can be summarized in four steps (figure 11.1):

1. Equipping school leaders through professional development and cycles of inquiry for planning, implementing, and evaluating family engagement activities will increase school teams' capacity to reach out to all families.
2. Better implementation of family engagement activities by schools will lead to improved family capacity to support students in the transition to high school and through grade 9.

FIGURE 11.1   Theory of change

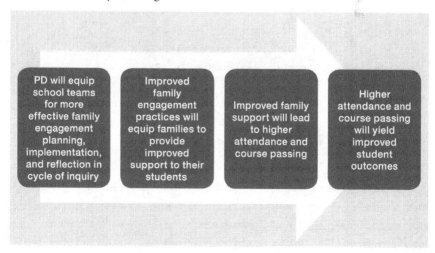

3. Increased family support, monitoring, and teacher-parent and student-parent interactions will lead to better student attendance and more homework completion in the first year of high school.

4. Students' improved attendance and homework completion will lead to increased course-passing rates in the ninth-grade year, which will lead to higher rates of on-time graduation from high school.

Building on an existing partnership between the National Network of Partnership Schools and the Seattle Public Schools, we began implementing this more focused partnership initiative in fall of 2015. The components of the initiative involve:

- recruiting K–8, middle, and high schools to send a small team to an all-day workshop in the fall about applying a continuous improvement approach to family engagement during the transition to high school

- conducting the fall workshop, during which teams apply what they have learned to reflect on their past family engagement efforts and construct a preliminary plan for their family engagement work in the coming year, with particular focus on activities relating specifically to the transition to high school

- follow-up coaching (approximately monthly) of school leaders/teams as they work to implement their plans

- follow-up coaching of school leaders/teams to reflect on their work in a cycle of inquiry process and to include analysis of school attendance data in their improvement process

- holding follow-up cluster meetings (two per year) in which school leaders share ideas about family engagement with each other

- encouraging systematic reflection by district leaders and their research partners in a cycle of inquiry process on how to improve the coaching process so that school leaders will grow in their ability to plan, implement, and critically reflect on their family engagement efforts and the impact of those efforts on student attendance and achievement outcomes.

The initiative is currently in its third year, and school participation in the initiative has evolved over time. A total of 15 schools (of 33 schools serving eighth- and ninth-grades in the district) participated to some extent during the first year, 21 schools during the second year, and 22 schools during the third year. Participating schools include both middle and high schools, together with a small number of K–8 schools. Some groups of feeder and receiving schools are all participating in the initiative, although some are more isolated and are participating without having their feeder or receiving schools also involved. As some schools have dropped out and others have joined, the initiative has thus far touched a total of 27 schools. Ten schools (6 high schools, 3 middle schools, and 1 K–8) have participated to some extent all three years. During the first year of implementation, 14 schools received coaching after the fall workshop, and a total of 9 schools went on to implement some sort of transition-focused family engagement activity for either eighth- or ninth-grade families. During the second year of implementation, 20 schools received coaching and went on to conduct at least two transition-focused family engagement activities during the year. Schools also reflected systematically on their transition-focused family engagement activities in a cycle of inquiry process. The planned evaluation of the initiative involves an interrupted time-series design with a similar comparison district not that is not receiving the intervention. In cases where it is not possible to use an experimental design, this design can control for differences in both the baseline mean of chronic absence and trends between the comparison and treatment groups.[17]

In light of arguments for multiple postintervention data time points for reliable interpretations of intervention effects, and to allow sufficient time for the intervention to be fully implemented, it is still too early to interpret the results of those analyses.[18] This chapter therefore focuses on describing practical implementation issues, including the types of family activities implemented by schools and some of the challenges involved in helping secondary schools emphasize student outcomes like attendance in their family engagement work.

Typical Transition-Focused Family Engagement Activities

Not surprisingly, schools in our study began their continuous improvement approach to family engagement by building on what they were already doing to involve families during the transition to high school. Many (though not all) high schools had a tradition of holding a spring welcome dinner for the eighth graders and their families who would be transitioning to the high school as ninth graders in the fall. Leaders at some of these schools began to think more strategically about how to communicate information to families that would support improved attendance and course performance. The initiative encouraged feeder middle schools and receiving high schools that had not worked closely together in the past to collaborate together on such activities as a high school information night or evening to help eighth-grade families understand the course registration process for high school and to be involved in that process. Some high schools improved on the orientation for new ninth-grade families at the beginning of the school year. Most schools, however, did not address the attendance issue directly with families at these activities.

Helping school leaders think beyond the typical events they planned for families and to focus more systematically on how to get information and important messaging to all families, including those unable to attend events, was one of the major goals of the initiative. More specifically, one of the goals was to encourage school leaders to begin thinking about how sharing information and supports with families prior to the start of ninth grade could actually help *prevent* problem attendance, rather than waiting until problems arose to begin interventions.

Motivating school leaders to take a preventative rather than reactive approach to chronic absenteeism proved challenging, but several schools embraced the idea. Over the first two years of the initiative, some participating schools were able to implement different proactive strategies to communicate information with incoming ninth-grade families (as well as other high school families in some cases) about the importance of attendance.

One of the high schools used an evidence-based "nudge" postcard approach to remind families about the importance of attendance (figure 11.2).[19] Designed with student-produced graphics, the postcard also included a graph showing the relationship between ninth-grade attendance and the rate of on-time graduation. It emphasized the importance of missing no more than a day per month and encouraged parents to contact the school's attendance office for support in addressing issues if their students missed more than a day that month. The high school is gearing up to adapt the card for another school year and to study potential attendance changes associated with the mailing of the postcards. As part of the continuous improvement process, the school will, ideally, monitor increases in the number of families reaching out for help in supporting their students' attendance.

FIGURE 11.2 Attendance "nudge" postcard used by a Seattle high school

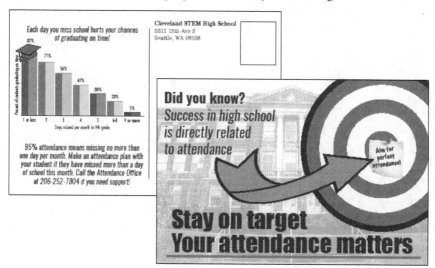

Similarly, in addition to communicating information on the district website, on school posters, and in person at school events, the district's Career and Technical Education Center sent postcards to all incoming ninth graders about its summer program in which students could earn a half-credit for a high school elective or a Career Technology Education (CTE) course. (Not all families have regular access to email, and because text-messaging requires an active opt-in process, that means of communication would miss a substantial number of families.) On the front of the postcard were tips for high school success, including a message about the importance of attendance: "Absences add up; Successful students miss no more than one day a month" (see figure 11.3). Another high school created a refrigerator magnet to distribute to families during a spring welcome event for rising ninth graders. The magnet was produced in English and Spanish and included important school phone numbers for families to contact, including the attendance office. On the magnet the school mascot emphasized the importance of attending school every day (figure 11.4).

Another approach for reaching all parents with information to help them support their teens in the transition to high school, including those who are unable to attend meetings at the school building, involved a research-based interactive homework intervention for grade 8 students and their families.

FIGURE 11.3   Tips for high school success on a postcard mailing to all incoming ninth graders at one Seattle high school

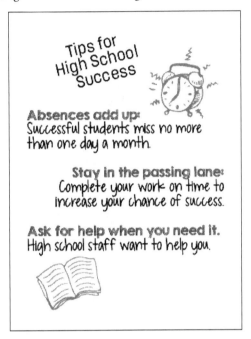

FIGURE 11.4   Refrigerator magnet with attendance information and encouragement in Spanish for incoming ninth-grade families in one Seattle high school

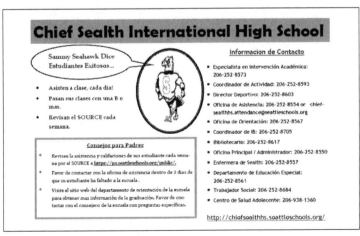

This intervention was based on the National Network of Partnership Schools (NNPS) Teachers Involve Parents in Schoolwork (TIPS) intervention with research-based evidence of positive emotional, behavioral, and achievement effects at the middle-school level.[20] Using the standard NNPS framework for TIPS, the team developed four interactive family activities for schools to pilot in the spring of 2016, including "Absences Add Up," an assignment about the impact of ninth-grade attendance on student success in high school (figure 11.5). Besides the four NNPS middle schools in different parts of the country that piloted the TIPS activities during the first year of the initiative, three Seattle middle schools implemented the TIPS activity with eighth graders during the spring of the second year of the initiative. Two of the schools used it as a homework activity, and one school had the TIPS activities as part of an evening high school information event for students and families.

Challenges to Implementing a Preventative Approach Districtwide

Although there were encouraging examples of a proactive, preventative approach to chronic absenteeism in some schools' family engagement efforts, there remain several challenges to expanding this more preventative approach districtwide. These challenges involve changing mind-sets and priorities of both district leaders and school leaders and contending with logistical challenges to implementing evidence-based practices.

Changing mind-sets about priorities. Even though the Seattle Public Schools was outwardly focused on reducing chronic absenteeism during the course of this initiative, the pressure of other district priorities often appeared to take this issue off school leaders' radar. While one in five ninth graders districtwide was chronically absent, this was still a minority of students (and a much smaller minority in some high schools than others). School leaders did not always appear to be receiving the message that reducing chronic absence rates, much less engaging families in preventative ways to achieve this, should be among their top priorities. The district was not actively reinforcing the message to high school leaders about the links among chronic absence, course failure, and graduation rates. This made efforts to promote family engagement around the importance of attendance seem optional.

Moving from a reactive to proactive perspective. We also observed that school leaders still tend to be reactive rather than proactive when it came

FIGURE 11.5   Example of a home activity for eighth-grade families focused on attendance in high school assigned by one Seattle middle school

TIPS-Transitions1 - ATTENDANCE

Name: _____   Class: _____   Date: _____

Absences Add Up

Dear Parent or Family Partner,

I am learning about high school and what I can do to make sure that I graduate on-time. Attending school every day helps a lot. I hope you enjoy this activity with me. This assignment is due _____.

Sincerely,

_____
Student Signature

SOMETHING TO REMEMBER

If you graduate on time from high school, you will have a better chance to prepare for the college or career that you really want.

PROCEDURE

With a family partner, look over the graph. Who is working with you? _____

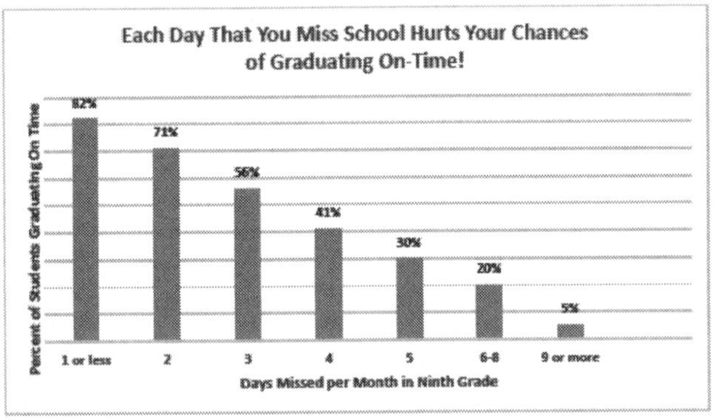

Each Day That You Miss School Hurts Your Chances of Graduating On-Time!

The graph shows data from students in a big city in the U.S. Data from other cities show the same trends. You can see that excellent attendance greatly increases a student's chance of success.

Talk with your family partner about the information in the graph.

Which information did you find interesting and important? (Mark one or more answers that you and your family partner agree on.)

○ Ninth graders who miss even two days of school per month are less likely to graduate from high school.

○ Ninth graders who miss just one day of school a month are two times more likely to graduate than students who miss four days a month.

○ Less than one third of the ninth graders who miss five days a month graduate on time.

○ [Something else:] _____

—Continue on the back page.—

to addressing issues of chronic absenteeism. Although some were aware of family challenges that could affect absenteeism rates, the educators we observed often viewed it as "not our responsibility" to anticipate attendance challenges

FIGURE 11.5 (continued)

TEXT MESSAGES FROM A MENTOR

Some schools provide some ninth graders with a mentor to coach them and help them have a successful start in high school. The mentor is usually a volunteer who communicates regularly with a student. **Pretend that YOU are mentoring 3 students during their first year in high school.**

Below are descriptions of the 3 students. Read each one aloud to your family partner. Then, check the graph on page 1 to see what the data say about the likely outcome of the student's attendance habits.

Together, create a text message to send to each student. YOU write the message that you and your family partner agree on. For example, you might write a message to warn, encourage, inspire, or offer assistance to the student.

Student 1. This ninth-grader often skips school on rainy days and Mondays. She is absent about 5 days a month. What message will you send to this student?

_____

_____

Student 2. This ninth-grader comes to school every day. He was absent just one day in the first semester when he had the stomach flu. What message will you send to this student?

_____

_____

Student 3. This ninth-grader misses 2 days of school per month. That adds up to 18 days across the whole school year. What message will you send to this student?

_____

_____

TWEET IT!

Every Student, Every Day is a project to improve student attendance across the country. Let's say that the leaders asked you to send a message about attendance to all students entering high school. Using the graph on page 1 and the ideas you discussed with your family partner, write a Tweet to tell 9th grade students about the importance of attendance (up to 140 characters including letters, spaces, and punctuation).

_ _

_ _

_ _

HOME-TO-SCHOOL COMMUNICATION

Dear Parent or Family Partner,
Please give your reactions to this activity. Write YES or NO for each statement.

1. _____ My teen understood the homework and was able to discuss it.

2. _____ My teen and I enjoyed the activity.

3. _____ This assignment helped us talk about the importance of attendance in grade 9 and in high school.

Comment: _____

Parent Signature: _____

© MacIver, D. & Epstein, J. 2017. Teachers Involve Parents in Schoolwork (TIPS). Seattle Transitions Project Series. Baltimore: Johns Hopkins University.

families might face (such as transportation or childcare) and help them plan in advance how to address them. Given the time challenges faced by school leaders, this is not surprising. They may need convincing evidence that time invested in preventative measures will actually reduce the consequences and time required to deal with chronic absence problems after they arise.

Keeping the focus on student outcome goals.   Even those leaders who might have been willing to help families proactively negotiate their attendance challenges often lost sight of the student outcome goals when planning and executing their family engagement activities. Helping busy school leaders to focus their family engagement efforts in the most effective ways requires ongoing and systematic effort. Our preliminary analyses of data from schools' cycle of inquiry reflection forms indicate that schools still approach family engagement primarily from an "event perspective" rather than devoting as much attention to the goal of sharing information and resources with families in multiple ways. When most attention is focused on events attended by families whose children are not chronically absent, there remains much less time to reach out in other ways to families more likely to face attendance challenges.

Addressing implementation challenges to evidence-based practices.   And even when we were able to persuade school leaders to consider effective, research-based interventions, they faced notable implementation challenges. Our discussions with school leaders during training and coaching sessions uncovered a significant challenge to the promising research-based intervention of texting families with updates about attendance and course performance. Even though school leaders may be enthusiastic about implementing the texting intervention, most school districts require an active "opt-in" by families to receive text messages because of the charges associated with such messages on many phone plans, particularly those used by low-income families. Families who attend events can be encouraged to opt-in during those face-to-face encounters, and schools can encourage families to opt-in through their websites. But, we learned, reaching the secondary school families who most need the texts to get them to opt-in to receive those texts is a significant challenge for schools that are typically underresourced. Using email does not require the same opt-in commitment from families (except for providing an email address), but low-income families do not always have regular access to email. Even those with smart phones may not have sufficient internet access or storage for apps to be able to access email. Finding ways to implement technology solutions for families most in need of them continues to be a challenge for school leaders.

In the short run, encouraging the use of low-tech research-based interventions, such as nudge postcards, appears to be a more promising strategy. In the next stages of this work, it will be important to equip and persuade school leaders to expand their messaging on such cards to include suggestions about planning ahead for transportation and family sickness issues that negatively affect attendance. Including contact information for support personnel and services is another important step. Helping school leaders find ways to mobilize community partnerships and leverage scarce resources to successfully implement these family engagement strategies will be the challenge.

Toward Building a Proactive Approach to Chronic Absences

Implementation of this continuous improvement initiative focused on increasing schools' engagement and equipping of families to understand how they can support their students' attendance and course performance during the critical first year of high school has yielded several key findings. It is possible to create a networked improvement community of schools willing to undertake the work of critically reflecting on how to improve their family engagement efforts during the high school transition. Schools progress at varying rates in understanding how to improve their effectiveness in engaging all families with the information and support they need to support their students well during this transition. Some schools have reached the stage of thinking proactively about preventing chronic absence before it erupts and are willing to consider implementing research-based initiatives, but not all schools are willing to undertake this work.

Including chronic absence as an accountability measure at the state level, as encouraged by the Every Student Succeeds Act, is certainly a first step.[21] Although this certainly encourages districts to give high priority to reducing chronic absence, it will be necessary to ensure that this message is clearly articulated to all schools in an effective way. High schools may vary greatly in the "degree of difficulty" they face, the number of entering students with a history of chronic absence. Schools with much smaller numbers of these students may be tempted to just let them slip through the cracks unnoticed, while schools with much larger numbers of these students need additional resources to cope with the challenge, not just accountability pressure.

And districts need to take the lead in inspiring and equipping school leaders, including high school principals, to view the work of engaging families as a core part of their mission and a key factor in helping to improve student attendance and other outcomes. District expectations about coordinated efforts between middle and high schools to engage families in multiple ways throughout the ninth-grade transition are needed. It should not be the luck of the draw whether or not one's zoned high school makes the effort to ensure that all families receive information and support that can help them more effectively help their students during the first year of high school. Clear district expectations for all schools to prioritize family engagement efforts, as well as supports equipping them to do so, are needed.

If high schools are to pursue more intentional family engagement strategies in a preventative rather than reactive way, in attempts to equip parents to support student attendance *before* chronic absence becomes a problem and begins to negatively affect ninth graders' course performance, they will need to have greater resources to support increased family engagement. The major sources of school funding for family engagement currently are Title I funds, which are disproportionately distributed to elementary schools in most districts. High schools, historically less focused on systematically engaging the families of their students, are also less likely to be designated as Title I schools and to be eligible for family engagement funding. Although the historical tendency for high schools to focus less attention on family engagement is unlikely to have been *caused* by less available funding, attempts to shift the practices of high schools would benefit greatly from additional human resources to assist in family engagement responsibilities.

Feedback from administrators in Seattle emphasized the difficulties they experience in adding family engagement to their already overloaded schedules. Even the small grant-funded honorariums for schools helped encourage participation in training and networked improvement community meetings as well as school leaders' decisions to try out new family engagement activities they had not considered in the past. Legislation introduced recently in several states related to funding family engagement work is an encouraging step.[22]

But districts do not need to wait for a large influx of resources to begin this work. They can leverage existing resources to begin networking middle and high schools to reflect on their family engagement work and how it can support the goal of reducing chronic absenteeism, particularly during the critical ninth-grade year. As schools that are doing remarkable work in family engagement share their stories and receive recognition from their own districts and larger organizations, like the National Association for Family, School and Community Engagement and the National Network of Partnership Schools, the work can begin to spread. Leveraging our best allies for regular school attendance—students' families—begins with district leaders taking the steps to make this happen.

12

Intervention Design Choices and Evaluation Lessons from Multisite Field Trials on Reducing Absenteeism

REKHA BALU

THE NEED FOR SOLUTIONS to address absenteeism is often higher in schools that serve a higher proportion of students at risk of not graduating. Even in Title I schools, which receive additional resources to support struggling students, there is a need to implement more systematic solutions and programs that have proven to work elsewhere. In addition, schools flagged as sites of chronic absence (either based on new Every Student Succeeds Act indicators or other metrics) do not have just one type of absenteeism problem. High schools with high chronic absence rates often contend with a mix of absenteeism patterns; students who are absent for long spells need different interventions than students who are intermittently absent throughout the year. The varying dynamics of absenteeism suggest that schools need to consider motivation, information, and coordination approaches that can change behavior for students across the absence spectrum.

In this chapter I briefly review evidence on solutions based on cases of four multisite randomized field trials implemented at scale across the country by MDRC.[1] Each experiment tested an evidence-based solution but with a different theory of change about what can boost attendance. For each case, I describe the theory of change—whose behavior is the intervention changing (parents, students, school leaders)—and the intensity and duration of the intervention, how it was delivered, and school structures that supported it. I note the staff and data required to implement the intervention and to assess both the implementation and impact and discuss how the intervention design choices addressed specific aspects of an absenteeism problem and the extent to which findings suggest that interventions work better for some types of students or absence patterns. In concluding the chapter, I synthesize what each of these cases suggests about areas for further descriptive study and lessons for future testing.

In reviewing the cases, it's helpful to consider the following decision points (table 12.1):

- *recipient:* Is the intervention engaging directly with students, parents, or both?
- *theory of change:* Is the intervention trying to address a single barrier to attendance or multiple challenges? Is the solution proactive (preventative) or reactive?
- *mode:* Is the intervention delivered across many school programs and partners or via a single mechanism? Is it individualized for some students or automated and generalized to all students?
- *data required:* How often does the intervention require attendance data to be pulled and reviewed? Are other types of data required to understand absenteeism (e.g., discipline data)?
- *staff involvement:* Does the intervention require staff input or engagement? If so, does it require management or front-line staff response? Does it require specialists to deliver services?
- *timing, grade span, and duration:* Does the intervention start at a transition grade? If yes, at the beginning of the year? Does it last for the entire year? Is the intervention responding in real time? Is the intervention dynamic and able to be adjusted midsemester?

TABLE 12.1

Attendance intervention descriptions

	Case 1 Information (2016)	Case 2 Financial incentives (2007–08)	Case 3 Coordinate support services (2012–13)	Case 4 Whole-school structures plus targeted student support (2011–12)
	ATTENDANCE INTERVENTION			
	INTERVENTION DESIGN			
Theory of change	Timely information engages parents.	Rewards encourage students to meet goals.	Struggling students need services that address multiple challenges; case workers coordinate with family needs.	Teacher teams and administrators review data, differentiate services accordingly; volunteers mentor/tutor struggling students.
Target/Unit	All parents/guardians	All students	Parents and struggling students	All students, with focus on struggling students
Mode	*Individual*: Weekly text messages to parents about attendance weekly and daily updates if an absence	*Individual*: Monthly financial incentives if students attend 95% of scheduled days	*Individual*: Case management/coordination of services to support attendance	*Whole-school and individualized*: Early-warning systems, near-peer mentoring, case management of outside services
Data required for intervention	Daily	Monthly	Monthly	Biweekly or monthly
Staff required	N/A (automated)	Clerical	Specialists	Specialists, school facilitator, volunteers
Timing and grade span	9th–12th grades, spring semester	9th grade, full year	9th and 10th grades, full year	9th and 10th grades, full year
	RESEARCH DESIGN			
Unit of analysis	Student			School
Sample size in high school	12 high schools, ~4,000 students	~1,970 students	10 high schools, ~1500 students	29 high schools, ~9,340 students
Average impact on attendance	No	Yes	No	No
Subgroup impacts	Grade: No High vs. low 1st-semester attendance: No	High-proficiency students: Yes	Grade: No High-risk students: No	Kept on-track students on track

- *subgroups:* Is the intervention likely to be more effective for some types of students? If so, is a different iteration of the intervention offered to those students?

CASE 1: Can Information Change Parent Engagement and Student Attendance?

For New York City high school students, just getting to school is a production. Because students can choose to attend high school anywhere in the city, many students cross boroughs. They travel for an average of forty-five minutes on public transit from home to school and contend with uncertain arrival times. Many parents cannot see or know in real time whether their students attend school, as they could with a neighborhood school if they personally dropped off their student. Meanwhile, the clerical staff in these large high schools' front offices are tasked with tracking attendance as well as contending with the chaos of school management, making it difficult to determine who arrives on time or not at all.

Given these many factors that contribute to absences, schools want to know how to engage parents around attendance. In addition, questions about the completeness or accuracy of attendance data prompt some schools to ask whether real-time absence information drawn from an updated database could better engage parents with more frequent, accurate updates. Another question relates to timing—absence information provided to parents might be more salient and actionable to shift attendance away from the typical second-semester slump, if parents see an absence pattern during the first semester and then recognize that the second semester represents a chance to change that pattern.

To explore these questions, a practitioner-researcher collaboration tested an informational intervention.[2] The school support organization New Visions for Public Schools, which works with district high schools serving low-income students in New York City, collaborated with MDRC to design a text message system to provide real-time alerts to parents of absent students and weekly attendance summaries to parents of all students. Messages were purely informational, such as "John was absent today. Please call [school and phone number] with questions." These messages were translated into one of the nine official languages in New York City, personalized for the guardian and student, and included the relevant school phone number that parents could autodial in case of questions.

The theory of change for this type of intervention is that discrete information without prescriptive action may be sufficient for parents to monitor their student's absence and address absenteeism. Some parents also may not notice their student's attendance pattern, even if they notice occasional absences, so weekly summaries throughout the semester were intended to identify patterns. In addition, the intervention sent messages to guardians of all students, rather than targeting chronically absent students, with the goal of boosting average attendance rates.

While the intervention may seem simple, any real-time information intervention requires a strong foundation of accurate, real-time attendance data; if parents are alerted to an absence when their student is present, or vice versa, they will ignore or opt out of message alerts. Accurate tracking of attendance requires schools to have a high degree of internal coordination and functioning to reconcile conflicting data between teachers in different periods of the day. As a result, a real-time informational intervention relies on teachers, school staff, central office staff, and data teams to maintain accurate attendance data systems. This intervention tried to avoid overburdening school staff alongside the need to minimize false positive or false negative reports to parents.

Within each grade at each school, MDRC randomly assigned households with authorized guardians and active cell phones to receive text messages. The intervention sent text messages to any identified parents and guardians of program group students in grades 9–12 in twelve New York City district high schools during the spring semester of the 2015–16 school year. These schools were selected for several reasons. In terms of data, New Visions reviewed fall semester data to determine how accurate the attendance data were (e.g., the proportion of students whose absence was later recorded as present, or vice versa). Schools that had at least 80 percent accuracy were eligible. In addition, schools needed to upload attendance data daily, ideally by midday, to permit same-day updates to parents that afternoon. Finally, these schools did not have existing text message outreach to parents, to ensure sufficient contrast and to avoid sending duplicate messages to parents.

MDRC found that the messages did not boost overall attendance rates in the second semester; both intervention and control groups had an attendance rate around 86 percent. Although attendance on certain days was higher for the text message group, the program and control group students both followed an overall pattern of attendance decline from the beginning to end of the second semester. While some students' attendance improved from the first to second semester, the proportion of "improvers" was similar in the two groups (29 percent in the program group versus 30 percent in the control group). The intervention did not reduce the proportion of chronically absent students either. Parents who responded to a survey said they would like to continue receiving the information, but their characteristics were not representative of all families in the study.

Future interventions could expand beyond what was tried here to include additional text message content or in-person services paired with text messaging. In text messages, providing links to additional resources to address student absence could make the messages feel more actionable and supportive. Information alone, without a prompt to action, is likely not sufficient.[3] Messages may also lose salience or novelty for guardians over time, especially for regularly absent students whose patterns do not change. However, messages that target ninth-grade students, that begin at the start of the year, and that are sent to both students and parents could set a more positive trajectory. School systems may want to consider how to improve the accuracy of attendance tracking and data, especially as districts invest more in early-warning systems that include attendance data.

CASE 2: Can Financial Incentives Change Student Attendance?

In another experiment in New York City, Mayor Michael Bloomberg's office considered in 2007 a more intensive intervention to support low-income families and boost attendance, but one that did not involve services or case management. The theory of change asserts that financial incentives, rather than services, can change behavior. The Family Rewards program provided payments to parents and students only if they demonstrated certain actions (a so-called conditional cash transfer).[4] While the attendance incentive was offered directly to students to change their behavior, the overall program included incentives paid directly to parents/guardians as well as to students.

Students may be absent for reasons related to complex challenges facing low-income families involved in multiple social programs and services. Parents in the study cited the challenges of keeping up with everyday responsibilities along with complying with government program requirements. "I have to manage those four lives plus my own. So I have five schedules to manage every day and basically keeping my head" related to social program require-ments, noted one parent.[5] In addition, for New York City high school stu-dents travel across boroughs, transportation costs and coordination are daily challenges. Another parent noted that the incentive could be noticeable for some families: "It's not a lot of money, but it does help. I'm sure it's an incen-tive . . . Even just taking your kid to school on a daily basis, it's not something people always do in this community."[6]

Low-income families in New York were randomly assigned by MDRC to receive the offer of the financial incentive or to a control group. About one-third lived in public housing, less than one-fourth received safety net income assistance, and about three-fifths received food stamps. Children of families in the program group were eligible for the incentives; children in the control group received no incentives. Within the family-level random assignment evaluation, there was an embedded study focused on ninth-grade students and their intermediate outcomes, including attendance. High school students directly received rewards for key academic behaviors: $50 a month if they attended 95 percent of scheduled days; $50 for taking the PSAT; $600 for accumulating enough credits to move to the next grade, paid in the summer; and $600 for each gateway exam (New York State Regents) passed, also paid in the summer. A nonprofit service organization helped set up bank accounts for families, collected data to keep track of activities or milestones completed, and coordinated payments.

At the end of two school years, MDRC found that students in the program group were more likely to attend 95 percent or more of scheduled days (28.9 percent of program students compared to 23.7 percent in the control group). Students who scored at or above proficiency on their eighth-grade math test attended at a higher rate at the end of two years, 51.1 percent of program group students compared to 36.2 percent of control group students. By con-trast, the students who scored below proficiency on their eighth-grade math test in the program group had statistically similar attendance rates as their control group counterparts (21 percent versus 19 percent, respectively). The impact on attendance for students in the study does not necessarily mean that overall school attendance rates improved where these students were enrolled. Because randomization occurred within families and not schools, school attendance rates were not analyzed.

Any program involving financial incentives raises questions of scalability and sustainability, since governments or foundations are unlikely to offer incentives continuously. Long-term behavior change comes from establishing a routine, and whether this happens via individual support or via community systems is a subject of much debate among practitioners and researchers.

The reward structure is worth exploring. The availability of the reward each month may have helped, as did the monthly dollar amount. Yet, asking students to meet a high standard—attending 95 percent of scheduled days—may make the reward less relevant or accessible for students who initially struggle with attendance. Instead, a reward for attendance improvement could have boosted the proportion of program group students with a higher overall attendance rate. It is unclear whether the incentives solved a specific financial barrier to attendance (e.g., lack of bus fare) or whether students lacked intrinsic motivation to attend and needed some external encouragement. However, the fact that attendance at the 95 percent standard was greater for incentive recipients than for control students suggests that students were both intrinsically motivated to reach a high standard and extrinsically motivated by the additional cash. If both extrinsic and intrinsic motivations matter for students' attendance, then it is not surprising that frequent and well-timed financial incentives can shift the behavior of students living with financial need.[7]

CASE 3: How Can Case Management Support Student Attendance?

In a midsized school district, Jesse regularly misses school because of chronic asthma, while Adam misses school because he is concerned about his safety. Each of these attendance challenges requires a different solution and coordination with the student's family. If Jesse needs an external clinic referral and Adam needs support resolving dynamics within the school, the varied and personalized service coordination required for each student may require more time and assistance than most teachers and administrators can provide, even though they may recognize the need.

This third case explores the question of whether an independent site coordinator can coordinate services to support struggling students and families to boost attendance. MDRC evaluated case management delivered by the national nonprofit Communities In Schools (CIS) to assess the impact of its case management services around attendance starting in 2012–13.[8] Among CIS coordinators across schools in the study, 90 percent listed poor attendance as one of their schools' high-priority problems.

The theory of change for the attendance intervention is that school coordinators can refer students to targeted services, which can address the underlying challenges related to absenteeism, poor academic performance, and other adverse outcomes. As with the earlier cases, CIS aims to relieve school staff of the work involved in service coordination. Teachers, administrators, after-school programs, or community agencies need to refer a student to CIS, and then CIS coordinators identify what intervention services the student may need (e.g., Tier 2 or Tier 3, or behavioral, financial, or family related) and connect students to those services, either at the school or off-site (e.g., family therapy). Among students referred for these intervention services in the participating schools, MDRC randomly assigned students either to receive case management from CIS coordinators at the high school in addition to existing services or to just continue with existing services. Student services related to attendance could include specific attendance check-ins and earning rewards for meeting attendance targets, as well as tutoring, home visits, and parent conferences and contacts, depending on the nature of the problem.

After two years of the program, MDRC found that case management did not reduce the percentage of absent students. For students assigned in the beginning of ninth grade, about 21 percent of both those who did and did not receive case management services were chronically absent; the average attendance rate among students in both groups was about 92 percent. The theorized mechanism for reducing absenteeism—students' participation rate in support services—did not operate as expected. Among all 701 program students, only 80 percent of students received any service. The tiered intervention model would suggest that high-risk students—those who had failed a course or who had attended less than 90 percent (were chronically absent) or suspended in the previous year—receive more, or more intensive, services than moderate-risk students. Yet the direction was reversed: 75 percent of high-risk students versus 85 percent of moderate-risk students received services. For attendance in particular, 10 percent of high-risk students compared to 14.6 percent of moderate-risk students received attendance-related supports. Moreover, the percentage of high-risk students participating in case management declined from the first to second year of the study (from 93 percent to 74 percent of high-risk students). As a result, the goal of providing more intensive services for higher-risk students was not fully achieved over the two years.

There are several possible reasons for poor service participation. With caseloads of about 115 students in need of at least Level/Tier 2 services per case manager, it may be difficult for case managers to devote extra attention to higher-risk students and ensure that those students receive ongoing services. To this end, the national CIS office is supporting affiliates in ways to make services distinct for high-risk versus moderate-risk students and to manage caseloads accordingly. While case management, especially in transition grades, such as ninth, can provide a single point of contact for students struggling with challenges associated with absenteeism, students still face time and coordination constraints related to attending services while juggling school and other obligations. Students may feel more comfortable pursuing or attending services they can access on their own. Survey research could reveal more about these intentions and motivations.

THE ROLE OF EARLY WARNING INDICATORS

The schools participating in the intervention trials in the cases 1, 3, and 4 used some version of early-warning indicators that included chronic absence. Many high schools use early-warning systems to identify students at risk of high school dropout based on a combination of attendance, behavior, and course performance data.[9] These systems create "on-track" indicators and help schools identify which students need support.[10] However, schools need to create or select which interventions could help specific students, such as those described in this chapter, and then deliver interventions within tiered systems of support:[11]

- Tier 1 services are those that all students receive and that are often intended to prevent students from needing more intensive services.

- Tier 2 interventions serve students at moderate risk of dropout, usually for a limited time. Sometimes students receive these services in small groups.

- Tier 3 services are more intensive for high-risk students who have not responded to general support or Tier 2 interventions.

Early-warning systems typically categorize higher-risk students in potential need of Tier 2 or 3 services, as a prompt to intervene before students have developed patterns of missing school.

CASE 4: Can Whole-School Reform Reduce Chronic Absence?

As the previous cases suggest, high school success involves multiple players and depends on teachers, students, and school leaders receiving intervention and support. In contrast to earlier cases that tested an intervention involving a single user or actor, this fourth case describes a more comprehensive and complex intervention designed to engage multiple stakeholders.[12] The theory of change is that all parties in a high school—from teachers to staff to students—need to improve the three early-warning indicators of attendance, behavior, and course performance to shift student outcomes. Chronic absence often flags students for the other two indicators and provides an independent warning of high school dropout risk, so regular monitoring of attendance is essential to the program model.[13]

Diplomas Now (DN) is a whole-school organizational and instructional reform effort that joined three organizations—Talent Development Secondary, City Year, and Communities In Schools—to reduce high school dropout in large urban districts.[14] This type of whole-school reform is inherently more challenging because it involves coordination between organizations and schools, buy-in from multiple school-level stakeholders, and multiple parties to monitor, interpret, and act on early-warning data.[15]

Beginning in the academic year 2011–12, schools from eleven large urban districts in different states began implementing this model. Schools with high poverty and dropout rates were randomly assigned within districts to implement DN or to continue using existing services, which could include other chronic absence initiatives. For schools to achieve program fidelity and impact, they needed to resolve a tension between addressing chronic absence within a larger reform effort versus creating a separate program just on attendance. While all schools in the study focused on chronic absence, their attention was spread across multiple other competing responsibilities related to DN to differing degrees. Of the nine program inputs, three addressed student support, including those related to absenteeism. Fidelity remained constant throughout four years of implementation and relatively high for elements related to student supports. In addition, contrast from the control schools increased during that time, suggesting that the DN structures represented a change from typical practice.

The program showed mixed results in high schools by the end of the second year.[16] It improved the percentage of ninth-grade students (in DN schools compared with non-DN schools) who had no early-warning indications of dropout risk (the percentage of students who maintained an 85 percent or greater attendance rate along with minimal suspensions and no failures in key courses), 52.6 percent in DN schools compared with 50 percent in non-DN schools. The program also helped keep those students at low risk of dropout in tenth grade. However, the program did not have an impact on the overall attendance rate, which was about 87 percent for DN and non-DN schools. In terms of the percentage of students who attended 90 percent of enrolled days (who were not chronically absent), the program did not have a statistically significant impact (60 percent in DN schools versus 62 percent in non-DN schools).

The comprehensive program may have required so much coordination on the part of schools that it made it difficult for administrators, volunteers, or case managers to focus primarily on absenteeism. Yet the integrated approach addresses many solutions identified in prior literature: data-driven identification of students, customizing intervention strategies by students' needs, tackling academic struggles with in-school tutoring, addressing family struggles with coordinated counseling and other social services.[17] This suggests an implementation tension—how many strategies can schools reasonably address? In 2019, MDRC will release results after following students for four years to see if absences declined. The fact that the program was slightly more effective at reducing absences for students who were already on-track than those who were not may suggest that more intensive services may be required for students at greater risk.

Why Was It Difficult to Boost Attendance in These Studies?

The answer to this question of why it was difficult to boost attendance relates in part to the research design, intervention design, and implementation of each study. First, in terms of research design, the level of randomization may influence the results. Family Rewards incentives were randomized to low-income families at the household level rather than school level or students within schools. Therefore, spillover within schools was less of a concern; and the typical within-school and between-school variation that staff need to address in intervention implementation was not as much a factor. The results discussed addressed two-year impacts, because ongoing (rather than temporary) attendance is what is associated with graduation. Note that comparing impacts across cases is difficult when each study uses a different threshold to define absenteeism and risk (DN and CIS used 90 percent to define chronic absence, Family Rewards used 95 percent attendance to reward students).

Second, for intervention design it is useful to consider what is easier to implement with fidelity. Whole-school reforms require multiple forms of coordinating people and services that can reduce fidelity. Individuals delivering support to students via counseling sessions or meetings also could vary in fidelity. By contrast, informational interventions and incentives rely on data systems to deliver the intervention as designed. However, communication interventions may still rely on people to raise awareness so that messages or incentive opportunities are more salient. Also, the intervention must provide a sufficient enhancement over usual practice. This may require more ex ante data collection and documentation of attendance outreach to determine whether a new intervention could add value. In addition, it is important to account for seasonal and grade-level variation in high school attendance (higher in fall, lower in spring; higher ninth than tenth grade, lower in twelfth). It is also useful to consider what hidden costs an intervention represents. Data warehouse construction and tracking, technological enhancements to communicate directly to parents or staff, and other automations require upfront time and resources. And a final intervention design consideration is the behavioral channel. For example, a reward operates differently than an intervention that problematizes student behavior.

Third, in terms of implementation, these were not pilot studies. Despite designing each of these interventions based on prior evidence, they were scaled to a larger population of schools or districts using existing school or district staff who faced real time and resource constraints. The quality of implementation varied across sites and within each program and over time. In addition, the dosage may not have been sufficient or may have been too diffused. Even in a comprehensive program like Diplomas Now, some students may need more of a few things than a little bit of many services. However, this type of differentiation of services tends to require more staff attention and, potentially, school resources. Also, addressing absence while changing other behaviors is difficult for school and program staff. Staff may perceive an opportunity cost: focusing on absences takes them away from addressing academic needs. And though this may be a false choice, interventions may need to account for the perception and balance any intervention burden on staff with the need to document, differentiate, and intensify services for higher-risk, chronically absent students. Differentiation seems particularly important given that each case showed better results for higher-achieving, higher-performing, lower-risk students. Students at greatest risk did not respond as well or at all. This suggests that further research could test targeted interventions for higher-risk students (rather than implementing the same intervention for all students and analyzing high-absence students as a subgroup).

Unfortunately, the cases do not answer the question "What intervention is best?" Interventions are best designed to answer "What is the problem?" "For whom are we changing behavior, and in what context?" No single intervention is best, and design needs to be adapted to type of student, need, and circumstance. However, a summary across these cases suggests that interventions can achieve implementation success and impact when they increase attention on absence, document that new attendance outreach and support extend far beyond existing services, consider and limit unintended consequences, and balance staff workload and decision making. These principles of intervention design can inform future testing as well.

Conclusion

ETHAN L. HUTT AND MICHAEL A. GOTTFRIED

AFTER THE PASSAGE of the federal Every Student Succeeds Act (ESSA) and the subsequent approval of state accountability plans by the US Department of Education, it seems likely that student absenteeism, as an accountability metric and policy lever, will receive a level of attention not seen since the Progressive Era. The decision by Congress to provide increased flexibility in states' selection of school quality metrics and the decision by lawmakers in a majority states to use that flexibility to introduce absence metrics is a key development in renewing a focus on missed school days. This revival has the potential to be significant; the rhetoric of education reform has long stressed the need to "get back to basics," and there is almost nothing more basic than focusing on getting students to school, into the classroom, and in front of a teacher. There are also few more straightforward deprivations of educational opportunity than students being absent from school.[1] Indeed, there is no question that unequal attendance is a source of inequitable educational opportunity, as is made plain by the contributing authors throughout this book. Likewise, there is no question that schools and districts can take concrete steps to close that opportunity gap, and several chapters provide concrete policies, specific interventions, and detailed advice on how to do just that. This gives us hope that a renewed focus on attendance in general, and chronic absenteeism in particular, have the power to generate positive change for American education.

But what gives us hope in education policy should also give us pause. As decades of reform failures should remind us, it takes more than good intentions or even good ideas to make meaningful educational change. School systems are complicated and the potential for unintended consequences or even backfire is ever present.[2] Even as we may applaud the diversification of school quality metrics that shrink the place of standardized test scores and make room for measures of absenteeism, we are aware of the many challenges that lie ahead. For instance, to the extent that many believed that holding schools accountable for student test scores was objectionable because test scores are a function of many factors beyond the control of schools, some might contend that this same argument should carry even more force when applied to holding schools accountable for student absence rates. That is, while a teacher can reasonably be expected to affect the learning of students present in the classroom through curriculum and instruction, can we expect schools—or teachers—to be held similarly accountable when it comes to securing high attendance rates? This is only one of many question that remain to be addressed if we are to develop a set of productive policies and practices for holding schools accountable for student absences.

In bringing together contributions on the full range of topics stemming from the renewed commitment to addressing absenteeism, we are taking the lead in addressing issues in a way that can help manage complexity, mitigate potential risks, and cultivate an optimism that a focus on chronic absenteeism can effect positive change in the lives of American schoolchildren. To that end, we aim to clear away some common misconceptions about the measurement, sources, and solutions to absenteeism. In place of those myths we offer a more complicated and nuanced story, one that is elaborated by each of the chapters in the volume.

It is certainly a cliché to say that things in education are complicated, but that does not make it any less true. When it comes to addressing absenteeism, the sources of measurement error are many; the causes of absences are multifaceted; and the effectiveness of policies is contingent. But while we do hope that readers will come away from this volume having added absenteeism to their "it's complicated" list, we do not think that is the only takeaway or even the unequivocal message of the book. Based on the evidence presented in this volume, we offer what we believe are as close to truisms as one can get in education. If not immutable truisms, they are, at the very least, waypoints that policy makers, practitioners, and scholars can use as they navigate this new policy space.

TRUISM 1: Measuring Absenteeism Is Both Easier and Harder Than You Thought

One of the most surprising findings—to us at least—was Gershenson, McBean, and Trann's demonstration that the effects of being absent from school are more or less the same for students regardless of where the student falls within the achievement distribution. This is an important insight, and it suggests that districts can focus on telling a simple and crucially important message with their communities: no matter who your student is or how well she is doing in school, her attendance matters. This message takes on even more weight when we consider, as Dougherty and Childs note, that the cumulative effects of attendance are essentially linear. Despite lawmakers' and district leaders' penchant for setting attendance thresholds, there is nothing magic about these targets. Again, generally speaking, the value of each day is equally important.

This uniformity also makes for an easy calculation—literal and metaphorical—for districts considering whether to implement district- or schoolwide efforts to reduce student absences. Those efforts will not exacerbate achievement gaps (provided they are equally effective on all students): a day of attendance regained is day of learning regained. Full stop. In an era when districts, schools, and teachers are responsible for the continued learning growth of all students—thereby demonstrating their "value-added"—knowing that attendance matters for all students should come as very welcome news.

While the effects of being absent are uniform, the number of times students experience those effects, of course, differs. And unfortunately, as several of our authors show, they differ in ways that disproportionately fall on already-disadvantaged low-income and minority students. This is where the story gets complicated and where lawmakers and practitioners would do well to tend to that complexity. As Gee, Hough, and Dougherty and Childs show in each of their chapters, the rates of absenteeism are anything but uniform:

most of the variation in school attendance exists at the level of the individual student not the classroom or school. And those looking at schoolwide attendance numbers should be aware that rates vary by both school levels and grade levels. This complexity should serve as a stern warning against rigidly uniform definitions for chronic absenteeism or targets for improved attendance. The failure to recognize the variation in attendance rates across school levels, schools, and grade levels in the use of chronic absentee measures for school accountability is almost certain to court failure or scandal, and very likely both.

The District of Columbia Public Schools (DCPS) learned this lesson recently when an investigation uncovered that 34 percent of high school graduates received their diplomas despite attendance policy violations.[3] A subsequent internal investigation found that that an overly rigid goal-setting process contributed to a culture in which attendance records were falsified and attendance policies were not properly enforced. Principals described a process in which they were "given a specific . . . promotion rate number" that was subsequently internalized by teachers who "spoke to limits on the number of students they felt comfortable failing" as well as by other DCPS employees who understood "that these goals established an expectation that only very few students could be marked as failing before either they or their supervisors would be rated as ineffective."[4]

We kid ourselves if we think there is something unique to DC—its principals or teachers—in this scandal. Indeed, in their chapter, Anderson, Egalite, and Mills provide another reminder about the challenges of top-down pronouncements to secure change. The effort to ban outright the use of out-of-school suspensions for truancy did not result in more student engagement or in increased student attendance. It did, however, likely result in schools engaging in more strategic behavior around the implementation of the ban and in reclassification of student behavior. The incorporation of attendance data into ESSA metrics will almost certainly lead to more attempts to legislate away certain challenges, to engage in strategic behavior (legal and illegal), and to develop routines for complying with the letter, if not the spirit, of the rules. Incidents of this sort will be for the first decade of ESSA what the district test-score cheating scandals were for the last decade of No Child Left Behind, unless lawmakers and districts take a realistic approach to the measurement and mitigation of chronic absenteeism. That approach should begin with the simple message that *every day of school matters* and proceed to a nuanced examination of the problem in each district, school, and grade level.

TRUISM 2: School Is Not a Silo

It bears repeating: student attendance is affected by many factors beyond the direct control of schools. Students miss school for health reasons (not just their own but also those of their family members), for housing reasons, for work reasons (again, theirs and their families'), and for reasons too idiosyncratic to list. There are quite a few mechanisms documented in this volume that can either reduce or increase the likelihood that these issues will result in missed school. These include access to school buses, as shown by Cordes, Leardo, Rick, and Schwartz, as well as Graves, Weisburd, and Salem's suggestion that access to health services plays a role and Sattin-Bajaj and Kirksey's discussion of attendance issues around immigration and deportation.

Many of our authors offer additional insights into the complexity of the issue, designing school supports as systems of resources intended to work in conjunction with communities. Too often we think of improving educational outcomes as strictly rooted in schools, such as improving teacher quality or changing curriculum, or as strictly targeted at students. Indeed, in the process of writing this book one of us proposed a project aimed at reducing rates of student absence by developing communication tools aimed at connecting schools with community players only to be met with a skeptical reply from the potential funder that "wouldn't it be better to build the tools for the students?" While student-focused solutions might also work, as Ehrlich and Johnson, Graves and colleagues, Sattin-Bajaj and Kirksey, Smythe-Leistico and Page, and Mac Iver and Sheldon show us, one important step schools can take is developing specific plans and specific capacities around engaging the entire community—within and beyond the school—in ways that address absenteeism.

To be effective, however, efforts will need to go beyond any siloed effort. Instead, as described by Ehrlich and Johnson, schools must develop comprehensive plans that engage administrators, teachers, and support staff in developing tailored strategies, capacities, and messages directed at executing a uniform plan to engage entire communities—ranging from social services to mentors to parents to religious organizations—on issues of student attendance. Specific interventions, like at-home activities, mentors, and two-way messaging, need to be carried out as expressions and extensions of this broader organizational commitment.

TRUISM 3: Not Your Dad's Intervention—or Is It?

Though Truism 2 touched on the role of parents, parents merit their own truism. Given that intervention work in the area of absenteeism reduction is still so new, it is, at present, difficult to develop a sense of what scalable policies and practices might be *most* efficacious at mitigating school absenteeism for our nation's students. However, based on the summaries in Balu's chapter, we propose that attendance interventions which focus on school-parent partnerships might be particularly salient. It has been documented that children benefit when a stronger link is made between parent and school, particularly in lower socioeconomic status families.[5]

Chapters like Smythe-Leistico and Page's and Mac Iver and Sheldon's highlight the important role parents play in school-based attendance interventions. Parents who do not fully understand the importance of daily attendance also may not understand the consequences of missing school, and without the proper information or supports and resources this may lead to even higher rates of child absenteeism. Hence, in one respect, school-parent attendance interventions can be especially important because they increase parental awareness, and, in turn, child absences may decline.

That said, the generic engagement between parents and schools—an extra announcement about the importance of school attendance at Back-to-School Night—is unlikely to do the trick. Old-school flyers and announcements do not connect absences to consequences, and statistics often get glossed over. However, when schools provide tools and tips to parents through more modern means like texting, we begin to see improvement. This underscores the role of the medium as well as the message. Interventions that have the potential to be the most efficacious invoke a change in attitudes and behavior for both parents and their children, but they do so in a way that provides support and in a way that feels very "now."

Identifying if school-parent programs help increase awareness around truancy and engagement about schooling and, ultimately, reduce student-level truancy will allow policy makers, practitioners, and community members to develop scalable programs to reduce absenteeism. Hence, as we continue to involve parents in absence reduction in ways that make sense for the next decade, this will enable multiple stakeholders to more efficiently channel funds and resources in ways that reduce this high-risk schooling behavior and in ways that properly reach parents.

*   *   *

There is exciting potential for addressing absenteeism. As such, *Absent from School* has numerous implications for policy, practice, and scholarship. High rates of absenteeism limit the potential of our nation's students and cost school districts and the state billions of dollars each year. The information presented here provides critical data regarding measuring patterns of attendance as well as mechanisms and potential interventions and innovations. This should prove useful to policy makers and school leaders throughout the country as they continue to develop truancy reduction programs, in terms of required future infrastructure, human capital, and financing.

This book also has important implications for practice and community support. Parents and community members are key partners in promoting good attendance because they have the ultimate responsibility for ensuring that their children get to school every day, particularly younger children. Many parents, however, do not recognize the adverse impact that poor attendance can have on learning as early as preschool or the importance of building a habit of good attendance from the beginning. To carry out their responsibility, parents need to be equipped with the correct information. Our intervention chapters highlight the importance of developing supports for parents. Similarly, the chapters on school-based programs highlight the role schools can play in supporting good attendance for both children and their families. Parent awareness and school supports are key components of effective and comprehensive approaches to reducing chronic absenteeism. Hence, intervention and school-based programs can make significant differences in reducing absenteeism by helping community members understand the importance of regular attendance and by helping develop programs to nurture a habit of regular attendance.

The book also holds implications for research and scholarship. In particular, it provides a unique opportunity to explore measurement issues as well as program evaluation, especially around the underresearched area of understanding how programs reduce absenteeism. Therefore, through exploring the development of various programs, the book begins to establish empirical links between data, program, and outcome and contributes to ongoing scholarship on the equity of education and its implications for access and success.

We believe *Absent from School* contributes these important findings at a time when our nation struggles with how to address the absenteeism crisis in our schools, and particularly in those schools serving at-risk student populations with multiple needs, and when waning budgets mean that fewer resources are being devoted to the improvement of student outcomes. The capacity for educational improvement continues to grow. The United States is a place where, budgets aside, reform can take hold and where, with the right results, policy makers and practitioners can drastically improve our youths' educational and life outcomes. We hope our book helps us all reach this goal.

AFTERWORD

THIS VOLUME ARRIVES at a critical time for American education. The Every Student Succeeds Act has resulted in a majority of states using absenteeism reduction as one of their core measures of school performance and improvement. This has created urgency for effective interventions to reduce absenteeism at scale and cost effectively. The contributors to this volume have reviewed and suggested several such promising intervention strategies. Here we highlight a handful of additional promising absence research projects that underscore the value and importance of using randomized controlled trials (RCTs) to inform the development of absence-reduction plans.

One such RCT was conducted by Todd Rogers and Avi Feller with the School District of Philadelphia (SDP).[1] They assessed the impact of an absence-reduction intervention modeled after the Home Energy Reports sent regularly to millions of homes around the world.[2] The RCT included parents of 28,080 K–12 students at risk of high absenteeism. These parents were randomly assigned to a control group or one of three treatment conditions that each received an average of four mail-based treatments. Treatments sent to the *reminder* condition emphasized the importance of attendance and the consequences of absences. Treatments sent to the *total absences* condition included the same content as those sent in the reminder condition with the addition of a graphic display of the total number of absences the student had accumulated so far in the school year. Treatments sent to parents in the *comparison* condition included the same content as those sent in the total absences condition with the addition of a graphic display of how their child's absences compared to their typical classmate.

The intervention reduced chronic absenteeism by 11 percent for students whose parents were assigned to the total absences and the comparison conditions. The absence-reducing effects were consistent across grades, races, genders, and socioeconomic statuses, and it also spilled over to other nontargeted siblings living in the same household. Consistent with an asset-based approach to family engagement, the intervention was useful to parents. They reported showing it to others in their homes and were more accurate about both their child's absences and the absences of their child's classmates. These personalized, mail-based attendance reports reduced absenteeism at a cost of $5–10 per net day generated. This intervention and impact has subsequently been replicated in a published RCT with 10,967 K–5 students across ten districts in California and several times by In Class Today, the organization we cofounded to help districts around the US implement the intervention at scale.[3]

Just as RCTs can teach which interventions work cost-effectively, they can also teach which (unexpectedly) do not. Carly Robinson, Jana Gallus, Monica Lee, and Todd Rogers studied an intervention involving giving awards to high school students for perfect attendance (N=15,329).[4] Students who had a perfect month of attendance during the preceding semester were randomly assigned to a control condition or one of two treatments. Those assigned to the retrospective award condition received a high-quality embossed placard congratulating them for having had at least one month of perfect attendance, while those assigned to the prospective award condition received a letter informing them that they would receive the same award if they had a perfect month of attendance in the subsequent semester. The researchers predicted that students in both the retrospective award and prospective award conditions would have fewer absences in the subsequent month than those in the control condition. To their surprise, those in the prospective award condition showed no absence reduction relative to control, while absences among those in the retrospective award condition increased by 8 percent in the month after awards were received. Subsequent survey experiments suggest that these awards may have inadvertently signaled to students that they had attended school more than their peers and more than their schools expected them to attend, potentially causing the unintended absence increase. This experiment studied a specific and stylized kind of award: unexpected, purely symbolic, and of no economic value. Other kinds of awards may be beneficial, but these experimental results suggest that educators should think carefully about what unintended signals are being sent when they offer students attendance awards.

We note two other important recent RCTs on absenteeism. In the first, Rekha Balu, Kristin Porter, and Brad Gunton found that sending weekly automated personalized SMS text messages to high school parents of students in New York City Public Schools about their children's attendance had no statistically reliable effect on subsequent attendance (N=3,957).[5] This was surprising given the apparent promise of SMS-based interventions in K–12 education.[6] However, in contrast to the intervention described by Kenneth Smythe-Leistico and Lindsay Page, in this study there were no school-affiliated individuals personally sending the SMS messages; the messages were automated.[7] It is likely that the perceived interpersonal element of Smythe-Leistico and Page's intervention increased its potency. Unless an SMS message prompts a specific and immediate action (e.g., complete a missing homework assignment tonight) or has a strong interpersonal accountability element, it may be at risk of entering and exiting attention before it can be acted on.

The second noteworthy recent RCT is by Jonathan Guryan and colleagues, who report the only RCT of which we are aware that examines the impact of attendance-focused mentors (N=765).[8] They found that mentors decreased absences by around three days among students in grades 5–7 but had no detectable effect on absenteeism in the other grades studied. Since the mentors cost around $1,500 per student, the researchers estimate that the intervention cost around $500 per net day generated among students in grades 5–7. We note that this is 50–100 times more expensive per net day generated than the mail-based, personalized absence reports described above and is significantly more time- and labor-intensive to implement.[9]

As the scholars in this volume demonstrate, absenteeism often results from deep personal and structural challenges facing students, families, and communities. As such, districtwide or even national-level absence reduction will require multiple effective interventions woven together over time. There is no single panacea; rather, districts will need comprehensive attendance plans that incorporate varied interventions that are supported by rigorous evidence. Some interventions, in particular, can be implemented cost-effectively at scale relatively quickly, such as the intervention built around attendance reports.[10]

Interventions like this are not substitutes for more intensive interventions but, rather, complements that could free schools and educators to direct their scarce resources toward more intensive and comprehensive efforts. We look forward to more (and more effective) interventions that empower and support all stakeholders to reduce student absenteeism in the future. The contributions in this book underscore the need for those interventions and clarify what the path toward their development may look like.

Todd Rogers
Professor of Public Policy, Harvard Kennedy
School of Government, and cofounder,
In Class Today

Johannes Demarzi
Cofounder and President, In Class Today

NOTES

INTRODUCTION

1. Henry May and Jonathan A. Supovitz, "Capturing the Cumulative Effects of School Reform: An 11-Year Study of the Impacts of America's Choice on Student Achievement," *Educational Evaluation and Policy Analysis* 28, no. 3 (2006): 231–57.
2. Michael A. Gottfried, "Peer Effects in Urban Schools: Assessing the Impact of Classroom Composition on Student Achievement," *Educational Policy* 28, no. 5 (2014): 607–47.
3. Mariajose Romero and Young-Sun Lee, *A National Portrait of Chronic Absenteeism in the Early Grades* (Washington, DC: National Center for Children in Poverty, 2007).
4. Hedy Chang and Rochelle Davis, *Mapping the Early Attendance Gap* (San Francisco: Attendance Works, 2015).
5. Phyllis W. Jordan and Raegen Miller, *Who's In* (Washington, DC: FutureEd, 2017).
6. *In School and On Track* (Sacramento: Office of the Attorney General of California, 2015).
7. David Tyack and Larry Cuban, *Tinkering Toward Utopia: A Century of Public School Reform* (Cambridge, MA: Harvard University Press, 1996); David F. Labaree, *Someone Has to Fail: The Zero Sum Game of Public Education* (Cambridge, MA: Harvard University Press, 2012).
8. Ethan L. Hutt, "Measuring Missed School: The Historical Precedents for the Measurement and Use of Attendance Records to Evaluate Schools," *Journal of Education for Students Placed at Risk (JESPAR)* 23, nos. 1–2 (2018): 5–8.
9. Walter S. Deffenbaugh, *Compulsory School Attendance* (Washington, DC: Government Printing Office, 1914); A. O. Heck, "A Measure of the Comparative Efficiency for Public-School Systems," *Educational Research Bulletin* 4, no. 14 (1925): 304–10; Arthur B. Moehlman, *Child Accounting: A Discussion of the General Principles Underlying Educational Child Accounting, Together with the Development of a Uniform Procedure* (Detroit: Friesema Bros. Press, 1924).
10. Hutt, "Measuring Missed School."
11. Moehlman, *Child Accounting.*
12. Kate McGee, "What Really Happened at the School Where Every Graduate Got into College," National Public Radio, November 28, 2017, https://www.npr.org/sections/ed/2017/11/28/564054556/what-really-happened-at-the-school-where-every-senior-got-into-

college; Alvarez and Marshall, *Interim Report District of Columbia Public Schools Audit and Investigation—Ballou High School* (Washington, DC: Office of the State Superintendent, 2018), https://osse.dc.gov/sites/default/files/dc/sites/osse/release_content/attachments/Analysis%20of%20Attendance%20and%20Graduation%20Outcomes%20at%20Public%20High%20Schools%20in%20DC%20-%20Jan%2016%202018%20-%20sm.pdf.

13. Michael Gottfried, "Excused versus Unexcused: How Student Absences in Elementary School Affect Academic Achievement," *Educational Evaluation and Policy Analysis* 31, no. 4 (2009): 392–415.

14. Kirsten J. Hancock, Michael Gottfried, and Stephen R. Zubrick, "Does the Reason Matter? How Student-Reported Reasons for School Absence Contribute to Differences in Achievement Outcomes Among 14–15 Year Olds," *British Educational Research Journal* (OnlineFirst, 2018), doi:10.1002/berj.3322.

15. Michael Gottfried, "Chronic Absenteeism and Its Effects on Students' Academic and Socioemotional Outcomes," *Journal of Education for Students Placed at Risk (JESPAR)* 19, no. 2 (2017): 53–75.

16. Jordan and Miller, *Who's In.*

17. Shaun M. Dougherty, "How Measurement and Modeling of Attendance Matter to Assigning Dimensions of Inequality," *Journal of Education for Students Placed at Risk (JESPAR)* 23, nos. 1–2 (2018): 9–23.

18. Stacy Ehrlich, Julia A. Gwynne, Amber Stitziel Pareja, and Elaine M. Allensworth, *Preschool Attendance in Chicago Public Schools: Relationships with Learning Outcomes and Reasons for Absences* (Chicago: University of Chicago Consortium on Chicago School Research, 2013).

19. Chang and Davis, *Mapping the Early Attendance Gap.*

20. Romero and Lee, *A National Portrait.*

21. Stacy B. Ehrlich, Julia A. Gwynne, and Elaine M. Allensworth, "Prekindergarten Attendance Matters: Early Chronic Absence Patterns and Relationships to Learning Outcomes," *Early Childhood Research Quarterly* 44 (2018): 136–51.

22. Hedy Chang and Mariajose Romero, *Present, Engaged, and Accounted For.* (New York: Columbia University, 2008).

23. Faith Connolly and Linda S. Olson, *Early Elementary Performance and Attendance in Baltimore City Schools' Pre-Kindergarten and Kindergarten* (Baltimore: Baltimore Education Research Consortium, 2012).

24. Gottfried, "Chronic Absenteeism."

25. Robert Balfanz and Vaughan Byrnes, "The Importance of Being in School: A Report on Absenteeism in the Nation's Public Schools" (report, Johns Hopkins University, Baltimore, 2012).

26. *Portraits of Change: Aligning School and Community Resources to Reduce Chronic Absenteeism* (San Francisco: AttendanceWorks and Everyone Graduates Center, 2017); Michael Gottfried, Leanna Stiefel, Amy Ellen Schwartz, and Bryant Hopkins, "Showing Up: Disparities in Chronic Absenteeism Between Students with and Without Disabilities in Traditional Public Schools," *Teachers College Record* (in press); Hancock et al., "Does the Reason Matter?"; Romero and Lee, *A National Portrait.*

27. Chang et al., *Portraits of Risk*; Ehrlich et al., "Prekindergarten Attendance Matters"; Kevin Gee, "Minding the Gaps in Absenteeism: Disparities in Absenteeism by Race/Ethnicity, Poverty, and Disability," *Journal of Education for Students Placed at Risk (JESPAR)* 19, no. 2 (2018): 204–8.

28. Ehrlich et al., "Prekindergarten Attendance Matters."
29. Gee, "Minding the Gaps in Absenteeism."
30. Michael Gottfried and Kevin Gee, "Identifying the Determinants of Chronic Absenteeism: A Bioecological Systems Approach," *Teachers College Record* 119, no. 7 (2017), https://eric.ed.gov/?id=EJ1144259.
31. Ehrlich et al., "Prekindergarten Attendance Matters."
32. Michael Gottfried, "Quantifying the Consequences of Missing School: Linking School Nurses to Student Absences to Standardized Achievement," *Teachers College Record* 115, no. 6 (2013): 1–30.
33. Michael Gottfried, "Linking Getting to School with Going to School," *Educational Evaluation and Policy Analysis* 39, no. 4 (2017): 571–92.
34. Chang and Romero, *Present, Engaged, and Accounted For.*
35. Gottfried, "Linking Getting to School."
36. Todd Rogers and Avi Feller, "Reducing Student Absences at Scale by Targeting Parents' Misbeliefs," *Nature Human Behavior* 2 (2018): 335–42.
37. Laura S. Abrams and Jewelle Taylor Gibbs, "Disrupting the Logic of Home-School Relations," *Urban Education* 37, no. 3 (2002): 384–407; Joyce L. Epstein, "Building Bridges of Home, School, and Community: The Importance of Design," *Journal of Education for Students Placed at Risk (JESPAR)* 6, nos. 1–2 (2001): 161–68; Annette Laureau, "Social Class Differences in Family-School Relationships: The Importance of Cultural Capital," *Sociology of Education* 60, no. 2 (1987): 73–85.
38. Sophia Catsambis and Andrew A. Beveridge, "Does Neighborhood Matter? Family, Neighborhood, and School Influence on Eighth-Grade Mathematics Achievement," *Sociological Focus* 34, no. 4 (2001): 435–57; Xitao Fan and Michael Chen, "Parental Involvement and Students' Achievement: A Meta-Analysis," *Educational Psychology Review* 13, no. 1 (2001): 1–22; William H. Jeynes, "A Meta-Analysis: The Effects of Parental Involvement on Minority Children's Academic Achievement," *Education and Urban Society* 35, no. 2 (2003): 202–18.
39. Gottfried, "Excused versus Unexcused."
40. Steven B. Sheldon, "Improving Student Attendance with School, Family, and Community Partnerships," *Journal of Educational Research* 100, no. 5 (2007): 267–75; Jane Graves Smith, "Parental Involvement in Education Among Low-Income Families: A Case Study," *School Community Journal* 16, no. 1 (2006): 43–56.
41. Lareau, "Social Class Differences."
42. Esteban M. Aucejo and Teresa Foy Romano, "Assessing the Effect of School Days and Absences on Test Score Performance," *Economics of Education Review* 55 (December 2016): 70–87; Douglas D. Ready, "Socioeconomic Disadvantage, School Attendance, and Early Cognitive Development: The Differential Effects of School Exposure," *Sociology of Education* 83, no. 4 (2010): 271–86.
43. Aucejo and Romano, "Assessing the Effect"; Seth Gershenson, Alison Jacknowitz, and Andrew Brannagan, "Are Student Absences Worth the Worry in U.S. Primary Schools," *Education Finance and Policy* 12, no. 2 (2017): 137–65.
44. Diane Whitmore Schanzenbach, *Does Class Size Matter?* (Boulder, CO: National Education Policy Center, 2014).
45. Gershenson et al., "Are Absences Worth the Worry?"

CHAPTER 1

1. David N. Figlio and Lawrence S. Getzler, "Accountability, Ability and Disability: Gaming the System" (report, National Bureau of Economic Research, Cambridge, MA, 2002); Brian A. Jacob and Steven D. Levitt, "Rotten Apples: An Investigation of the Prevalence and Predictors of Teacher Cheating," *Quarterly Journal of Economics* 118, no. 3 (2003): 843–77; Douglas Lee Lauen and S. Michael Gaddis, "Accountability Pressure, Academic Standards, and Educational Triage," *Educational Evaluation and Policy Analysis* 38, no. 1 (2016): 127–47; Derek Neal and Diane Whitmore Schanzenbach, "Left Behind by Design: Proficiency Counts and Test-Based Accountability," *Review of Economics and Statistics* 92, no. 2 (2010): 263–83.

2. Hedy N. Chang and Mariajose Romero, "Present, Engaged, and Accounted for: The Critical Importance of Addressing Chronic Absence in the Early Grades" (report, National Center for Children in Poverty, New York, 2008); Alan Ginsburg, Phyllis Jordan, and Hedy N. Chang, *Absences Add Up: How School Attendance Influences Student Success* (Portland, OR: Attendance Works, 2014).

3. Phyllis Jordan and Raegen Miller, "Who's In: Chronic Absenteeism Under the Every Student Succeeds Act," FutureEd, September 26, 2017, https://www.future-ed.org/whos-in-chronic-absenteeism-under-the-every-student-succeeds-act/

4. The six districts are Fresno, Long Beach, Los Angeles, Oakland, San Francisco, and Santa Ana. With the passage of ESSA, the districts are no longer formally implementing the accountability system that they developed under the waiver. Now they are leveraging their shared measurement system as a networked improvement community, using the tools of improvement science to collectively improve math achievement. Other publications detail measurement use and collaboration within the CORE districts. See Julie A. Marsh, Susan Bush-Mecenas, and Heather J. Hough, "Learning from Early Adopters in the New Accountability Era," *Educational Administration Quarterly* 53, no. 3 (2017); Heather J. Hough, Demetra Kalogrides, and Susanna Loeb, *Using Surveys of Students' Social-Emotional Skills and School Climate for Accountability and Continuous Improvement* (Palo Alto: Policy Analysis for California Education, 2017); Michelle Nayfack, Vicki Park, Heather Hough, and Larkin Willis, *Building Systems Knowledge for Continuous Improvement: Early Lessons from the CORE Districts* (Palo Alto: Policy Analysis for California Education, 2016).

5. The data used in this paper are from only seven of the CORE districts, as one district's data weren't available yet for 2016–17. When doing analyses across time, data are from five districts, since two did not have valid data from 2014–15.

6. Analysis based on data from the National Center on Education Statistics (NCES), https://nces.ed.gov/pubs2016/2016076/tables/table_03.asp.

7. Mark Hugo Lopez, Jeffrey S. Passel, and Molly Rohal, "Modern Immigration Wave Brings 59 Million to US, Driving Population Growth and Change Through 2065: Views of Immigration's Impact on US Society Mixed" (report, Hispanic Trends Project, Pew Research Center, Washington, DC, 2015), http://www.pewhispanic.org/files/2015/09/2015-09-28_modern-immigration-wave_REPORT.pdf.

8. California Department of Education, 2016–17, https://dq.cde.ca.gov/dataquest/; National Center for Education Statistics, 2014–15, https://nces.ed.gov/programs/digest/current_tables.asp.

9. This is a subset of the measures that CORE districts utilize in their data system. For more detail on the full set of metrics, see http://coredistricts.org/our-data-research/improvement-

measures/. Analysis is limited to these indicators to reflect what states are required to collect under ESSA.

10. See California Department of Education, https://www.cde.ca.gov/fg/aa/pa/lcffitfaq.asp.

11. CORE's measure of EL proficiency is slightly different than what is specified in ESSA. Rather than using only test score results to determine progress on English proficiency, the CORE districts chose to report reclassification rates, which are a combination of language proficiency scores and academic performance. For more on this see Richard Carranza, "How Best to Measure Success with English Learners," EdSource (September 20, 2015), https://edsource.org/2015/holding-school-districts-accountable-for-success-with-english-learners/87121.

12. Phyllis Jordan and Raegen Miller, "Who's In: Chronic Absenteeism Under the Every Student Succeeds Act," Future Ed, September 2017, https://www.future-ed.org/wp-content/uploads/2017/09/REPORT_Chronic_Absenteeism_final_v5.pdf.

13. Robert Balfanz, Liza Herzog, and Douglas J. Mac Iver, "Preventing Student Disengagement and Keeping Students on the Graduation Path in Urban Middle-Grades Schools: Early Identification and Effective Interventions," *Educational Psychologist* 42, no. 4 (2007).

14. It is important to note that this definition of *attendance*—counting only full days of absence rather than portions of any day—may understate chronic problems of attendance within the school day in high schools (i.e., ditching periods).

15. Here I use a logistic regression model, which is the preferred approach when the outcome is binary (chronically absent/not chronically absent). This model controls for student grade level, thus predicting the probability of being chronically absent in the current year based on prior year status, comparing students in the same grade.

16. The interquartile range (IQR) is calculated as 1.5 times the distance between the third and first quartiles. Outliers are those schools with chronic absenteeism rates higher than 1.5 IQR above the third quartile or lower than 1.5 IQR below the first quartile.

17. This category combines Alternative Schools of Choice, Continuation High Schools, District Community Day Schools, and Opportunity Schools. For more, see Paul Warren, *Accountability for California's Alternative Schools* (San Francisco: Public Policy Institute of California, 2016).

18. Zachary Malter, "ESSA and Understanding Accountability in Alternative Education" (paper, American Youth Policy Forum, Washington, DC, July 2016), http://www.aypf.org/resources/essa-and-understanding-accountability-in-alternative-education/.

19. Note that subgroups within a school are only reported if there are twenty or more students in that group.

20. Note that this analysis can only be conducted for schools that have two or more racial/ethnic groups.

21. Sara B. Krachman, Rebecca Arnold, and Robert LaRocca, *Expanding Our Definition of Student Success: A Case Study of the CORE Districts* (Boston: Transforming Education, 2016).

22. Recent work demonstrating the effect of teachers on attendance provides useful information about the in-school factors affecting chronic absenteeism. See Seth Gershenson, "Linking Teacher Quality, Student Attendance, and Student Achievement," *Education Finance and Policy* 11, no. 2 (2016).

23. Every Student Succeeds Act, Pub. L. No. 114-95 (2015) §1111(c)(4)(D)(1).

24. For more on the identification of schools under ESSA, see Heather J. Hough, Emily Penner, and Joe Witte, *Identity Crisis: Multiple Measures and the Identification of Schools Under ESSA* (Palo Alto: Policy Analysis for California Education, 2016).

25. Jason A. Okonofua, Gregory M. Walton, and Jennifer L. Eberhardt, "A Vicious Cycle: A Social-Psychological Account of Extreme Racial Disparities in School Discipline," *Perspectives on Psychological Science* 11, no. 3 (2016); Harriet R. Tenenbaum and Martin D. Ruck, "Are Teachers' Expectations Different for Racial Minority Than for European American Students? A Meta-Analysis," *Journal of Educational Psychology* 99, no. 2 (2007).

26. Ruth Berkowitz, Hadass Moore, Ron Avi Astor, and Rami Benbenishty, "A Research Synthesis of the Associations between Socioeconomic Background, Inequality, School Climate, and Academic Achievement," *Review of Educational Research* 87, no. 2 (2017): 425–69, doi:10.3102/0034654316669821; Adam Voight, Thomas Hanson, Meagan O'Malley, and Latifah Adekanye, "The Racial School Climate Gap: Within-School Disparities in Students' Experiences of Safety, Support, and Connectedness," *American Journal of Community Psychology* 56, nos. 3–4 (2015); Annette Lareau and Erin McNamara Horvat, "Moments of Social Inclusion and Exclusion Race, Class, and Cultural Capital in Family-School Relationships," *Sociology of Education* 72, no. 1 (1999): 37–53; Amanda Lewis, *Race in the Schoolyard: Negotiating the Color Line in Classrooms and Communities* (New Brunswick, NJ: Rutgers University Press, 2003).

27. http://coredistricts.org/calif-core-districts-pilot-accountability-measures/.

28. Heather J. Hough, Jason Willis, Alicia Grunow, Kelsey Krausen, Sylvia Kwon, Laura Steen Mulfinger, and Sandra Park, *Continuous Improvement in Practice* (Palo Alto: Policy Analysis for California Education, 2017); Linda Darling-Hammond and David N. Plank, *Supporting Continuous Improvement in California's Education System* (Palo Alto: Policy Analysis for California Education, 2015).

29. Heather J. Hough, Erika Byun, and Laura Mulfinger, *Using Data for Improvement: Learning from the CORE Data Collaborative* (Palo Alto: Policy Analysis for California Education, 2018).

30. David N. Figlio and Lawrence S. Getzler, "Accountability, Ability and Disability: Gaming the System" (report, National Bureau of Economic Research, Cambridge, MA, 2002); Brian A. Jacob and Steven D. Levitt, "Rotten Apples: An Investigation of the Prevalence and Predictors of Teacher Cheating," *Quarterly Journal of Economics* 118, no. 3 (2003).

31. Andrew Dean Ho, "The Problem with 'Proficiency': Limitations of Statistics and Policy Under No Child Left Behind," *Educational Researcher* 37, no. 6 (2008); Jennifer Booher-Jennings, "Rationing Education in an Era of Accountability," *Phi Delta Kappan* 87, no. 10 (2006).

32. This was the case with NCLB's well-documented effect of school focus on the "bubble kids." See Susan Brookhart, "The Many Meanings of 'Multiple Measures,'" *Educational Leadership* 67, no. 3 (2009); Charles A. DePascale, "Managing Multiple Measures," *Principal* 91, no. 5 (2012).

CHAPTER 2

This work was conducted with financial support from the Spencer Foundation. This article reflects the work of the author and not of the granting agency.

1. Based on data from EdSource's *Database on Chronic Absenteeism in California Schools 2016–17*, https://edsource.org/2017/database-on-chronic-absenteeism-in-california-schools-2016-17.

2. National Center for Education Statistics (NCES), *ECLS-K:2011 Restricted-Use Kindergarten-Second Grade Data File and Electronic Codebook* (2015).

3. Rounded to the nearest 10 per NCES requirements.

4. Michael A. Gottfried, "Chronic Absenteeism and Its Effects on Students' Academic and Socioemotional Outcomes," *Journal of Education for Students Placed at Risk (JESPAR)* 19, no. 2 (2014): 53–75; Michael A. Gottfried and Kevin A. Gee, "Identifying the Determinants of Chronic Absenteeism: A Bioecological Systems Approach," *Teachers College Record* 119, no. 7 (2017): 1–34; Michael A. Gottfried, Leanna Stiefel, Amy Ellen Schwartz, and Bryant Hopkins, "Showing Up: Disparities in Chronic Absenteeism Between Students with and Without Disabilities" (Working Paper No. 03-17, Institute for Education and Social Policy, New York University, New York, 2017).

5. Hedy N. Chang and Mariajosé Romero, "Present, Engaged, and Accounted For: The Critical Importance of Addressing Chronic Absence in the Early Grades" (report, National Center for Children in Poverty, Mailman School of Public Health, Columbia University, New York, 2008).

6. US Department of Education, "Chronic Absenteeism in the Nation's Schools," https://ed.gov/datastory/chronicabsenteeism.html.

7. Gottfried, "Chronic Absenteeism."

8. Gottfried and Gee, "Identifying the Determinants."

9. Ibid.

10. Brandy R. Maynard, Katherine Tyson McCrea, Terri D. Pigott, and Michael S. Kelly, "Indicated Truancy Interventions for Chronic Truant Students: A Campbell Systematic Review," *Research on Social Work Practice* 23, no. 1 (2013): 1–17.

11. Kevin A. Gee, "Minding the Gaps in Absenteeism: Disparities in Absenteeism by Race/Ethnicity, Poverty and Disability," *Journal of Education for Students Placed at Risk (JESPAR)* 23, no. 2 (2018): 204–8.

12. For models predicting chronic absenteeism in the spring of first and second grades, I included chronic absenteeism in the prior year. For the model predicting second grade absenteeism, I included first-grade absenteeism, and for the first-grade model, I included kindergarten absenteeism. The kindergarten model contained no prior absenteeism information.

13. Richard D. McKelvey and William Zavoina, "A Statistical Model for the Analysis of Ordinal Level Dependent Variables," *Journal of Mathematical Sociology* 4, no. 1 (1975): 103–20; Tom A. B. Snijders and Roel J. Bosker, *Multilevel Analysis: An Introduction to Basic and Advanced Multilevel Modeling* (Thousand Oaks, CA: Sage, 2012).

14. Stephen W. Raudenbush and Anthony S. Bryk, *Hierarchical Linear Models: Applications and Data Analysis Methods* (Thousand Oaks, CA: Sage, 2002); Judith D. Singer and John B. Willett, *Applied Longitudinal Data Analysis: Modeling Change and Event Occurrence* (New York: Oxford University Press, 2003).

15. In some cases variances can increase, leading to negative values, so only those models with variance declines are reported.

16. Spyros Konstantopoulos, "Trends of School Effects on Student Achievement: Evidence from NLS:72, HSB: 82, and NELS: 92" (Discussion Paper No. 1749, Institute for the Study of Labor, Bonn, Germany, September 2005).

17. Robert Balfanz and Hedy N. Chang, "Preventing Missed Opportunity: Taking Collective Action to Confront Chronic Absence" (report, Attendance Works and Everyone Graduates Center, Baltimore, 2016).

CHAPTER 3

1. Seth Gershenson, "Linking Teacher Quality, Student Attendance, and Student Achievement," *Education Finance and Policy* 11, no. 2 (2016): 125–49, doi:10.1162/EDFP_a_00180; Seth Gershenson, Alison Jacknowitz, and Andrew Brannegan,. "Are Student Absences Worth the Worry in U.S. Primary Schools?" *Education Finance and Policy* 12, no. 2 (2017): 137–65, doi:10.1162/EDFP_a_00207; Michael A. Gottfried, "Chronic Absenteeism and Its Effects on Students' Academic and Socioemotional Outcomes," *Journal of Education for Students Placed at Risk (JESPAR)* 19, no. 2 (2014): 53–75, doi:10.3102/0162373709342467; Rebecca A. London, Monika Sanchez, and Sebastian Castrechini, "The Dynamics of Chronic Absence and Student Achievement," *Education Policy Analysis Archives* 24 (2016), doi:10.14507/epaa.24.2741; Taryn W. Morrissey, Lindsey Hutchinson, and Adam Winsler, "Family Income, School Attendance, and Academic Achievement in Elementary School," *Developmental Psychology* 50, no. 3 (2014): 741, doi:10.1037/a0033848; Todd Rogers and Avi Feller, "Intervening Through Influential Third Parties: Reducing Student Absences at Scale via Parents" (working paper, John F. Kennedy School of Government, Harvard University, Cambridge, MA, 2017).

2. Michael Gottfried, Leanna Stiefel, Amy Ellen Schwartz, and Bryant Hopkins, "Showing Up: Disparities in Chronic Absenteeism Between Students with and Without Disabilities in Traditional Public Schools," *Teachers College Record* (in press); Gottfried, "Chronic Absenteeism," 53; Morrissey et al., "Family Income," 741; Gershenson et al., "Are Student Absences Worth the Worry in US Primary Schools?" 137.

3. Gottfried, "Chronic Absenteeism," 53; Douglas D. Ready, "Socioeconomic Disadvantage, School Attendance, and Early Cognitive Development: The Differential Effects of School Exposure," *Sociology of Education* 83, no. 4 (2010): 271–86, doi:10.1177/0038040710383520; Morrissey et al. "Family Income," 741; Greg J. Duncan and Richard J. Murnane, eds., *Whither Opportunity? Rising Inequality, Schools, and Children's Life Chances* (New York: Russell Sage Foundation, 2011); Vonnie C. McLoyd, "Socioeconomic Disadvantage and Child Development," *American Psychologist* 53, no. 2 (1998): 185, http://dx.doi.org.ezproxy.lib.uconn.edu/10.1037/0003-066X.53.2.185.

4. Robert Balfanz, Liza Herzog, and Douglas J. Mac Iver, "Preventing Student Disengagement and Keeping Students on the Graduation Path in Urban Middle-Grades Schools: Early Identification and Effective Interventions," *Educational Psychologist* 42, no. 4 (2007): 223–35, doi:10.1080/00461520701621079; Russell W. Rumberger, "High School Dropouts in the United States," in *School Dropout and Completion*, ed. Stephen Lamb, Eifred Markussen, Richard Teese, Nina Sandberg, and John Polesel (Amsterdam: Springer Netherlands, 2011), 275–94.

5. Lauren Bauer, Patrick Liu, Diane Whitmore Schanzenbach, and Jay Shambaugh, *Reducing Chronic Absenteeism Under the Every Student Succeeds Act* (Washington, DC: Brookings Institute, 2018).

6. Hedy N. Chang and Mariajose Romero, *Present, Engaged, and Accounted For: The Critical Importance of Addressing Chronic Absence in the Early Grades* (New York, NY: National Center for Children in Poverty and the Mailman School of Public Health at Columbia, 2008); Camilla A. Lehr, Mary F. Sinclair, and Sandra L. Christenson, "Addressing Student Engagement and Truancy Prevention During the Elementary School Years: A Replication Study of the Check & Connect Model," *Journal of Education for Students Placed at Risk* 9, no. 3 (2004): 279—301, doi:10.1207/s15327671espr0903_4.

7. Robert Balfanz and Nettie Legters, "Locating the Dropout Crisis: Which High Schools Produce the Nation's Dropouts? Where Are They Located? Who Attends Them?" (Report No. 70, Center for Research on the Education of Students Placed at Risk, Johns Hopkins University, Baltimore, 2004); Ruth C. Neild and Robert Balfanz, "An Extreme Degree of Difficulty: The Educational Demographics of Urban Neighborhood Schools," *Journal of Education for Students Placed at Risk* 11, no. 2 (2006): 123–41, doi:10.1207/s15327671espr1102_1; Ruth C. Neild, Scott Stoner-Eby, and Frank Furstenberg, "Connecting Entrance and Departure: The Transition to Ninth Grade and High School Dropout," *Education and Urban Society* 40, no. 5 (2008): 543–69, doi:10.1177/0013124508316438; Philip J. Cook, Kenneth A. Dodge, Elizabeth J. Gifford, and Amy B. Schulting, "A New Program to Prevent Primary School Absenteeism: Results of a Pilot Study in Five Schools," *Children and Youth Services Review* 82 (2017): 262–70, doi:10.1016/j.childyouth.2017.09.017; Michael A. Gottfried, "Can Center-Based Childcare Reduce the Odds of Early Chronic Absenteeism?" *Early Childhood Research Quarterly* 32, no. 3 (2015): 160–73, doi:10.1016/j.ecresq.2015.04.002; Rogers and Feller, "Intervening," 2017; Steven B. Sheldon and Joyce L. Epstein, "Getting Students to School: Using Family and Community Involvement to Reduce Chronic Absenteeism," *School Community Journal* 14, no. 2 (2004): 39.
8. Robert Balfanz, and Vaughan Byrnes, "The Importance of Being in School: A Report on Absenteeism in the Nation's Public Schools," *Education Digest* 78, no. 2 (2012): 4; Gottfried, "Chronic Absenteeism," 53.
9. Gottfried et al., "Showing Up."
10. Ready, "Socioeconomic Disadvantage," 171.
11. Gershenson et al., "Are Student Absences Worth the Worry in U.S. Primary Schools?" 137; Morrissey et al., "Family Income," 741; Ready, "Socioeconomic Disadvantage," 171.
12. Gershenson et al., "Are Student Absences Worth the Worry in U.S. Primary Schools?" 137.
13. Morrissey et al., "Family Income," 741.
14. Phyllis W. Jordan and Raegen Miller, "Who's In? Chronic Absenteeism Under the Every Student Succeeds Act" (report, McCourt School of Public Policy, Georgetown University, Washington, DC, https://www.future-ed.org/wp-content/uploads/2017/09/REPORT_Chronic_Absenteeism_final_v5.pdf; Gottfried, "Chronic Absenteeism," 53.
15. Andrew Dean Ho, "The Problem with 'Proficiency': Limitations of Statistics and Policy Under No Child Left Behind," *Educational Researcher* 37, no. 6 (2008): 351–60, doi:10.3102/0013189X08323842.
16. Carolyn Phenicie, "37 States Are Using Their ESSA Plans to Crack Down on Chronic Absences: So How Will They Do It?" The 74Million, last modified September 26, 2017, https://www.the74million.org/article/37-states-are-using-their-essa-plans-to-crack-down-on-chronic-student-absences-so-how-will-they-do-it/.
17. Jeffrey C. Wayman, Vincent Cho, Jo Beth Jimerson, and Daniel D. Spikes, "District-Wide Effects on Data Use in the Classroom," *Education Policy Analysis Archives/Archivos Analíticos de Políticas Educativas* 20 (2012), doi:10.14507/epaa.v20n25.2012.
18. Chang and Romero, *Present, Engaged, and Accounted For.*
19. Gottfried, "Chronic Absenteeism," 83.
20. Joshua Childs and Ain A. Grooms, "Improving School Attendance Through Collaboration: A Catalyst for Community Involvement and Change," *Journal of Education for Students Placed at Risk (JESPAR)* 23, nos. 1–2 (2018): 122–38, https://www.tandfonline.com/doi/full/10.1080/10824669.2018.1439751.

CHAPTER 4

1. Esteban M. Aucejo and Teresa Foy Romano, "Assessing the Effect of School Days and Absences on Test Score Performance," *Economics of Education Review* 55 (2016): 70–87; Seth Gershenson, Alison Jacknowitz, and Andrew Brannegan, "Are Student Absences Worth the Worry in U.S. Primary Schools?" *Education Finance & Policy* 12, no. 2 (2017): 137–65; Joshua Goodman, "Flaking Out: Student Absences and Snow Days as Disruptions of Instructional Time" (Working Paper No. w20221, National Bureau of Economic Research, Cambridge, MA, 2014); Michael A. Gottfried, "Excused Versus Unexcused: How Student Absences in Elementary School Affect Academic Achievement," *Educational Evaluation and Policy Analysis* 31, no. 4 (2009): 392–419; Michael A. Gottfried, "The Detrimental Effects of Missing School: Evidence from Urban Siblings," *American Journal of Education,* 117, no. 2 (2011): 147–82.

2. Marianne Bitler, Thurston Domina, Emily Penner, and Hilary Hoynes, "Distributional Analysis in Educational Evaluation: A Case Study from the New York City Voucher Program," *Journal of Research on Educational Effectiveness* 8, no. 3 (2015): 419–50; Eric Eide and Mark H. Showalter, "The Effect of School Quality on Student Performance: A Quantile Regression Approach," *Economics Letters* 58 (1998): 345—50; Michael S. Hayes and Seth Gershenson, "What Differences a Day Can Make: Quantile Regression Estimates of the Distribution of Daily Learning Gains," *Economics Letters* 141 (2016): 48–51.

3. Gershenson et al., "Are Student Absences Worth the Worry?"

4. Roger Koenker and Kevin F. Hallock, "Quantile Regression," *Journal of Economic Perspectives* 15, no. 4 (2001): 143–56.

5. Gershenson et al., "Are Student Absences Worth the Worry?"

6. Alan B. Krueger, "Experimental Estimates of Education Production Functions," *Quarterly Journal of Economics* 114, no. 2 (1999): 497–532.

7. Ibid.

8. Susan Dynarski, Joshua Hyman, and Diane Whitmore Schanzenbach, "Experimental Evidence on the Effect of Childhood Investments on Postsecondary Attainment and Degree Completion," *Journal of Policy Analysis and Management* 32, no. 4 (2013): 692–717.

9. Diane Whitmore Schanzenbach, "What Have Researchers Learned from Project STAR?" *Brookings Papers on Education Policy* 9 (2006): 205–28.

10. Thomas S. Dee, "Teachers, Race, and Student Achievement in a Randomized Experiment," *Review of Economics and Statistics* 86, no. 1 (2004): 195–210; Raj Chetty, John N. Friedman, Nathaniel Hilger, Emmanuel Saez, Diane Whitmore Schanzenbach, and Danny Yagan, "How Does Your Kindergarten Classroom Affect Your Earnings? Evidence from Project Star," *Quarterly Journal of Economics* 126, no. 4 (2011): 1593–660; Bryan S. Graham, "Identifying Social Interactions Through Conditional Variance Restrictions," *Econometrica* 76, no. 3 (2008): 643–60.

11. Seth Gershenson, "Linking Teacher Quality, Student Attendance, and Student Achievement," *Education Finance and Policy* 11, no. 2 (2016): 125–49.

12. Michael A. Gottfried, "Absent Peers in Elementary Years: The Negative Classroom Effects of Unexcused Absences on Standardized Testing Outcomes," *Teachers College Record* 113, no. 8 (2011): 1597–632.

13. Gershenson et al., "Are Student Absences Worth the Worry?"

14. Robert Balfanz and Vaughan Byrnes, *Chronic Absenteeism: Summarizing What We Know from Nationally Available Data* (Baltimore: Johns Hopkins University Center for Social Organization of Schools, 2012).

15. The analogous figure for reading achievement is qualitatively similar.
16. Gershenson et al., "Are Student Absences Worth the Worry?"
17. We refer to grades rather than years because the STAR experiment follows a cohort of students, so grades are perfectly collinear with years. The classroom FE directly control for issues of test timing and testing conditions, since all students in a classroom take the test on the same day.
18. Gershenson et al., "Are Student Absences Worth the Worry?"
19. Seth Gershenson, "Linking Teacher Quality, Student Attendance, and Student Achievement," *Education Finance & Policy* 11, no. 2 (2016): 125–49.
20. Two technical points are worth mentioning here. First, to conduct statistical inference, we cluster the standard errors at the school level to allow for a common error structure among students in a given school. We compute these standard errors via 500 blocked (by school) bootstrap replications. Second, conditioning on FE in a quantile regression model is nontrivial. We include FE in the quantile regressions by implementing the nonadditive quantile FE estimator proposed by David Powell in "Quantile Regression with Nonadditive Fixed Effects" (unpublished paper), 2016, http://works.bepress.com/david_powell/1.
21. Gershenson et al., "Are Student Absences Worth the Worry?"
22. Ibid.

CHAPTER 5

1. Elaine Allensworth and John Q. Easton, *What Matters for Staying On-Track and Graduating in Chicago Public Schools* (Chicago: University of Chicago Consortium on School Research, 2007); Ruth C. Neild, Robert Balfanz, and Liza Herzog, "An Early Warning System," *Educational Leadership* 65, no. 2 (2007): 28–33.
2. Allensworth and Easton, *What Matters*; Robert Balfanz, Liza Herzog, and Douglas J. Mac Iver, "Preventing Student Disengagement and Keeping Students on the Graduation Path in Urban Middle-Grades Schools: Early Identification and Effective Interventions," *Educational Psychologist* 42, no. 4 (2007): 223–35, doi:10.1080/00461520701621079; *Destination Graduation: Sixth Grade Early Warning Indicators for Baltimore City Schools: Their Prevalence and Impact* (Baltimore: Baltimore Education Research Consortium, 2011).
3. See www.attendanceworks.org for an overview of research.
4. Phyllis W. Jordan and Raegen Miller, *Who's In: Chronic Absenteeism Under the Every Student Succeeds Act* (Washington, DC: FutureEd at Georgetown University, 2017).
5. Stacy B. Ehrlich, Julia A. Gwynne, and Elaine M. Allensworth, "Pre-Kindergarten Attendance Matters: Early Chronic Absence Patterns and Relationships to Learning Outcomes," *Early Childhood Research Quarterly* 44, no. 3 (2018): 136—51; Todd M. Rosenkranz, Marisa de la Torre, W. David Stevens, and Elaine M. Allensworth, *Why Grades Drop When Students Enter High School and What Adults Can Do About It* (Chicago: Consortium on Chicago School Research, 2014).
6. Sara E. Rimm-Kaufman, Robert C. Pianta, and Martha J. Cox, "Teachers' Judgments of Problems in the Transition to Kindergarten," *Early Childhood Research Quarterly* 15, no. 2 (2000): 147–66.
7. Kyle DeMeo Cook and Rebekah Levine Coley, "School Transition Practices and Children's Social and Academic Adjustment in Kindergarten," *Journal of Educational Psychology* 109, no. 2 (2017): 166–77.
8. Faith Connolly and Linda S. Olsen, *Early Elementary Performance and Attendance in Baltimore City Schools' Pre-Kindergarten and Kindergarten* (Baltimore: Baltimore Education

Research Consortium, 2012); Lisa Dubay and Nikhil Holla, *Absenteeism in DC Public Schools Early Education Program: An Update for School Year 2013–14* (Washington, DC: Urban Institute, 2015); Lisa Dubay and Nikhil Holla, *Does Attendance in Early Education Predict Attendance in Elementary School? An Analysis of DCPS's Early Education Program* (Washington, DC: Urban Institute, 2016); Ehrlich et al., "Pre-Kindergarten Attendance Matters."

9. Hedy Chang and Mariajosé Romero, *Present, Engaged, and Accounted For* (New York: National Center for Children in Poverty, 2008); Connolly and Olsen, *Early Elementary Performance*; Ehrlich et al., "Pre-Kindergarten Attendance Matters"; Michael A. Gottfried, "Excused Versus Unexcused: How Student Absences in Elementary School Affect Academic Achievement," *Educational Evaluation and Policy Analysis* 31, no. 4 (2009): 392—419, doi:10.3102/0162373709342467.

10. Rosenkranz et al., *Why Grades Drop*.

11. Ibid.

12. Allensworth and Easton, *What Matters*; Russell W. Rumberger and Scott L. Thomas, "The Distribution of Dropout and Turnover Rates Among Urban and Suburban High Schools," *Sociology of Education* 73, no. 1 (2000): 39–67, doi:10.2307/2673198.

13. Steven B. Sheldon and Joyce L. Epstein, "Getting Students to School: Using Family and Community Involvement to Reduce Chronic Absenteeism," *School Community Journal* 14, no. 2 (2004): 39–56.

14. Stacy B. Ehrlich, Julia A. Gwynne, and Elaine M. Allensworth, *Preschool Attendance in Chicago Public Schools: Relationships with Learning Outcomes and Reasons for Absences* (Chicago: Consortium on Chicago School Research, 2014); Douglas D. Ready, "Socioeconomic Disadvantage, School Attendance, and Early Cognitive Development," *Sociology of Education* 83, no. 4 (2010): 271–86, doi:10.1177/0038040710383520; Michael A. Gottfried, "The Spillover Effects of Grade-Retained Classmates: Evidence from Urban Elementary Schools," *American Journal of Education* 119, no. 3 (2013): 405–44, doi:10.1086/669851; Sheldon Rothman, "School Absence and Student Background Factors: A Multilevel Analysis," *International Education Journal* 2, no. 1 (2001): 59–68.

15. For example, see chapters in this volume by Smythe-Leistico and Page, "Ready . . . Set . . . Text! Reducing School Absenteeism Through Parent-School Two-Way Text Messaging," and Balu, "Intervention Design Choices and Evaluation Lessons from Multisite Field Trials on Reducing Absenteeism."

16. Stacy B. Ehrlich, David W. Johnson, and Molly F. Gordon, *Improvements in Chicago's Pre-Kindergarten Attendance: Who Is Attending School More and How Are Schools Supporting Better Attendance?* (Chicago: University of Chicago Consortium on School Research, forthcoming).

17. Stacy B. Ehrlich, Debra M. Pacchiano, Amanda G. Stein, and Maureen Wagner, *Organizing Early Childhood Education for Improvement: Testing a New Survey Tool* (Chicago: University of Chicago Consortium on School Research and the Ounce of Prevention Fund, 2018).

18. Elaine M. Allensworth, Kaleen Healey, Julia A. Gwynne, and René Crespin, *High School Graduation Rates Through Two Decades of District Change: The Influence of Policies, Data Records, and Demographic Shifts* (Chicago: University of Chicago Consortium on School Research, 2016); Melissa Roderick, Thomas Kelley-Kemple, David W. Johnson, and Nicole O. Beechum, *Preventable Failure: Improvements in Long-Term Outcomes When High*

Schools Focused on the Ninth Grade Year (Chicago: University of Chicago Consortium on School Research, 2014).

19. Elaine M. Allensworth, Paul T. Moore, Lauren Sartain, and Marisa de la Torre, *The Educational Benefits of Attending Higher Performing Schools: Evidence from Chicago High Schools* (Chicago: University of Chicago Consortium on School Research, 2014).

20. We focus on two specific transition points—pre-kindergarten and ninth grade—because in Chicago elementary schools serve students through eighth grade. Other locales face similar challenges when students transition from elementary school to middle school. Whether to focus on pre-kindergarten or kindergarten as the first transition into school may rest on how many pre-kindergarten students a system/school serves and how reliable data systems are around pre-kindergarten attendance. CPS serves large numbers of pre-kindergarten students, and attendance has been collected in the same system as for K–12 students. In other districts, the transition of focus may be kindergarten, given the large number of students entering the school system at that moment. See Debra Lou Duaro, "Solutions to Chronic Absenteeism: An Evaluation of a Kindergarten Attendance Improvement Program in LAUSD" (PhD diss., University of California, Los Angeles, 2013).

21. See CPS "Stats and Facts," https://cps.edu/About_CPS/At-a-glance/Pages/Stats_and_facts.aspx.

22. Elaine M. Allensworth, Stacy Ehrlich, Julia Gwynne, Stuart Luppescu, Paul Moore, Amber Stitziel Pareja, Todd Rosenkranz, David Stevens, and Marisa de la Torre, *Absenteeism from Preschool to High School* (Chicago: Consortium on School Research, 2013), https://consortium.uchicago.edu/page/presentations.

23. Ehrlich et al., *Improvements in Chicago's Pre-Kindergarten Attendance*.

24. The on-track indicator is a measure of students' successful progression through ninth grade. According to this indicator, a ninth grader student is considered on-track to graduate if they or she has no more than one course failure in a core subject and has accumulated five or more credits by the end of ninth grade. Students who were on-track in ninth grade were nearly four times more likely to graduate high school on time than their off-track peers. Allensworth and Easton, *What Matters*; Allensworth, *High School Graduation*.

25. Pre-kindergarten attendance was added to school accountability metrics in 2018–19.

26. Roderick et al., *Preventable Failure*.

27. Elaine Allensworth and John Q. Easton, *The On-Track Indicator as a Predictor of High School Graduation* (Chicago: Consortium on Chicago School Research, 2005).

28. Allensworth and Easton, *What Matters*.

29. Roderick et al., *Preventable Failure*.

30. Ehrlich et al., *Improvements in Chicago's Pre-Kindergarten Attendance*.

31. Allensworth and Easton, *What Matters*.

32. Janet A. Weiss, "Data for Improvement, Data for Accountability," *Teachers College Record* 114, no. 11 (2012): 1.

33. Network for College Success, housed in the School of Social Service Administration at the University of Chicago, works directly with high school leadership teams on using data to improving outcomes. For more information, see https://ncs.uchicago.edu. Mary Ann Pitcher, Sarah J. Duncan, Jenny Nagaoka, Eliza Moeller, Latesha Dickerson, and Nicole O. Beechum, *The Network for College Success: A Capacity-Building Model for School Improvement* (Chicago: Network for College Success, University of Chicago, 2016). However, this does not preclude a simultaneous focus on improving instructional quality. See

Network for College Success, *Freshman On-Track Toolkit* (Chicago: Network for College Success, University of Chicago, 2017), 8.

34. See NCS, *Freshman On-Track Toolkit.*
35. Ibid.
36. Pitcher et al., *The Network for College Success.*
37. Stacy B. Ehrlich, David W. Johnson, and Molly F. Gordon, *Improvements in Chicago's Pre-Kindergarten Attendance: Who Is Attending School More and How Are Schools Supporting Better Attendance?* (Chicago: University of Chicago Consortium on School Research, forthcoming); Michael Katz, Martha Johnson, and Gina Adams, *Improving Prekindergarten Attendance: School-Level Strategies for Messaging, Engaging Parents, and Responding to Absences in Four DC Public Schools* (Washington, DC: Urban Institute, 2016).
38. Rosenkranz et al., *Why Grades Drop.*
39. Ibid, 6.
40. Allensworth and Easton, *What Matters.*
41. Rosenkranz et al., *Why Grades Drop.*
42. Roderick et al., *Preventable Failure.*
43. Lauren Bauer, Patrick Liu, Diane Whitmore Shanzenbach, and Jay Shambaugh, *Reducing Chronic Absenteeism Under the Every Student Succeeds Act,* The Hamilton Project (Washington, DC: Brookings Institution, 2018).
44. Bauer et al., *Reducing Chronic Absenteeism.*

CHAPTER 6

1. Jeffrey S. Passel and D'Vera Cohn, "Size of U.S. Unauthorized Immigrant Workforce Stable After the Great Recession" (report, Hispanic Trends Project, Pew Research Center, Washington, DC, November 3, 2016, http://www.pewhispanic.org/2016/11/03/size-of-u-s-unauthorized-immigrant-workforce-stable-after-the-great-recession/; Jeffrey S. Passel, D'Vera Cohn, Jens Manuel Krogstad, and Ana Gonzalez-Barrera, "As Growth Stalls, Unauthorized Immigrant Population Becomes More Settled" (report, Hispanic Trends Project, Pew Research Center, Washington, DC, September 3, 2014), http://www.pewhispanic.org/2014/09/03/as-growth-stalls-unauthorized-immigrant-population-becomes-more-settled/.
2. Passel and Cohn, "Size of the U.S. Unauthorized Immigrant Workforce."
3. Joanna Dreby, *Everyday Illegal: When Policies Undermine Immigrant Families (Berkeley: University of California Press, 2015); Ajay* Chaudry, Randy Capps, Juan Manuel Pedroza, Rosa Maria Castaneda, Robert Santos, and Molly M. Scott, "Facing Our Future: Children in the Aftermath of Immigration Enforcement" (report, The Urban Institute, Washington, DC, February 2010), https://www.urban.org/sites/default/files/publication/28331/412020-Facing-Our-Future.PDF; Randolph Capps, Rosa Maria Castaneda, Ajay Chaudry, and Robert Santos, "Paying the Price: The Impact of Immigration Raids on America's Children" (report, The Urban Institute and National Council of La Raza, Washington, DC, October 2007), https://www.urban.org/sites/default/files/publication/46811/411566-Paying-the-Price-The-Impact-of-Immigration-Raids-on-America-s-Children.PDF.
4. Jonathan Blitzer, "After an Immigration Raid, a City's Students Vanish," *New Yorker,* March 23, 2017, https://www.newyorker.com/news/news-desk/after-an-immigration-raid-a-citys-students-vanish.
5. One of the few studies on the topic of the educational impacts of immigration enforcement combined data from the Current Population Survey with information on the timing

and geographic scope of interior immigration enforcement policies to examine grade rep-
etition and dropout. They found that among children of "likely unauthorized immigrants,"
the probability of repeating a grade increases by 6 percent and the probability of dropping
out increases by 25.2 percent with increases in immigration enforcement. See Catalina
Amuedo-Dorantes and Mary J. Lopez, "Falling Through the Cracks? Grade Retention and
School Dropout Among Children of Likely Unauthorized Immigrants," *American Economic Review* 105, no. 5 (2015): 598–603. Another recent study found that the average
yearly increase in immigration enforcement between 2005 and 2011 was associated with a
4 percent increase in the likelihood that US-born children living with at least one undocumented immigrant parent would be living in poverty. See Catalina Amuedo-Dorantes,
Esther Arenas-Arroyo, and Almudena Sevilla, "Immigration Enforcement and Economic
Resources of Children with Likely Unauthorized Parents," *Journal of Public Economics*
158 (February 2018): 63–78. For research on the educational and developmental challenges associated with being undocumented and/or living in mixed-status families, see
Chaudry et al., "Facing Our Future"; Jens Hainmueller, Duncan Lawrence, Linna Martén,
Bernard Black, Lucila Figueroa, Michael Hotard, Tomás R. Jiménez, Fernando Mendoza,
Maria I. Rodriguez, Jonas J. Swartz, and David D. Laitin, "Protecting Unauthorized Immigrant Mothers Improves Their Children's Mental Health," *Science* 357, no. 6355 (2017):
1041–44; Hirokazu Yoshikawa and Jenya Kholoptseva, "Unauthorized Immigrant Parents and Their Children's Development" (report, Migration Policy Institute, Washington,
DC, March 2013), https://www.migrationpolicy.org/research/unauthorized-immigrant-
parents-and-their-childrens-development; Roberto G. Gonzales, Carola Suárez-Orozco,
and Maria Cecilia Dedios-Sanguineti, "No Place to Belong," *American Behavioral Scientist*
57, no. 8 (2013): 1174–99; Caitlin Patler, "Citizen Advantage, Undocumented Disadvan-
tage, or Both? The Comparative Educational Outcomes of Second and 1.5 Generation
Latino Young Adults," *International Migration Review* (2017), doi:10.1111/imre.12347;
Carola Suárez-Orozco, Hirokazu Yoshikawa, Robert Teranishi, and Marcelo Suárez-
Orozco, "Growing Up in the Shadows: The Developmental Implications of Unauthorized
Status," *Harvard Educational Review* 81, no. 3 (2011): 438–73; Luis H. Zayas, Kalina M.
Brabeck, Laurie Cook Heffron, Joanna Dreby, Esther J. Calzada, J. Rubén Parra-Cardona,
Alan J. Dettlaff, Lauren Heidbrink, Krista M. Perreira, and Hirokazu Yoshikawa, "Chart-
ing Directions for Research on Immigrant Children Affected by Undocumented Status,"
Hispanic Journal of Behavioral Sciences 39, no. 4 (2017): 412–35; Roberto G. Gonzalez,
Lives in Limbo: Undocumented and Coming of Age in America. (Berkeley: University of
California Press, 2015).

6. Sarah Pierce and Andrew Selee, "Immigration Under Trump: A Review of Policy Shifts
in the Year Since the Election" (report, Migration Policy Institute, Washington, DC,
December 2017), https://www.migrationpolicy.org/research/immigration-under-trump-
review-policy-shifts.

7. Joanna Dreby, "The Burden of Deportation on Children in Mexican Immigrant Families,"
Journal of Marriage and Family 74, no. 4 (2012): 829–45; Capps et al., "Implications
of Immigration Enforcement"; Heather Koball, Randy Capps, Krista Perreira, Andrea
Campetella, Sarah Hooker, Juan Manuel Pedroza, William Monson, and Sandra Huerta,
"Health and Social Service Needs of US-Citizen Children with Detained or Deported
Immigrant Parents" (report, The Urban Institute and Migration Policy Institute, Washing-
ton, DC, September 2015), https://www.migrationpolicy.org/research/health-and-social-
service-needs-us-citizen-children-detained-or-deported-immigrant-parents; Edward D.

Vargas, "Latinos' Connections to Immigrants: How Knowing a Deportee Impacts Latino Health" (paper, Association for Public Policy Analysis and Management, Chicago, November 2017); Consuelo Arbona, Norma Olvera, Nestor Rodriguez, Jacqueline Hagan, Adriana Linares, and Margit Wiesner, "Acculturative Stress Among Documented and Undocumented Latino Immigrants in the United States," *Hispanic Journal of Behavioral Sciences* 32, no. 3 (2010): 362–84.

8. Hirokazu Yoshikawa, *Immigrants Raising Citizens: Undocumented Parents and Their Young Children* (New York: Russell Sage Foundation, 2012); Koball et al., "Health and Social Service Needs."

9. Marjorie S. Zatz and Nancy Rodriguez, *Dreams and Nightmares: Immigration Policy, Youth and Families (Berkeley: University of California Press, 2015).*

10. Muzaffar Chishti, Sarah Pierce, and Jessica Bolter, "The Obama Record on Deportations: Deporter in Chief or Not?" Migration Policy Institute, January 26, 2017, https://www.migrationpolicy.org/article/obama-record-deportations-deporter-chief-or-not; Jie Zong, Jeanne Batalova, and Jeffrey Hallock, "Frequently Requested Statistics on Immigrants and Immigration in the United States," Migration Policy Institute, February 8, 2018, https://www.migrationpolicy.org/article/frequently-requested-statistics-immigrants-and-immigration-united-states.

11. "Secure Communities," US Immigration and Customs Enforcement, January 3, 2018, https://www.ice.gov/secure-communities.

12. Jeh Johnson, "Exercising Prosecutorial Discretion with Respect to Individuals Who Came to the United States as Children and with Respect to Certain Individuals Who Are the Parents of U.S. Citizens or Permanent Residents," US Department of Homeland Security, November 20, 2014, http://www.dhs.gov/sites/default/files/publications/14_1120_memo_deferred_action.pdf.

13. Amuedo-Dorantes and Lopez, "Falling Through the Cracks?"; Randy Capps, Michael Fix, and Jie Zong, "A Profile of Children with Unauthorized Immigrant Parents in the United States" (report, Migration Policy Institute, Washington, DC, January 13, 2016), https://www.migrationpolicy.org/multimedia/profile-children-unauthorized-immigrant-parents-united-states; Julia Gelatt, Heather Koball, Hamutal Bernstein, Charmaine Runes, and Eleanor Pratt, "State Immigration Enforcement Policies: How They Impact Low-Income Households" (report, The Urban Institute, Washington, DC, May 2017), https://www.urban.org/research/publication/state-immigration-enforcement-policies.

14. Caitlin Dickerson, "Immigration Arrests Rise Sharply as a Trump Mandate Is Carried Out," *New York Times*, May 17, 2017, https://www.nytimes.com/2017/05/17/us/immigration-enforcement-ice-arrests.html.

15. "Justice Department Demands Documents and Threatens to Subpoena 23 Jurisdictions as Part of 8 U.S.C. 1373 Compliance Review," US Department of Justice, January 24, 2018, https://www.justice.gov/opa/pr/justice-department-demands-documents-and-threatens-subpoena-23-jurisdictions-part-8-usc-1373; John Burnett, "Border Patrol Arrests Parents While Infant Awaits Serious Operation," *NPR*, September 20, 2017, https://www.npr.org/2017/09/20/552339976/border-patrol-arrests-parents-while-infant-awaits-serious-operation; Erica Meltzer, "New Videos Show ICE Arresting Immigrants at Denver Courthouse, Despite Local Leaders Requests," *Denverite*, May 9, 2017, https://www.denverite.com/new-videos-show-ice-arresting-immigrants-denver-county-court-something-local-officials-asked-not-35314/; Sophie Nieto-Munoz, "Gov. Murphy Races to Sanctuary Church After ICE Detains 2 in N.J.," *NJcom*, January 26, 2018, http://www.nj.com/

middlesex/index.ssf/2018/01/hold_murphy_shows_up_at_church_that _houses_immigra.html.

16. Zatz and Rodriguez, *Dreams and Nightmares.*

17. Robert Balfanz and Vaughan Byrnes, "Closing the Mathematics Achievement Gap in High-Poverty Middle Schools: Enablers and Constraints," *Journal of Education for Students Placed at Risk (JESPAR)* 11, no. 2 (2006): 143–59; Michael A. Gottfried, "Evaluating the Relationship Between Student Attendance and Achievement in Urban Elementary and Middle Schools," *American Educational Research Journal* 47, no. 2 (2010): 434–65; Rebecca Giallo, Karli Treyvaud, Jan Matthews, and Mandy Kienhuis, "Making the Transition to Primary School: An Evaluation of a Transition Program for Parents," *Australian Journal of Educational and Developmental Psychology* 10 (2010): 1–17; Ken Reid, "Institutional Factors and Persistent School Absenteeism," *Educational Management and Administration* 11, no. 1 (1983): 17–27.

18. For some of the first evidence of how students are being impacted by increased polarization and xenophobia under the Trump presidency, see John Rogers, Megan Franke, Jung-Eun Yun, Michael Ishimoto, Claudia Diera, Rebecca C. Geller, R, Anthony Berryman, and Tizoc Brenes, "Teaching and Learning in the Age of Trump: Increasing Stress and Hostility in America's High Schools" (white paper, Institute for Democracy, Education, and Access, University of California, Los Angeles, October 2017), https://idea.gseis.ucla.edu/publications/teaching-and-learning-in-age-of-trump; Patricia Gándara and Jongyeun Ee, "U.S. Immigration Enforcement Policy and Its Impact on Teaching and Learning in the Nation's Schools" (report, The Civil Rights Project, University of California, Los Angeles, February 2018), https://www.civilrightsproject.ucla.edu/research/k-12-education/integration-and-diversity/u.s.-immigration-enforcement-policy-and-its-impact-on-teaching-and-learning-in-the-nations-schools.

19. Zatz and Rodriguez, *Dreams and Nightmares.*

20. Amuedo-Dorantes and Lopez, "Falling Through the Cracks?"

21. Stephanie Potochnick, Jen-Hao Chen, and Krista Perreira, "Local-Level Immigration Enforcement and Food Insecurity Risk Among Hispanic Immigrant Families with Children: National-Level Evidence," *Journal of Immigrant and Minority Health* 19, no. 5 (2016): 1042–49; Edward D. Vargas, "Immigration Enforcement and Mixed-Status Families: The Effects of Risk of Deportation on Medicaid Use," *Children and Youth Services Review* 57 (July 2015): 83–89; Edward D. Vargas and Maureen A. Pirog, "Mixed-Status Families and WIC Uptake: The Effects of Risk of Deportation on Program Use," *Social Science Quarterly* 97, no. 3 (2016): 555–72; Tara Watson, "Inside the Refrigerator: Immigration Enforcement and Chilling Effects in Medicaid Participation," *American Economic Journal: Economic Policy* 6, no. 3 (2014): 313–38.

22. See Christopher A. Kearney, "School Absenteeism and School Refusal Behavior in Youth: A Contemporary Review," *Clinical Psychology Review* 28, no. 3 (2008): 451–71.

23. Karen Tourangeau, Christine Nord, Thanh Lê, Alberto G. Sorongon, Mary C. Hagedorn, Peggy Daly, and Michelle Najarian, *Early Childhood Longitudinal Study, Kindergarten Class of 2010–11 (ECLS-K:2011): User's Manual for the ECLS-K:2011 Kindergarten Data File and Electronic Codebook, Public Version* (Washington, DC: National Center for Education Statistics, 2015).

24. Patrick Royston, "Multiple Imputation of Missing Values," *The Stata Journal* 4, no. 3 (2004): 227–41.

25. Seth Gershenson, Alison Jacknowitz, and Andrew Brannegan, "Are Student Absences Worth the Worry in U.S. Primary Schools?" *Education Finance and Policy* 12, no. 2 (2017): 137–65; Joshua Goodman, "Flaking Out: Student Absences and Snow Days as Disruptions of Instructional Time" (Working Paper No. w20221, National Bureau of Economic Research, Cambridge, MA, June 2014); Michael A. Gottfried, Anna Egalite, and J. Jacob Kirksey, "Does the Presence of a Classmate with Emotional/Behavioral Disabilities Link to Other Students' Absences in Kindergarten?" *Early Childhood Research Quarterly* 36, no. 3 (2016): 506–20; Taryn W. Morrissey, Lindsey Hutchison, and Adam Winsler, "Family Income, School Attendance, and Academic Achievement in Elementary School," *Developmental Psychology* 50, no. 3 (2014): 741–53; Douglas D. Ready, "Socioeconomic Disadvantage, School Attendance, and Early Cognitive Development," *Sociology of Education* 83, no. 4 (2010): 271–86.

26. Gottfried et al., "Does the Presence of a Classmate . . . ?"; Cassandra M. Guarino, Steven Dieterle, Anna E. Bargagliotti, and William M. Mason, "What Can We Learn About Effective Mathematics Teaching? A Framework for Estimating Causal Effects Using Longitudinal Survey Data," *Journal of Research on Educational Effectiveness* 6, no. 2 (2013): 164–98.

27. Rebecca Brown and Joe Jackson, "Attending School Every Day: Making Progress, Taking Action in Oakland Schools," Oakland Achieves Partnership, 2014, https://oakland-achieves.files.wordpress.com/2014/09/oakachattendancefinal.pdf.

28. Hainmueller et al., "Protecting Unauthorized Immigrant Mothers."

29. Dickerson, "Immigration Arrests Rise"; Pierce and Selee, "Immigration Under Trump"; Randolph Capps, Heather Koball, Andrea Campetella, Krista Perreira, Sarah Hooker, and Juan Manuel Pedroza, "Implications of Immigration Enforcement Activities for the Well-Being of Children in Immigrant Families" (report, The Urban Institute and Migration Policy Institute, Washington, DC, September 2015), https://www.migrationpolicy.org/research/implications-immigration-enforcement-activities-well-being-children-immigrant-families.

30. Potochnick et al., "Local-Level Immigration Enforcement and Food Insecurity Risk"; Vargas, "Immigration Enforcement and Mixed-Status Families"; Vargas and Pirog, "Mixed-Status Families and WIC Uptake"; Watson, "Inside the Refrigerator."

31. Jonathan Blitzer, "An ICE Raid Has Turned the Lives of Hundreds of Tennessee Kids Upside Down," *New Yorker*, April 24, 2018, https://www.newyorker.com/news/dispatch/an-icesmall-raid-has-turned-the-lives-of-hundreds-of-tennessee-kids-upside-down; Kelli Kennedy, "Deportation Fears Have Legal Immigrants Avoiding Health Care," *Chicago Tribune*, January 23, 2018, http://www.chicagotribune.com/news/sns-bc-us--health-overhaul-immigration-20180121-story.html; James Queally, "Fearing Deportation, Many Domestic Violence Victims Are Steering Clear of Police and Courts," *Los Angeles Times*, October 9, 2017, http://www.latimes.com/local/lanow/la-me-ln-undocumented-crime-reporting-20171009-story.html.

32. Balfanz and Byrnes, "Closing the Mathematics Achievement"; Gottfried, "Evaluating the Relationship Between Student Attendance and Achievement"; Michael A. Gottfried, "Chronic Absenteeism and Its Effects on Students' Academic and Socioemotional Outcomes," *Journal of Education for Students Placed at Risk* 19, no. 2 (2014): 53–75.

33. Jean A. Baker, "Assessing School Risk and Protective Factors," in *Transforming School Mental Health Services: Population-Based Approaches to Promoting the Competency and Wellness of Children*, ed. Beth Doll and Jack A. Cummings (Thousand Oaks, CA: Corwin Press, 2008), 43–65; US Department of Health and Human Services, *Protective*

Factors Approaches in Child Welfare (Washington, DC: Child Welfare Information Gateway, 2014).

34. Balfanz and Byrnes, "Closing the Mathematics Achievement"; Gottfried, "Evaluating the Relationship Between Student Attendance and Achievement"; Gottfried, "Chronic Absenteeism and Its Effects."

35. Emily R. Crawford, "When Boundaries Around the 'Secret' Are Tested: A School Community Response to the Policing of Undocumented Immigrants," *Education and Urban Society* 50, no. 2 (2018): 155–82; Ariana Mangual Figueroa, "Speech or Silence: Undocumented Students' Decisions to Disclose or Disguise Their Citizenship Status in School," *American Educational Research Journal* 54, no. 3 (2017): 485–523.

36. Emily R. Crawford, "The Ethic of Community and Incorporating Undocumented Immigrant Concerns into Ethical School Leadership," *Educational Administration Quarterly* 53, no. 2 (2017): 147–79; Emily Crawford and Fernando Valle, "Educational Justice for Undocumented Students: How School Counselors Encourage Student Persistence in Schools," *Education Policy Analysis Archives* 98/99, no. 24 (2016): 1–28.

37. "NCFL Boosts Attendance, Family Bonds and Literacy in SW Detroit," Attendance Works, September 2016, http://www.attendanceworks.org/boosting-literacy-attendance-sw-detroit/; Peter Bergman and Eric W. Chan, "Leveraging Parents Through Technology: The Impact of High-Frequency Information on Student Achievement" (working paper, Department of Education Policy and Social Analysis, Teachers College, Columbia University, New York, September 2017), http://www.columbia.edu/~psb2101/Parent-RCT.pdf; Todd Rogers and Avi Feller, "Reducing Student Absences at Scale by Targeting Parents' Misbeliefs," *Nature Human Behaviour* 2 (2018): 1; Ann-Marie Faria, Nicholas Sorensen, Jessica Heppen, Jill Bowdon, Suzanne Taylor, Ryan Eisner, and Shandu Foster, "Getting Students on Track for Graduation: Impacts of the Early Warning Intervention and Monitoring System After One Year" (report no. 2017-272, Regional Educational Laboratory Midwest, Washington, DC, 2017), http://ies. ed.gov/ncee/edlabs; Robert Balfanz and Vaughan Byrnes, "Meeting the Challenge of Combating Chronic Absenteeism: Impact of the NYC Mayor's Interagency Task Force on Chronic Absenteeism and School Attendance and Its Implications for Other Cities" (report, Everyone Graduates Center, Johns Hopkins University School of Education, Baltimore, 2013), https://files.eric.ed.gov/fulltext/ED544570.pdf.

38. Capps et al., "Paying the Price"; Chaudry et al., "Facing Our Future"; Dreby, "Everyday Illegal"; Dreby, "The Burden of Deportation"; Hainmueller et al., "Protecting Unauthorized Immigrant Mothers"; Yoshikawa and Kholoptseva, "Unauthorized Immigrant Parents"; Zayas et al., "Charting Directions"; Koball et al., "Health and Social Service Needs."

CHAPTER 7

This research was supported by the Institute of Education Sciences, US Department of Education, through Grant R305A170270. The opinions expressed are those of the authors and do not represent views of the US Department of Education. We thank the New York City Department of Education's Office of Pupil Transportation, and particularly Alexandra Robinson and Tim Calabrese, for providing data and feedback.

1. Michael A. Gottfried, "Linking Getting to School with Going to School," *Educational Evaluation and Policy Analysis* 39, no. 4 (2017): 571–92, doi:10.3102/0162373717699472.

2. Crystal Cook and Douglas Shinkle, "School Bus Safety," National Conference of State Legislatures, July 10, 2018, http://www.ncsl.org/research/transportation/school-bus-safety.

aspx; Bruce B. Henderson, "The School Bus: A Neglected Children's Environment," *Journal of Rural Community Psychology* 12, no. 1 (2009): 1–11; Jennifer J. McGeehan, Joseph L. Annest, Madhavi Vajani, Marilyn J. Bull, Phyllis E. Agran, and Gary A. Smith, "School Bus–Related Injuries Among Children and Teenagers in the United States, 2001–2003," *Pediatrics* 118, no. 5 (2006): 1978–84, doi:10.1542/peds.2006-1314; National Safety Council, "School Buses Are Students' Safest Mode of Transportation," *Status Report* 37, no. 8 (2002); Robbin M. Rittner-Heir, "School Bus Safety," *School Planning & Management* 40, no. 3 (2001): 53; Ellen W. deLara, "Bullying and Aggression on the School Bus: School Bus Drivers' Observations and Suggestions," *Journal of School Violence* 7, no. 3 (2008): 48–70, doi:10.1080/15388220801955554; Lisa M. Krueger, "The Implementation of an Anti-Bullying Program to Reduce Bullying Behaviors on Elementary School Buses" (doctoral diss., D'Youville College, 2010); Robert F. Putnam, Marcie W. Handler, Christina M. Ramirez-Platt, and James K. Luiselli, "Improving Student Bus-Riding Behavior Through a Whole-School Intervention," *Journal of Applied Behavior Analysis* 36, no. 4 (2003): 583–90; Juliana Raskauskas, "Bullying on the School Bus," *Journal of School Violence* 4, no. 3 (2005): 93–107, doi:10.1300/j202v04n03_08; Leo Floyd, Walter F. Abbott, and Charles F. Faber, "Additional Evidence on the Impact of Busing on Student Achievement," *Growth and Change* 14, no. 4 (1983): 37–45, doi:10.1111/j.1468-2257.1983.tb00420.x; Yaochi Lu, "The Impact of Busing on Student Achievement: Retort," *Growth and Change* 7, no. 3 (1976): 52–52, doi:10.1111/j.1468-2257.1976.tb00319.x; Dan A. White, "Effects of Bussing on Urban School Students," *Dissertation Abstracts* 31, no. 7 (1971): 3430A–31A; Barbara S. Zoloth, "The Impact of Busing on Student Achievement: Reanalysis," *Growth and Change* 7, no. 3 (1976): 43–47.

3. Gerald Dunlop, Richard Harper, and Steven Hunka, "The Influence of Transporting Children to Centralized Schools upon Achievement and Attendance," *Educational Administration and Supervision* 44 (1968): 191–98; Craig B. Howley, Aimee A. Howley, and Steve Shamblen, "Riding the School Bus: A Comparison of the Rural and Suburban Experience in Five States," *Journal of Research in Rural Education* 17, no. 1 (2001): 41–63; Kieran Killeen and John Sipple, "School Consolidation and Transportation Policy: An Empirical and Institutional Analysis" (report, Rural School and Community Trust, Arlington, VA, 2000); Beth Spence, "Long School Bus Rides: Stealing the Joy of Childhood" (opinion paper, Covenant House, Charleston, WV, 2000); Mark Witham, "The Economics of [Not] Closing Small Rural Schools" (paper, A Focus on Rural Issues symposium, Townsville, Queensland, Australia, July 1997); Belle Zars, "Long Rides, Tough Hides: Enduring Long School Bus Rides" (Rural Challenge Policy Program Report, Randolph, VT, 1998).

4. Lee H. Harrison, Carl W. Armstrong, Suzanne R. Jenkins, Maurice W. Harmon, Gloria W. Ajello, Grayson B. Miller, and Claire V. Broome, "A Cluster of Meningococcal Disease on a School Bus Following Epidemic Influenza," *Archives of Internal Medicine* 151, no. 5 (1991): 1005–9; Ken Reid, "The Causes, Views and Traits of School Absenteeism and Truancy," *Research in Education* 74, no. 1 (2005): 59–82, doi:10.7227/rie.74.6; Reid Ewing, William Schroeer, and William Greene, "School Location and Student Travel Analysis of Factors Affecting Mode Choice," *Transportation Research Record: Journal of the Transportation Research Board* 1895 (2004): 55–63, doi:10.3141/1895-08; Christopher A. Kearney, "School Absenteeism and School Refusal Behavior in Youth: A Contemporary Review," *Clinical Psychology Review* 28, no. 3 (2008): 451–71, doi:10.1016/j.cpr.2007.07.012;

Amith K. Yarlagadda and Sivaramakrishnan Srinivasan, "Modeling Children's School Travel Mode and Parental Escort Decisions," *Transportation* 35, no. 2 (2008): 201–18.

5. Michael A. Gottfried, "Linking Getting to School with Going to School," *Educational Evaluation and Policy Analysis* 39, no. 4 (2017): 571–92, doi:10.3102/016237371769 9472; Tori Rhoulac, "Bus or Car? The Classic Choice in School Transportation," *Transportation Research Record: Journal of the Transportation Research Board* 1922 (2005): 98–104, doi:10.3141/1922-13.

6. Gottfried, "Linking Getting to School with Going to School."

7. This discretion does not extend to special education bus service, but we exclude full-time special education students from our sample.

8. There are "special circumstances due to historic and geographic considerations" in how this rule is applied (Tim Calabrese, personal communication, July 13, 2016).

9. We focus on K–6, because students in grades 7–12 generally take public transit (subsidized) rather than school buses.

10. Students in charter schools are not included because data on their transportation is not available.

11. To be specific, bus services for special education students are typically mandated by an Individualized Education Program (IEP) and are "door to door" rather than "stop to school." Special education students often also receive additional services, including a bus attendant (in addition to the driver) to help students on and off the bus and to prevent disciplinary issues.

12. Students are classified as "poor" if they were eligible for free or reduced-price lunch while we observed them.

13. Gottfried, "Linking Getting to School with Going to School."

14. American Academy of Pediatrics Adolescent Sleep Working Group, "School Start Times for Adolescents," *Pediatrics* 134 (2014): 642–49; Christopher Drake, Chelsea Nickel, Eleni Burduvali, Thomas Roth, Catherine Jefferson, and Pietro Badia, "The Pediatric Daytime Sleepiness Scale (PDSS): Sleep Habits and School Outcomes in Middle-School Children," *Sleep–New York Then Westchester–* 26, no. 4 (2003): 455–60; Finley Edwards, "Early to Rise? The Effect of Daily Start Times on Academic Performance," *Economics of Education Review* 31, no. 6 (2012): 970–83; Judith A. Owens, Katherine Belon, and Patricia Moss, "Impact of Delaying School Start Time on Adolescent Sleep, Mood, and Behavior," *Archives of Pediatrics and Adolescent Medicine* 164, no. 7 (2010): 608–14; Kyla Wahistrom, "Changing Times: Findings from the First Longitudinal Study of Later High School Start Times," *NASSP Bulletin* 86, no. 633 (2002): 3–21; Amy R. Wolfson and Mary A. Carskadon, "Understanding Adolescents' Sleep Patterns and School Performance: A Critical Appraisal," *Sleep Medicine Reviews* 7, no. 6 (2003): 491–506; Amy R. Wolfson, Noah L. Spaulding, Craig Dandrow, and Elizabeth M. Baroni, "Middle School Start Times: The Importance of a Good Night's Sleep for Young Adolescents," *Behavioral Sleep Medicine* 5, no. 3 (2007): 194–209.

15. Robson Tigre, Breno Sampaio, and Tatiane Menezes, "The Impact of Commuting Time on Youths's School Performance," *Journal of Regional Science* 57, no. 1 (2016): 28–47, doi:10.1111/jors.12289.

16. An important impediment to this research is the dearth of detailed data on transportation outside of New York City. Data for this study has been graciously provided by the OPT. School districts and policy makers elsewhere might do well to follow their lead.

CHAPTER 8

1. Jill Kerr, Marva Price, Jonathan Kotch, Stephanie Willis, Michael Fisher, and Susan Silva, "Does Contact by a Family Nurse Practitioner Decrease Early School Absence?" *Journal of School Nursing* 28, no. 1 (2012): 38–46.

2. "10 Facts About School Attendance," Attendance Works, August 31, 2014, http://www .attendanceworks.org/facts-stats-school-attendance/.

3. L. L. Dock, "School-Nurse Experiment in New York," *American Journal of Nursing* 3, no. 2 (1902): 108–10.

4. USDA, "Nutrition Standards in the National School Lunch and School Breakfast Programs," *Federal Register* 77, no. 17 (2012): 4088–167.

5. "Redefining Health for Kids and Teens: 2012–2013 Annual Report," School-Based Health Alliance, 2013, http://www.sbh4all.org/.

6. Ibid.

7. Olga Acosta Price, "School-Centered Approaches to Improve Community Health: Lessons from School-Based Health Centers," *Brookings* (blog), November 30, 2001, https:// www.brookings.edu/research/school-centered-approaches-to-improve-community-health-lessons-from-school-based-health-centers/.

8. Ibid.

9. Julia Graham Lear, Hope Burness Gleicher, Anne St. Germaine, and Philip J. Porter, "Reorganizing Health Care for Adolescents: The Experience of the School Based Adolescent Health Care Program," *Journal of Adolescent Health* 12, no. 6 (1991): 450–58.

10. Julia Graham Lear, Nancy Eichner, and Jane Koppelman, "The Growth of School-Based Health Centers and the Role of State Policies: Results of a National Survey," *Archives of Pediatrics and Adolescent Medicine* 153, no. 11 (1999): 1177–80

11. Lear et al., "Reorganizing Health Care."

12. "2013–14 Census of SBHCs Report," School-Based Health Alliance, May 2015, http:// censusreport.sbh4all.org/.

13. *Making the Grade: State and Local Partnership to Establish School-Based Health Centers* (Princeton, NJ: Robert Wood Johnson Foundation, 2007).

14. "The Mission of the LA Trust," Los Angeles Trust for Children's Health, https://thelatrust .org/about-landing-page/about/.

15. "Whole School, Whole Community, Whole Child," Centers for Disease Control and Prevention, 2014, https://www.cdc.gov/healthyyouth/wscc/.

16. Ibid.

17. "School Health Index: A Self-Assessment and Planning Guide: Elementary School Version," Centers for Disease Control and Prevention, 2017, https://www.cdc.gov/healthy schools/shi/pdf/Elementary-Total-2017.pdf.

18. School Health Services Program, "State of Florida 2016–2017 Summary of School Health Services," Florida Department of Health, December 4, 2017, http://www.floridahealth .gov/programs-and-services/childrens-health/school-health/2016_2017_data_summary.pdf.

19. School Health Program, "School-Based Health Centers Fact Sheet," New York Department of Health, March 1, 2018, https://www.health.ny.gov/statistics/school/skfacts.htm.

20. "2013–14 Census of SBHCs Report."

21. Health Resources and Services Administration, "Budget Overview," Department of Health and Human Services, May 23, 2017, https://www.hhs.gov/about/budget/fy2018/ budget-in-brief/hrsa/index.html.

22. Price, "School-Centered Approaches to Improve Community Health."

23. "2013–14 Census of SBHCs Report."

24. Kerr et al., "Contact by a Family Nurse Practitioner"; Amy Wiseman and Susan Dawson, "The Central Texas Absence Reasons Study" (report, E3 Alliance, Austin, TX, 2015), http://e3alliance.org/wp-content/uploads/2015/06/E3-Alliance-Absence-Reasons-Study-Summary-vH.pdf; "Why Chronic Absence Matters," Attendance Works, http://www.attendanceworks.org/chronic-absence/the-problem/.

25. "Common Cold," Centers for Disease Control and Prevention, March 3, 2016, https://www.cdc.gov/dotw/common-cold/index.html.

26. The CDC notes that 14 percent of US children have been diagnosed with asthma, a chronic condition that requires regular medical attention (https://www.cdc.gov/asthma/). Kyla Boyse, Lina Boujaoude, and Jennifer Laundy, "Children with Chronic Conditions," *Michigan Medicine* (blog), November 2012, http://www.med.umich.edu/yourchild/topics/chronic.htm; Michael E. Rezaee, "Multiple Chronic Conditions Among Outpatient Pediatric Patients, Southeastern Michigan, 2008–2013," *Preventing Chronic Disease* 12, no. 18, (2015): 1–5 .

27. Nancy G. Murray, Barbara J. Low, Christine Hollis, Alan W. Cross, and Sally M. Davis, "Coordinated School Health Programs and Academic Achievement: A Systematic Review of the Literature," *Journal of School Health* 77, no. 9 (2007): 589–600.

28. Mayris P. Webber, Kelly E. Carpiniello, Tosan Oruwariye, Yungtai Lo, William B. Burton, and David K. Appel, "Burden of Asthma in Innercity Elementary Schoolchildren: Do School Based Health Centers Make a Difference?" *Pediatric Adolescent Medicine* 157, no. 2 (2003): 111–18; J. J. Guo, R. Jang, K. N. Keller, A. L. McCracken, W. Pan, and R. J. Cluxton, "Impact of School-Based Health Centers on Children with Asthma," *Journal of Adolescent Health* 37, no. 4 (2005): 266–74.

29. Michael Lovenheim, Randall Reback, and Leigh Wedenoja, "How Does Access to Health Care Affect Teen Fertility and High-School Drop Out Rates? Evidence from School-Based Health Centers" (Working Paper No. 22030, National Bureau of Economic Research, Cambridge, MA, 2016).

30. Randall Reback, "School Mental Health Services and Young Children's Emotions, Behavior and Learning," *Journal of Policy Analysis and Management* 29, no. 4 (2010), 698–725.

31. Jenni Jennings, Glen Pearson, and Mark Harris, "Implementing and Maintaining School-Based Mental Health Services in a Large, Urban School District," *Journal of School Health* 70, no. 5 (2000): 201–5; Paul Hutchinson, Thomas Carton, Marsha Broussard, Lisanne Brown, and Sarah Chrestman, "Improving Adolescent Health Through School-Based Health Centers in Post-Katrina New Orleans," *Children and Youth Services Review* 34, no. 2 (2012): 360–68; S. U. Kerns, M. D. Pullmann, S. Walker, A. R. Lyon, T. J. Cosgrove, and E. J. Bruns, "Adolescent Use of School-Based Health Centers and High School Dropout," *Archives of Pediatrics and Adolescent Medicine* 165, no. 7 (2011): 617–23.

32. Maureen Van Cura, "The Relationship Between School Based Health Centers, Rates of Early Dismissal from School, and Loss of Seat Time," *Journal of School Health* 80, no. 8 (2010): 3717.

33. Sarah Walker, Suzanne Cusworth, E. U. Kerns, Aaron Lyon, Eric Bruns, and T. J. Cosgrove, "Impact of School-Based Health Center Use on Academic Outcomes," *Journal of Adolescent Health* 46, no. 3 (2010): 251–57.

34. Guo et al., "Impact of School-Based Health Centers"; Murray et al., "Coordinated School Health Programs and Academic Achievement; Webber et al., "Burden of Asthma."

35. Sara Peterson Geierstanger, Gorette Amaral, Mona Mansour, and Susan Russell Walters, "School-Based Health Centers and Academic Performance: Research, Challenges and Recommendations," *Journal of School Health* 74, no. 9 (2004): 351, 352.

36. Center for Disease Control, *Summary of Health Statistics for US Children: National Health Interview Survey, 2016* (Hyattsville, MD: NCHS, 2016), https://ftp.cdc.gov/pub/Health_Statistics/NCHS/NHIS/SHS/2016_SHS_Table_C-8.pdf.

37. Ryan Yeung, Bradley Gunton, Dylan Kalbacher, Jed Seltzer, and Hannah Wesolowski, "Can Health Insurance Reduce School Absenteeism?" *Education and Urban Society* 43, no. 6 (2011): 696–721.

38. "Chronic Absenteeism," School-Based Health Alliance, http://www.sbh4all.org/school-health-care/health-and-learning/chronic-absenteeism/.

CHAPTER 9

1. Allison J. Bell, Lee A. Rosen, and Dionne Dynlacht, "Truancy Intervention," *Journal of Research and Development in Education* 57, no. 3 (1994): 203–11. See also Marcell I. Lee and Raymond G. Miltenberger, "School Refusal Behavior: Classification, Assessment, and Treatment Issues," *Education and Treatment of Children* 19, no. 4 (1996): 474–86; Michael A. Gottfried, "Chronic Absenteeism in the Classroom Context: Effects on Achievement," *Urban Education* (2015): 1–32, http://journals.sagepub.com/doi/pdf/10.1177/0042085915618709.

2. Dinah Frey, *Truancy and Habitual Truancy: Examples of State Definition* (Denver: Education Commission of the States, 2011).

3. Carolyn Gentle-Genitty, Isaac Karikari, Haiping Chen, Eric Wilka, and Jangmin Kim, "Truancy: A Look at Definitions in the USA and Other Territories," *Educational Studies* 41, nos. 1–2 (2015): 62–90.

4. Jim Siegel, "Ohio Lawmakers Question School Suspensions for Truancy," *Columbus Dispatch*, December 20, 2015.

5. See, for example, Kaitlin Anderson, "Inequitable Compliance: Implementation Failure of a Statewide Student Discipline Reform," *Peabody Journal of Education* 93, no. 2 (2018): 244–63. See also Siegel, "Ohio Lawmakers."

6. Siegel, "Ohio Lawmakers."

7. For up-to-date statistics on this and other indicators, see the 2013–14 civil rights data snapshot provided by the US Department of Education's Office for Civil Rights, https://www2.ed.gov/about/offices/list/ocr/docs/2013-14-first-look.pdf.

8. See, for example, Jay Smink and Joanna Zorn Heilbrunn, *The Legal and Economic Implications of Truancy* (Clemson, SC: National Dropout Prevention Center/Network, 2005). See also US Department of Education and US Department of Justice, "Joint 'Dear Colleague' Letter," Office for Civil Rights, January 8, 2014, https://www2.ed.gov/about/offices/list/ocr/letters/colleague-201401-ttle-vi.html.

9. In Maryland, for example, legislation signed into law in April 2017 prohibits the suspension or expulsion of students in grades preK–2 except under rare circumstances. In Arkansas, Act 1059, signed into law in April 2017, bans out-of-school suspensions for students in grades K–5 except in cases when children pose a physical risk to themselves or others or cause a disruption so serious it cannot be addressed by other strategies. In Texas, Senate Bill 370 and House Bill 674, both passed in May 2017, focus on students in grade 3 and younger, whereas a wide-reaching bill in California, Senate Bill 607, bans suspensions for "defiant" and "disruptive" behavior for students in the full range of grade levels, K–12.

10. Lauren Sartain, Elaine M. Allensworth, and Shanette Porter, with Rachel Levenstein, David W. Johnson, Michelle Hanh Huynh, Eleanor Anderson, Nick Mader, and Matthew P. Steinberg, *Suspending Chicago's Students: Differences in Discipline Practices Across Schools* (Chicago: University of Chicago Consortium on Chicago Schools Research, 2015).

11. Max Eden, *School Discipline Reform and Disorder: Evidence from New York City Public Schools, 2012–16* (New York: Manhattan Institute, 2017).

12. Matthew Steinberg and Johanna Lacoe, *The Academic and Behavioral Consequences of Discipline Policy Reform: Evidence from Philadelphia* (Washington, DC: Thomas B. Fordham Institute, 2017).

13. RI Gen L § 16-19-1 (2012); Ohio Rev. Code Ann. § 3313.668 (2016).

14. K. Darling-Churchill, V. Stuart-Cassel, R. Ryberg, H. Schmitz, J. Balch, A. Bezinque, and J. Conway-Turner, *Compendium of School Discipline Laws and Regulations for the 50 States* (Washington, DC: National Center on Safe Supportive Learning Environments, 2013).

15. "2011–12 State and National Estimations," Office for Civil Rights, https://ocrdata.ed.gov/StateNationalEstimations/Estimations_2011_12.

16. Edward Smith and Shaun Harper, *Disproportionate Impact of K–12 School Suspension and Expulsion on Black Students in Southern States* (Philadelphia: University of Pennsylvania, Center for the Study of Race and Equity in Education, 2015).

17. Arkansas Rev. Code § 6-18-507.

18. For a full discussion of the data and methods used, see Kaitlin Anderson, Anna Egalite, and Jonathan Mills, "Discipline Reform: The Impact of a Statewide Ban on Suspensions for Truancy" (working paper).

19. Infractions recorded in the "other" category are simply those that do not fit neatly in a state-designated reporting category, such as dress code violations or violations of cell phone policies.

20. Although very limited, interviews of employees in school districts with frequent use of "other" consequences for truancy suggest these "other" consequences are primarily non-exclusionary. One superintendent and former principal indicated that truancy is typically handled with ISS but that "other" consequences include students losing course credit or being required to recover missed instructional time. A high school principal indicated that his school primarily uses afterschool suspensions or Saturday school as a consequence for truancy. While these two reports indicate primarily nonexclusionary responses, a former high school teacher indicated that the "other" consequences are likely a mix of morning detentions (nonexclusionary) and students being "sent home" for part of the day (exclusionary). Unfortunately, this is sparse evidence, and there is also the potential for social desirability bias, limiting our ability to draw strong conclusions from this qualitative evidence.

21. "SWPBIS for Beginners," PBIS, 2018, https://www.pbis.org/school/swpbis-for-beginners.

22. To ensure that prior-year truancy is a good proxy for actual treatment exposure, or current-year truancy, we estimate the likelihood of being truant as a function of (1) a variety of prior-year truancy, (2) our full set of student characteristics, and (3) school or district fixed effects. Prior-year truancy is clearly the strongest predictor of current-year truancy; a student is approximately fourteen to eighteen percentage points more likely to be truant at least once in a school year if they were truant at least once in the previous year. This is a substantial increase given the relatively low rate of truancy overall (only about 3.5 percent of students in grades 7–12 in Arkansas are truant at least once in any given year).

23. Steinberg and Lacoe, *The Academic and Behavioral Consequences of Discipline Policy Reform: Evidence from Philadelphia* (Washington, DC: Thomas B. Fordham Institute, 2017).

24. Ibid., 7.

25. On positive behavior interventions and supports, see K. B. Flannery, K. B. P. Fenning, M. M. Kato, and K. McIntosh, "Effects of School-Wide Positive Behavioral Interventions and Supports and Fidelity of Implementation on Problem Behavior in High Schools," *American Psychological Association* 29, no. 2 (2014): 111–24. See also Jennifer Freeman, Brandi Simonsen, Betsy McCoach, George Sugai, Allison Lombardi, and Robert Horner, "Relationship Between School-Wide Positive Behavior Interventions and Supports and Academic, Attendance, and Behavior Outcomes in High Schools," *Journal of Positive Behavior Interventions* 18, no. 2 (2015): 41–51. On restorative justice, see Trevor Fronius, Hannah Persson, Sarah Guckenburg, Nancy Hurley, and Anthony Petrosino, *Restorative Justice in U.S. Schools: A Research Review* (San Francisco: West Ed, 2016); Steinberg and Lacoe, *The Academic and Behavioral Consequences.*

26. Brandy R. Maynard, Katherine Tyson McCrea, Terri D. Pigott, and Michael S. Kelly, "Indicated Truancy Interventions for Chronic Truant Students: A Campbell Systematic Review," *Research on Social Work Practice* 23, no. 1 (2013): 5–21.

CHAPTER 10

1. "Back to School Statistics," National Center for Education Statistics, https://nces.ed.gov/fastfacts/display.asp?id=372.

2. Sara Rimm-Kaufman, Robert Pianta, and Martha Cox, "Teachers' Judgments of Problems in the Transition to Kindergarten," *Early Childhood Research Quarterly* 15, no. 2 (2000): 147–66.

3. Amy Schulting, Patrick Malone, and Kenneth Dodge, "The Effect of School-Based Transition Policies and Practices on Child Academic Outcomes," *Developmental Psychology* 41, no. 6 (2005): 860–71.

4. Hedy Change and Mariajose Romero, "Present, Engaged, and Accounted For: The Critical Importance of Addressing Chronic Absence in the Early Grades," National Center for Children in Poverty, 2008, http://www.nccp.org/publications/pdf/text_837.pdf; Joyce Epstein and Steven Sheldon, "Present and Accounted For: Improving Student Attendance Through Family and Community Involvement," *Journal of Education Research* 95, no. 5 (2002): 308–18.

5. Diane Early, Robert Pianta, Lorraine Taylor, and Martha Cox, "Transition Practices: Findings from a National Survey of Kindergarten Teachers," *Early Childhood Education Journal* 28, no. 3 (2001): 199–206.

6. Epstein and Sheldon, "Present and Accounted For."

7. We replace all parent, child, and individual school names with pseudonyms to ensure confidentiality.

8. "The Attendance Imperative: How States Can Advance Achievement by Reducing Chronic Absence," Attendance Works, 2014, http://attendanceworks.org/wp-content/uploads/2017/08/AAM-Policy-Brief-091214-2.pdf.

9. Ad Council, "California School Attendance Research Project," June 2015, available at https://oag.ca.gov/sites/all/files/agweb/pdfs/tr/toolkit/QualitativeResearchReport.pdf.

10. Todd Rogers and Avi Feller, "Reducing Student Absences at Scale by Targeting Parents' Misbeliefs," *Nature Human Behaviour* 2 (2018): 335–42.

11. Douglas Ready, "Socioeconomic Disadvantage, School Attendance, and Early Cognitive Development: The Differential Effects of School Exposure," *Sociology of Education* 83, no. 4 (2010): 271–86; Mariajose Romero and Young-Sun Lee, "A National Portrait of Chronic Absenteeism in the Early Grades," National Center for Children in Poverty, 2007, http://www.nccp.org/publications/pdf/text_771.pdf; Faith Connolly and Linda Olson, "Early Elementary Performance and Attendance in Baltimore City Schools' Pre-Kindergarten and Kindergarten" (report, Baltimore Education Research Consortium, Baltimore, 2012), https://www.baltimore-berc.org/pdfs/PreKKAttendanceFullReport.pdf; Epstein and Sheldon, "Present and Accounted For"; Stacy Ehrlich, Julia Gwynne, Amber Stitziel Pareja, and Elaine Allensworth, "Preschool Attendance in Chicago Public Schools," University of Chicago Consortium on Chicago School Research, 2014, https://consortium.uchicago.edu/sites/default/files/publications/Pre-K%20Attendance%20Report.pdf.
12. Romero and Lee, "A National Portrait."
13. Ibid.
14. Charlie Bruner, Anne Discher, and Hedy Chang, "Chronic Elementary Absenteeism: A Problem Hidden in Plain Sight" (report, Attendance Works and Child and Family Policy Center, Washington, DC, 2011), http://www.attendanceworks.org/wp-content/uploads/2017/04/Chronic-Elementary-Absenteeism-A-Problem-Hidden-in-Plain-Sight.pdf.
15. Epstein and Sheldon, "Present and Accounted For."
16. Robert Balfanz and Vaughan Byrnes, "Meeting the Challenge of Combating Chronic Absenteeism: Impact of the NYC Mayor's Interagency Task Force on Chronic Absenteeism and School Attendance and Its Implications for Other Cities," (report, Everyone Graduates Center, Baltimore, 2013), http://solaris.techlab360.org/sites/default/files/document_library/NYC-Chronic-Absenteeism-Impact-Report%20(1).pdf.
17. Rogers and Feller, "Reducing Student Absences."
18. "Mobile Fact Sheet," Pew Research Center, February 5, 2018, http://www.pewinternet.org/fact-sheets/mobile-technology-fact-sheet/.
19. Benjamin York, Susanna Loeb, and Christopher Doss, "One Step at a Time: The Effects of and Early Literacy Text Messaging Program for Parents of Preschoolers," *Journal of Human Resources* (OnlineFirst, 2018), doi:10.3368/jhr.54.3.0517-8756R.
20. The two-way text service Remind reports that its messaging system is used in 70 percent of US public schools. See www.remind.com.
21. Benjamin Castleman and Lindsay Page, "Summer Nudging: Can Personalized Text Messages and Peer Mentoring Outreach Increase College Going Among Low-Income High School Graduates?" *Journal of Economic and Organization* 115 (2015): 144–66; Benjamin Castleman and Lindsay Page, "Freshman Year Financial Aid Nudges: An Experiment to Increase Financial Aid Renewal and Sophomore Year Persistence," *Journal of Human Resources* 51, no. 2 (2016): 389–415; Benjamin Castleman and Lindsay Page, "Parental Influences on Postsecondary Decision-Making: Evidence from a Text Messaging Experiment," *Educational Evaluation and Policy Analysis* 39, no. 2 (2017): 361–77; Lindsay Page and Hunter Gehlbach, "How an Artificially Intelligent Virtual Assistant Helps Students Navigate the Road to College," *AERA Open* 3, no. 4 (2017): 1–12.
22. York et al., "One Step at a Time"; Peter Bergman, "Parent-Child Information Frictions and Human Capital Investment: Evidence from a Field Experiment" (Working Paper 5391, CESifo, Columbia University, New York, 2015), http://www.cesifo-group.de/DocDL/cesifo1_wp5391.pdf.

23. Matthew Kraft and Todd Rogers, "The Underutilized Potential of Teacher-to-Parent Communication: Evidence from a Field Experiment," *Economics of Education Review* 47 (2015): 49–63.

24. York et al., "One Step at a Time."

25. We implemented this effort with technology partner Signal Vine. For more information about Signal Vine, see www.signalvine.com.

26. Ken Smythe-Leistico, Colleen Young, Laurie Mulvey, Robert McCall, Margaret Petruska, Carole Barone-Martin, Renata Capozzoli, Tiffani Best, and Barbara Coffee, "Blending Theory with Practice: Implementing Kindergarten Transition Using the Interactive Systems Framework," *American Journal of Community Psychology* 50, nos. 3–4 (2012): 357–69.

27. We sought to personalize the recruitment letter by including a photo of the AmeriCorps member who was staffing the outreach.

28. For technical details, see Ken Smythe-Leistico and Lindsay Page, "Connect-Text: Leveraging Text-Message Communication to Mitigate Chronic Absenteeism and Improve Parental Engagement in the Earliest Years of School," *Journal of Education for Students Placed at Risk* 23, nos. 1–2 (2018): 139–52. Our synthetic control approach follows that laid out in Alberto Abadie, Alexis Diamond, and Jens Hainmueller, "Synthetic Control Methods for Comparative Case Studies: Estimating the Effects of California's Tobacco Control Program," *Journal of the American Statistical Association* 105 (2010): 493–505.

29. We use the Stata package synth for the construction of our synthetic control. For additional technical details, see Abadie et al., "Synthetic Control Methods."

30. Heather Hough, Emily Penner, and Joe Witte, "Identify Crisis: Multiple Measures and the Identification of Schools Under ESSA" (policy memo, CORE-PACE Research Partnership, Stanford, CA, 2016), http://edpolicyinca.org/sites/default/files/PACE_PolicyMemo_1603.pdf.

31. Diane Whitmore Schanzenbach, Lauren Bauer, and Megan Mumford, "Lessons for Broadening School Accountability Under the Every Student Succeeds Act" (strategy paper, The Hamilton Project, Washington, DC, 2016), http://www.hamiltonproject.org/assets/files/lessons_broadening_school_accountability_essa.pdf.

32. Schanzenbach et al., "Lessons for Broadening School Accountability."

33. Hedy Chang, Charlene Russell-Tucker, and Kari Sullivan, "Chronic Early Absence: What States Can Do," *Phi Delta Kappan* 98, no. 2 (2016): 22; Peter Chen and Cynthia Rice, "Showing Up Matters: Newark Chronic Absenteeism in the Early Years" (report, Advocates for Children of New Jersey, Newark, 2016), http://acnj.org/downloads/2016_01_21_newark__chronic_absenteeism_rprt.pdf.

34. Change et al., "Chronic Early Absence."

35. Shannon Wanless, "The Role of Psychological Safety in Human Development," *Research in Human Development* 13, no. 1 (2016): 6–14.

36. Jonathan Davis, Jonathan Guryan, Kelly Hallberg, and Jens Ludwig, "The Economics of Scale Up" (Working Paper w23925, National Bureau of Economic Research, Cambridge, MA, 2017): http://www.nber.org/papers/w23925.

CHAPTER 11

1. See Elaine Allensworth and John Easton, *What Matters for Staying On-Track and Graduating in Chicago Public High Schools: A Close Look at Course Grades, Failures, and Attendance in the Freshman Year* (Chicago: Consortium on Chicago School Research, 2007); Martha Abele Mac Iver and Matthew Messel, "Predicting High School Outcomes in the Baltimore

City Public Schools: The Senior Urban Education Research Fellowship Series, Volume VII" (report, Council of the Great City Schools, Washington, DC, 2012).

2. Beth S. Simon, "High School Outreach and Family Involvement," *Social Psychology of Education* 7, no. 2 (2004): 185–209; Christopher Spera, "A Review of the Relationship Among Parenting Practices, Parenting Styles, and Adolescent School Achievement," *Educational Psychology Review* 17, no. 2 (2005): 125–46; Kathleen V. Hoover-Dempsey, Christa L. Ice, and Manya Whitaker, "'We're Way Past Reading Together': Why and How Parental Involvement in Adolescence Makes Sense," in *Families, Schools, and the Adolescents: Connecting Research, Policy, and Practice,* ed. Nancy Hill and Ruth Chao (New York: Teachers College Press, 2009), 19–36.

3. Aime T. Black, Richard C. Seder, and Wendy Kekahio, "Review of Research on Student Nonenrollment and Chronic Absenteeism" (report REL2015-054, Regional Educational Laboratory Pacific, National Center for Education Evaluation and Regional Assistance, US Department of Education, Washington, DC, 2014), http://ies.ed.gov/ncee/edlabs; Christopher A. Kearney, "School Absenteeism and School Refusal Behavior in Youth: A Contemporary Review," *Clinical Psychology Review* 28, no. 3 (2008): 451–71.

4. Claudia Galindo and Steven B. Sheldon, "School and Home Connections and Children's Kindergarten Achievement Gains: The Mediating Role of Family Involvement," *Early Childhood Research Quarterly* 27, no. 1 (2012): 90–103; Amy B. Schulting, Patrick S. Malone, and Kenneth A. Dodge, "The Effect of School-Based Kindergarten Transition Policies and Practices on Child Academic Outcomes," *Developmental Psychology* 41, no. 6 (2005): 860; Steven B. Sheldon and Joyce L. Epstein, "Involvement Counts: Family and Community Partnerships and Mathematics Achievement," *Journal of Educational Research* 98, no. 4 (2005): 196–207; Steven B. Sheldon, Joyce L. Epstein, and Claudia L. Galindo, "Not Just Numbers: Creating a Partnership Climate to Improve Math Proficiency in Schools," *Leadership and Policy in Schools* 9, no. 1 (2010): 27–48.

5. Joyce L. Epstein and Steven B. Sheldon, "Present and Accounted For: Improving Student Attendance Through Family and Community Involvement," *Journal of Educational Research* 95, no. 5 (2002): 308–18; Joyce L. Epstein and Steven B. Sheldon, "Necessary but Not Sufficient: The Role of Policy for Advancing Programs of School, Family, and Community Partnerships," *Russell Sage Foundation Journal of the Social Sciences* 2 (2016): 202–19; Steven B. Sheldon and Joyce L. Epstein, "Getting Students to School: Using Family and Community Involvement to Reduce Chronic Absenteeism," *School Community Journal* 14, no. 2 (2004): 39.

6. Steven B. Sheldon, "Improving Student Attendance with a School-Wide Approach to School, Family, and Community Partnerships," *Journal of Educational Research* 100, no. 5 (2007): 267–75.

7. Steven B. Sheldon and Sol Bee Jung, *The Family Engagement Project: Year 2 Student Achievement Outcomes* (Washington, DC: Flamboyan Foundation, 2015).

8. Katherine McKnight, Nitya Venkateswaran, Jennifer Laird, Jessica Robles, and Talia Shalev, "Mindset Shifts and Parent Teacher Home Visits" (report, RTI International for Parent Teacher Home Visits, Berkeley, CA, 2017).

9. Peter Bergman and Eric Chen, "Leveraging Parents: The Impact of High-Frequency Information on Student Achievement" (white paper, Teachers College, Columbia University, New York, 2017), http://www.columbia.edu/~psb2101/ParentRCT.pdf.

10. Todd Rogers and Avi Feller, "Reducing Student Absences at Scale" (working paper, 2016), http://scholar.harvard.edu/files/todd_rogers/files/reducing.pdf; Todd Rogers and

Avi Feller, "Reducing Student Absences at Scale by Targeting Parents' Misbeliefs" (working paper, 2017), https://scholar.harvard.edu/files/todd_rogers/files/sdp_revision .10.30.2017_final.pdf.

11. Carly Robinson, Monica Ga Lim Lee, Eric Dearing, and Todd Rogers, "Reducing Student Absenteeism in the Early Grades by Targeting Parental Beliefs" (Faculty Research Working Paper Series RWP17-011, Harvard Kennedy School, Cambridge, MA, March 2017).

12. Simon, "High School Outreach and Family Involvement"; Spera, "A Review of the Relationship."

13. United Way Worldwide and Harvard Family Research Project, *The Family Engagement for High School Success Toolkit: Planning and Implementing an Initiative to Support the Pathway to Graduation for At-Risk Students*, 2011, http://www.hfrp.org/ family-involvement/publications-resources/the-family-engagement-for-high-school-success-toolkit-planning-and-implementing-an-initiative-to-support-the-pathway-to-graduation-for-at-risk-students; Terrinieka Williams and Bernadette Sánchez, "Parental Involvement (and Uninvolvement) at an Inner-City High School," *Urban Education* 47, no. 3 (2012): 625–52; Matt Wallace, "High School Teachers and African American Parents: A (Not So) Collaborative Effort to Increase Student Success," *The High School Journal* 96, no. 3 (2013): 195–208.

14. Robert Crosnoe, "Family-School Connections and the Transitions of Low-Income Youths and English Language Learners from Middle School to High School," *Developmental Psychology* 45, no. 4 (2009): 1061–76.

15. Martha Abele Mac Iver, Joyce Epstein, Steven Sheldon, and Ean Fonseca, "Engaging Families to Support Students' Transition to High School: Evidence from the Field," *The High School Journal* 99, no. 1 (2015): 27–45.

16. Joyce L. Epstein, "Links in a Professional Development Chain: Preservice and Inservice Education for Effective Programs of School, Family, and Community Partnerships," *The New Educator* 1, no. 2 (2005): 125–41; Joyce L. Epstein, *School, Family, and Community Partnerships: Preparing Educators and Improving Schools*, 2nd ed. (Boulder, CO: Westview Press, 2011); Darcy J. Hutchins and Steven B. Sheldon, *Summary 2012 School Data: Annual Report from the National Network of Partnership Schools* (Baltimore: Center on School, Family and Community Partnerships at Johns Hopkins University, 2013); Mavis G. Sanders, "Schools, Families, and Communities Partnering for Middle Level Students' Success," *NASSP Bulletin* 85, no. 627 (2001): 53–61; Mavis G. Sanders and Karla C. Lewis, "Building Bridges Toward Excellence: Community Involvement in High Schools," *The High School Journal* 88, no. 3 (2005): 1–9; Mavis G. Sanders, Steven Sheldon, and Joyce Epstein, "Improving Schools' Partnership Programs in the National Network of Partnership Schools," *Journal of Educational Research & Policy Studies* 5, no. 1 (2005): 24–47; Mavis G. Sanders and Beth S. Simon, "A Comparison of Program Development at Elementary, Middle, and High Schools in the National Network of Partnership Schools," *School Community Journal* 12, no. 1 (2002): 7; Joyce L. Epstein, Mavis G. Sanders, Steven B. Sheldon, Beth S. Simon, Karen Clark Salinas, Natalie Rodriguez Jansorn, Frances L. Van Voorhis, Cecelia S. Martin, Brenda G. Thomas, Marsha D. Greenfeld, Darcy J. Hutchins, and Kenyatta J. Williams, *School, Family, and Community Partnerships: Your Handbook for Action* (Thousand Oaks, CA: Corwin Press, 2009); Steven B. Sheldon, "Linking School-Family-Community Partnerships in Urban Elementary Schools to Student Achievement to State Tests," *Urban Review* 35, no. 2 (2003): 149–65; Steven B. Sheldon, "Testing a Structural Equation Model of Partnership Program

Implementation and Parent Involvement," *The Elementary School Journal* 106, no. 2 (2005): 171–87; Steven B. Sheldon and Frances L. Van Voorhis, "Partnership Programs in US Schools: Their Development and Relationship to Family Involvement Outcomes," *School Effectiveness and School Improvement* 15, no. 2 (2004): 125–48; Epstein and Sheldon, "Present and Accounted For"; Sheldon and Epstein, "Getting Students to School"; Sheldon, "Improving Student Attendance with a School-Wide Approach"; Allensworth and Easton, *What Matters for Staying On-Track and Graduating in Chicago Public High Schools*; Elaine Allensworth, "The Use of Ninth-Grade Early Warning Indicators to Improve Chicago Schools," *Journal of Education for Students Placed at Risk (JESPAR)* 18, no. 1 (2013): 68–83.

17. Marie-Andree Somers, Pei Zhu, Robin Jacob, and Howard Bloom, "The Validity and Precision of the Comparative Interrupted Time Series Design and the Difference-in-Difference Design in Educational Evaluation" (Working Paper on Research Methodology, MDRC, New York, September 2013).

18. See, for example, Howard S. Bloom, "Using 'Short' Interrupted Time-Series Analysis to Measure the Impacts of Whole-School Reforms, with Applications to a Study of Accelerated Schools," *Evaluation Review* 27, no. 1 (2003): 3–49; Howard S. Bloom and James A. Riccio, "Using Place-Based Random Assignment and Comparative Interrupted Time-Series Analysis to Evaluate the Jobs-Plus Employment Program for Public Housing Residents," *Annals of the American Academy of Political and Social Science* 599, no. 1 (2005): 19–51; Robert Penfold and Fang Zhang, "Use of Interrupted Times Series Analysis in Evaluation Health Care Quality Improvements," *Academic Pediatrics* 13, no. 6S (2013): S38–S44.

19. Todd Rogers, Teresa Duncan, Tonya Wolford, John Ternavoski, Shruthi Subramanyam, and Adrienne Reitano, "A Randomized Experiment Using Absenteeism Information to 'Nudge' Attendance" (report, Regional Educational Laboratory Mid-Atlantic, National Center for Education and Regional Evaluation, US Department of Education, Washington, DC, 2017), http://ies.ed.gov/ncee/edlabs.

20. Frances L. Van Voorhis, "Interactive Homework in Middle School: Effects on Family Involvement and Science Achievement," *Journal of Educational Research* 96, no. 6 (2003): 323–38; Frances L. Van Voorhis, "Costs and Benefits of Family Involvement in Homework," *Journal of Advanced Academics* 22, no. 2 (2011): 220–49.

21. Phyllis W. Jordan and Raegen Miller, "Who's In: Chronic Absenteeism Under the Every Student Succeeds Act" (report, FutureEd, Washington, DC, September 2017), https://www.future-ed.org/wp-content/uploads/2017/09/REPORT_Chronic_Absenteeism_final_v5.pdf.

22. Matt Weyer, "Engaging Families in Education," National Conference of State Legislatures, 2015, http://www.ncsl.org/Portals/1/Documents/educ/Engaging_Families_Education.pdf.

CHAPTER 12

I am extremely grateful to William Corrin and other colleagues at MDRC for their insights and for the discussions that led to this chapter. MDRC thanks the many schools and districts that participated in these studies and shared their experiences over the past decade. All opinions and errors are my own.

1. MDRC is a nonprofit, nonpartisan research firm that evaluates social programs and policies. The firm served as the independent evaluator, executing random assignment and analyzing implementation and impacts.

2. Rekha Balu, Kristin Porter, and Brad Gunton, "Can Informing Parents Help High School Students Show Up for School?" (report, MDRC, New York, 2016), https://www.mdrc.org/publication/can-informing-parents-help-high-school-students-show-school.

3. Lashawn Richburg-Hayes, Caitlin Anzelone, Nadine Dechausay, Saugato Datta, Alexandra Fiorillo, Louis Potok, Matthew Darling, and John Balz, "Behavioral Economics and Social Policy: Designing Innovative Solutions for Programs Supported by the Administration for Children and Families: Technical Supplement: Commonly Applied Behavioral Interventions" (Report No. 2014-16b, Office of Planning, Research and Evaluation, Administration for Children and Families, US Department of Health and Human Services, Washington, DC, 2014).

4. Pamela Morris, Lawrence Aber, Sharon Wolf, and Justine Berg, "Using Incentives to Change How Teenagers Spend Their Time: The Effects of New York City's Conditional Cash Transfer Program" (report, MDRC, New York, 2012), https://www.mdrc.org/sites/default/files/ONYC_for_web_Final.pdf.

5. James A. Riccio, Nadine Dechausay, David M. Greenberg, Cynthia Miller, Zawadi Rucks, & Nandita Verma, "Toward Reduced Poverty Across Generations: Early Findings from New York City's Conditional Cash Transfer Program" (report, MDRC, New York, 2010), 114.

6. Ibid., 100.

7. Rekha Balu and Stacy B. Ehrlich, "Making Sense out of Incentives: A Framework for Considering the Design, Use, and Implementation of Incentives to Improve Attendance," *Journal of Education for Students Placed at Risk (JESPAR)* 23, nos. 1–2 (2018): 93–106.

8. Leigh Parise, William Corrin, Kelly Granito, Zeest Haider, Marie-Andree Somers, and Oscar Cerna, "Two Years of Case Management: Final Findings from the Random Assignment Evaluation of Communities in Schools" (report, MDRC, New York, 2017), https://www.mdrc.org/publication/two-years-case-management.

9. Sarah Frazelle and Aisling Nagel, "A Practitioner's Guide to Implementing Early Warning Systems (REL 2015–056)," National Center for Education Evaluation and Regional Assistance, Regional Educational Laboratory Northwest, 2015, http://ies.ed.gov/ncee/edlabs; Ruth Curran Neild, Robert Balfanz, and Liza Herzog, "An Early Warning System," *Educational Leadership* 65, no. 2 (2007): 28–33; Robert Balfanz, Liza Herzog, and Douglas J. Mac Iver, "Preventing Student Disengagement and Keeping Students on the Graduation Path in Urban Middle-Grade Schools: Early Identification and Effective Interventions," *Educational Psychologist* 42, no. 4 (2007): 223–35.

10. Elaine M. Allensworth and John Q. Easton, *The On-Track Indicator as a Predictor of High School Graduation* (Chicago: University of Chicago Consortium on Chicago School Research, 2005).

11. Rekha Balu and Joshua Malbin, "Tiered Systems of Support: Lessons from MDRC Evaluations: MDRC Issue Focus" (report, MDRC, New York, 2017).

12. William Corrin, Susan Sepanik, Rachel Rosen, and Andrea Shane et al., "Addressing Early Warning Indicators: Interim Impact Findings from the Investing in Innovation Evaluation of Diplomas Now" (report, MDRC, New York, 2016), https://www.mdrc.org/publication/addressing-early-warning-indicators.

13. Elaine M. Allensworth and John Q. Easton, *What Matters for Staying On-Track and Graduating in Chicago Public Schools: A Close Look at Course Grades, Failures, and Attendance in the Freshman Year* (Chicago: Consortium on Chicago School Research at the University of Chicago, 2007).

14. Talent Development Secondary employs a school facilitator who manages an early warning system and collaborates with administrators and teachers to review early warning data to identify students for tiered intervention services. The facilitator also may identify patterns across groups of students that warrant schoolwide changes. City Year volunteers, who are near-peers to high school students, tutor and mentor those in need of Tier 2 services. Communities in Schools coordinates school and community resources (academic and behavioral support) for students at risk of dropping out.

15. Talent Development Secondary also reorganizes schools into small learning communities, assigns coaches and teachers to deliver critical math and ELA courses, and provides college and career preparatory content.

16. Corrin et al., "Addressing Early Warning Indicators."

17. Joyce L. Epstein and Steven B. Sheldon, "Present and Accounted For: Improving Student Attendance Through Family and Community Involvement," *Journal of Educational Research* 95 (May/June 2002): 308–18; Geoffrey D. Borman, Gina M. Hewes, Laura T. Overman, and Shelly Brown, "Comprehensive School Reform and Achievement: A Meta-Analysis," *Review of Educational Research* 73, no. 2 (2003): 125–230.

CONCLUSION

1. Michael Gottfried and J. Jacob Kirksey, "When Students Miss School: The Role of Timing of Absenteeism on Students' Test Performance," *Educational Researcher* 46, no. 3 (2017): 119–30.

2. Michael Gottfried and Gilberto Conchas, *When School Policies Backfire* (Cambridge, MA: Harvard Education Press, 2016).

3. Alvarez and Marsal, "Interim Report District of Columbia Public Schools Audit and Investigation—Ballou High School" (report, Office of the State Superintendent, Washington, DC, 2018), 4, https://osse.dc.gov/sites/default/files/dc/sites/osse/release_content/attachments/Analysis%20of%20Attendance%20and%20Graduation%20Outcomes%20at%20Public%20High%20Schools%20in%20DC%20-%20Jan%2016%202018%20-%20sm.pdf.

4. Ibid.

5. Steven B. Sheldon, "Improving Student Attendance with School, Family, and Community Partnerships," *Journal of Educational Research* 100, no. 5 (2007): 267–75; Jane Graves Smith, "Parental Involvement in Education Among Low-Income Families: A Case Study," *School Community Journal* 16, no. 1 (2006): 43–56.

AFTERWORD

1. Todd Rogers and Avi Feller, "Reducing Student Absences at Scale by Targeting Parents' Misbeliefs," *Nature Human Behaviour* 2, no. 5 (2018): 335–432.

2. See Hunt Allcott, "Social Norms and Energy Conservation," *Journal of Public Economics* 95, nos. 9–10 (2011): 1082–95; Hunt Allcott and Todd Rogers, "The Short-Run and Long-Run Effects of Behavioral Interventions: Experimental Evidence from Energy Conservation," *American Economic Review* 104, no. 10 (2014): 3003–37.

3. Carly Robinson, Monica Lee, Eric Dearing, and Todd Rogers, "Reducing Student Absenteeism in the Early Grades by Targeting Parental Beliefs," *American Educational Research Journal* (OnlineFirst, 2018), doi:10.3102/0002831218772274.

4. Carly D. Robinson, Jana Gallus, Monica G. Lee, and Todd Rogers, "The Demotivating Effect (and Unintended Message) of Retrospective Awards" (HKS Faculty Research Working Paper Series RWP18-020, Harvard Kennedy School, Cambridge, MA, July 2018).

5. Rekha Balu, Kristin Porter, and Brad Gunton, "Can Informing Parents Help High School Students Show Up for School?" (policy brief MDRC, New York, 2016), https://www .mdrc.org/sites/default/files/NewVisionsRCT_2016_Brief.pdf.

6. See, for example, Ken Smythe-Leistico and Lindsay Page, "Connect-Text: Leveraging Text-Message Communication to Mitigate Chronic Absenteeism and Improve Parental Engagement in the Earliest Years of Schooling," *Journal of Education for Students Placed at Risk* 23, nos. 1–2 (2018): 139–52; Peter Bergman, "Parent-Child Information Frictions and Human Capital Investment: Evidence from a Field Experiment" (Working Paper Series No. 5391, CESifo, Munich, 2015), https://papers.ssrn.com/sol3/papers.cfm?abstract _id=2622034; Peter Bergman and Eric Chan, "Leveraging Technology to Engage Parents at Scale: Evidence from a Randomized Controlled Trial" (Working Paper Series No. 6493, CESifo, Munich, 2017), http://www.columbia.edu/~psb2101/ParentRCT. pdf; Peter Bergman, Jessica Lasky-Fink, and Todd Rogers, "Simplification and Defaults Affect Adoption and Impact of Technology, but Decision Makers Do Not Realize This" (HKS Faculty Research Working Paper Series RWP17-021, Harvard Kennedy School, Cambridge, MA, updated July 2018), https://scholar.harvard.edu/files/todd_rogers/files/ simplification_defaults_affect_adoption.pdf.

7. Smythe-Leistico and Page, "Connect-Text."

8. There is also promising research on a mentoring program in New York City that estimates a larger effect on reducing absenteeism, though is not an RCT. See Robert Balfanz and Vaughn Byrnes, "Meeting the Challenge of Combating Chronic Absenteeism: Impact of the NYC Mayor's Interagency Task Force on Chronic Absenteeism and School Attendance and Its Implications for Other Cities" (report, Johns Hopkins School of Education, Baltimore, 2013). Jonathan Guryan, Sandra Christenson, Amy Claessens, Mimi Engel, Ijun Lai, Jens Ludwig, Ashley Cureton Turner, and Mary Clair Turner, " The Effect of Mentoring on School Attendance and Academic Outcomes: A Randomized Evaluation of the Check & Connect Program" (Working Paper Series WP-16-18, Northwestern Institute for Policy Research, Evanston, IL, 2017), https://www.ipr.north western.edu/publications/docs/workingpapers/2016/WP-16-18.pdf.

9. Rogers and Feller, "Reducing Student Absences at Scale."

10. Ibid.; Robinson et al., "Reducing Student Absences in the Early Grades."

ACKNOWLEDGMENTS

WE WOULD LIKE TO THANK the Smith Richardson Foundation for its generous financial support for a convening of the editors and contributing authors during the book writing process. While such a gathering is not a standard part of producing volumes like this one, in our case this meeting played a crucial role in helping to shape and improve early drafts of all the chapters in the book. We would also like to thank Hedy Chang as well as the organization she directs, Attendance Works, for advice, support, and guidance throughout the conception and execution of this project.

ABOUT THE EDITORS

MICHAEL A. GOTTFRIED is an associate professor in the Gevirtz Graduate School of Education at University of California, Santa Barbara. He received his PhD and MA in applied economics from the University of Pennsylvania and his BA in economics from Stanford University. Gottfried has conducted numerous research studies in the area of school absenteeism, ranging from estimating the effects of absences on achievement and socioemotional development to identifying school factors and programs that can reduce chronic absenteeism, and has lectured domestically and internationally on the subject.

ETHAN L. HUTT is an assistant professor in the Department of Teaching and Learning, Policy and Leadership at the University of Maryland, College Park. He received his MA in history and PhD in the history of education from Stanford University. His research focuses on the historical relationship between quantification, education policy, and the law. In particular, he looks at the numbers and metrics that are used to describe, define, and regulate American school systems and has explored such topics as the history of the GED, grading practices, standardized test use, value-added measures, and longitudinal datasets.

ABOUT THE CONTRIBUTORS

KAITLIN ANDERSON is a postdoctoral research associate with the Education Policy Innovation Collaborative at Michigan State University. Her research focuses on improving access to high-quality educational opportunities for all students regardless of socioeconomic background. Her work includes evaluations of student discipline policies, teacher labor market reforms, and school choice policies, as well as methodological studies pertaining to causal inference from quasi-experimental methods.

REKHA BALU directs MDRC's Center for Applied Behavioral Science. Since 2011, she has led research studies and designed interventions tackling challenges in K–12 education and parenting, often deploying technology-driven solutions such as apps, text message campaigns, and online tools. She has partnered with institutions around the country to support more data-driven decision-making, incorporate predictive analytics, design interventions to solve process challenges, and test those interventions in randomized field trials or other rigorous research designs.

JOSHUA CHILDS is an assistant professor of educational policy and planning in the Department of Educational Leadership and Policy at the University of Texas at Austin. His research focuses on the role of interorganizational networks, cross-sector collaborations, and strategic alliances to address complex educational issues. Specifically, his work examines collaborative approaches involving community organizations and stakeholders that have the potential to improve academic achievement and reduce opportunity gaps for students in urban and rural schools.

SARAH A. CORDES is an assistant professor of educational leadership at the Temple University College of Education. She holds a PhD in public policy from the Robert F. Wagner Graduate School of Public Service at New York University. Her research focuses on the ways in which the urban context, including neighborhoods, housing, transportation, and school choice, affects student outcomes.

SHAUN M. DOUGHERTY is an associate professor of public policy and education in the Peabody College of Education and Human Development at Vanderbilt University. His research focuses on the use of quantitative research methods to evaluate the impact of educational policies and to understand how the requirements, incentives, and behaviors that policies produce develop human capital and promote equitable outcomes. In particular, he looks at on how family income, race, and disability status impact the implementation and outcomes of policies and programs.

ANNA J. EGALITE is an assistant professor in the Department of Educational Leadership, Policy, and Human Development at North Carolina State University. Her research focuses on the evaluation of education policies and programs intended to close racial and economic achievement gaps. Her studies have examined school choice policy, school size, the influence of family background on intergenerational economic mobility, and the diversification of the teacher labor force.

STACY B. EHRLICH is a senior research scientist at NORC at the University of Chicago. She holds a PhD in developmental psychology from the University of Chicago and has substantive expertise in the areas of early attendance and the measurement of early education program/school climate. Her work focuses on supporting improvements in early childhood education policy and practice through the use of high-quality research and data analytics. She takes a collaborative approach to her research, focusing on research-practice partnerships to ensure the work is directly relevant to practice and policy decisions.

KEVIN A. GEE is an associate professor in the School of Education at the University of California, Davis. His primary research agenda focuses on the role that schooling systems can play in influencing the health and well-being of children. In addition, he investigates how school policies and programs can help promote the well-being and educational outcomes of children who face a broad array of adverse conditions and experiences, including school bullying, food insecurity, and abuse and neglect. He holds a doctorate in quantitative policy analysis from the Harvard Graduate School of Education.

SETH GERSHENSON is an associate professor of public policy at American University. He works broadly on topics of relevant to domestic K–12 education policy and sociodemographic gaps in educational outcomes. His current research investigates the causes and consequences of student absences, summer learning loss, the short- and long-run impacts of having a same-race teacher, the formation and role of expectations in the education production function, and teachers' mental health.

JENNIFER GRAVES is an associate professor of economics at Autónoma University of Madrid (Universidad Autónoma de Madrid). With a focus on the economics of education and labor economics, she has studied topics related to classroom peer effects, year-round school calendars, and maternal labor market outcomes. Her ongoing research looks at topics such as labor performance under pressure and gender differences in the labor market.

HEATHER HOUGH is the executive director of the research partnership between Policy Analysis for California Education (PACE) and the CORE Districts, a collaborative of eight California school districts that have developed a robust measurement and accountability system that represents nearly a million students. Before joining PACE, she was an improvement adviser with the Carnegie Foundation for the Advancement of Teaching, helping education system leaders use research and data to support continuous improvement. She has also worked as a researcher with the Public Policy Institute of California, the Center for Education Policy Analysis at Stanford University, and the Center for Education Policy at SRI International. Hough's area of expertise is in district- and state-level policy making and implementation, with a particular focus on policy coherence, system improvement, and school and teacher accountability. She holds a PhD in education policy and a BA in public policy from Stanford University.

DAVID W. JOHNSON is a senior research analyst at the UChicago Consortium on School Research. His research emphasizes understanding schools as organizations and explores how adults use data to learn professionally, build relationships, and improve outcomes for historically underserved children in public schools. He holds a doctorate in social service administration from the University of Chicago and is a former kindergarten and first grade teacher in the District of Columbia Public Schools.

JACOB KIRKSEY is a PhD candidate in the Gevirtz Graduate School of Education and a graduate research fellow with the National Science Foundation. Drawing from various perspectives and interdisciplinary frameworks in educational policy, his research examines unintended consequences in educational policy and focuses on frequently forgotten student populations (e.g. students with special needs). Trained as an economist, Kirksey primarily uses quasi-experimental methods with large, secondary datasets. As an instructor, he seeks to expand the way in which practitioners and policy makers use and interpret data in their decision-making.

MICHELE LEARDO is a researcher at New York University's Steinhardt School of Education, Culture, and Human Development. Her interests span a variety of topics related to education, health, and social policy. Her current projects include examining the relationship between pupil transportation and student outcomes and how school and neighborhood built environments shape student health.

MARTHA ABELE MAC IVER is an associate professor in the Johns Hopkins University School of Education and its Center for Social Organization of Schools. Her recent research has focused on on early warning indicators and the effectiveness of numerous school and district educational interventions designed to improve student engagement and achievement.

JESSICA RAE MCBEAN is a PhD candidate in the Department of Government at American University. Her research interests center around statistical political methodology, particularly in local politics and public policy.

JONATHAN N. MILLS is a senior research associate at the Department of Education Reform at the University of Arkansas and a non-resident research fellow with the Education Research Alliance for New Orleans. His research focuses on policies designed to expand educational opportunities for students, especially those from disadvantaged backgrounds. He is currently examining the effects of school choice programs on student outcomes, as well as the benefits and unintended consequences of programs designed to improve college access and retention among disadvantaged student populations.

LINDSAY C. PAGE is an assistant professor of research methodology at the University of Pittsburgh School of Education, a research scientist at Pitt's Learning Research and Development Center, and a faculty research fellow of the National Bureau of Economic Research. Her work focuses on quantitative methods and their application to questions regarding the effectiveness of educational policies and programs across the preschool-to-postsecondary spectrum. She holds a doctorate in quantitative policy analysis and master's degrees in statistics and education policy from Harvard University.

CHRISTOPHER RICK is a doctoral student in public administration and international affairs at the Maxwell School of Citizenship and Public Affairs at Syracuse University. His research interests include urban policy and transportation.

CHRISTOPHER SALEM is a PhD student at the University of California, Santa Barbara. His research interests include education policy and the intersection of community resources and school outcomes. He has eight years of experience in public sector education, including six years as a fifth-grade teacher.

CAROLYN SATTIN-BAJAJ is an associate professor in the Department of Education Leadership, Management, and Policy at Seton Hall University, where she is also director of the Center for College Readiness. She uses a range of qualitative research methodologies to study issues of educational access and equity for immigrant-origin youth and other historically underserved student populations, with an emphasis on school choice policies and points of educational transition.

Amy Ellen Schwartz is the Daniel Patrick Moynihan Professor of Public Affairs and Economics at Syracuse University's Maxwell School and is rofessor Emeritus Professor of Public Policy, Education and Economics at New York University's Wagner School. Since earning a PhD in economics at Columbia University, she has investigated a wide range of issues in urban economics, economics of education, and public policy. She is the editor of the journal *Education Finance and Policy.*

Steven B. Sheldon is an associate professor in the Johns Hopkins University School of Education and a faculty affiliate in the Center on School, Family, and Community Partnerships. His research focuses on the predictors and impact of family engagement in children's education. He is the author of numerous peer reviewed articles and books on the topics and teaches about leadership and the implementation of school, family, and community partnership programs.

Ken Smythe-Leistico is an assistant professor and field coordinator in the School of Education and Applied Social Sciences at Seton Hill University. His applied research merges evidence-based approaches with practical service delivery to foster innovative practice. He holds a master's degree in social work from the University of Alabama and a doctorate in education from the University of Pittsburgh.

Long Tran is a PhD candidate in the Department of Public Administration and Policy at American University. He specializes in public and nonprofit management.

Sarit Weisburd is a tenure-track lecturer of economics at Tel Aviv University and a research affiliate with the Centre for Economics Policy Research Industrial Organization Programme. Her research focuses on applied microeconomics and aims to better understand the extent to which people respond to changes in incentives across a range of environments.

INDEX